15.00 T.

THE NATURE AND DESTINY OF MAN
VOLUME II. HUMAN DESTINY

The Nature and Destiny of Man

A CHRISTIAN INTERPRETATION

VOLUME II. HUMAN DESTINY

By

Reinhold Niebuhr

GIFFORD LECTURES

CHARLES SCRIBNER'S SONS
New York

To my wife
URSULA

who helped, and

To my children
CHRISTOPHER *and* ELIZABETH

*who frequently interrupted me
in the writing of these pages*

PREFACE FOR THE
SCRIBNER LIBRARY EDITION

THE GIFFORD LECTURES, delivered in Edinburgh about a quarter century ago and embodied in the two volumes entitled "Human Nature" and "Human Destiny," were devoted to the thesis that the two main emphases of Western culture, namely the sense of individuality and the sense of a meaningful history, were rooted in the faith of the Bible and had primarily Hebraic roots. It was my purpose to trace the growth, corruption and purification of these two concepts in the ages of Western history in order to create a better understanding between the historic roots and the several disciplines of our modern culture which were concerned with the human situation.

In regard to the Western emphasis on the individual, my thesis, which I still hold, was that individual selfhood is expressed in the self's capacity for self-transcendence and not in its rational capacity for conceptual and analytic procedures. Thus a consistent idealism and a consistent naturalism both obscure the dimension of selfhood, the former by equating the self with universal reason (as in Plato and Hegel) and the latter by reducing the self to an unfree nature not capable of viewing itself and the world from the position transcending the flow of events, causes and sequences.

The second Biblical-Hebraic emphasis about human selfhood was the unity of the self in its body, mind and spirit, in its freedom from natural necessity and in its involvement as creature in all these necessities. This unity was obscured in all forms of dualism, of which that of Descartes is a convenient example, which cut the self into two entities, body and mind, or body and spirit. The unity of the self can only be expressed in poetic, religious and metaphorical symbols.

Since the delivery of these lectures modern "ego-psychology," particularly as elaborated by my friend Erik Erikson, has developed this paradoxical position of the self scientifically. I agree with this position, but it would have prompted some changes in my statement of the reality.

The third problem about human selfhood has to do with its moral stature. I believed and still believe that human evil, primarily expressed in undue self-concern, is a corruption of its essential freedom and grows with its freedom. Therefore, every effort to equate evil purely with the ignorance of the mind and with the passions of the body is confusing and erroneous. I used the traditional religious symbols of the "Fall" and of "original sin" to counter these conceptions. My only regret is that I did not realize that the legendary character of the one and the dubious connotations of the other would prove so offensive to the modern mind, that my use of them obscured my essential thesis and my "realistic" rather than "idealistic" interpretation of human nature.

The second main emphasis of Biblical and Hebraic faith consists in the hazardous assertion of a meaningful history. The effort to discern meaning in all the confusions and cross purposes of history distinguishes Western culture and imparts historical dynamic to its striving. It must be distinguished from all religions, mystical or rationalistic, which equate "salvation" with flight from the confusions and responsibilities of man's historic existence. But Western culture has paid for this boon of historical dynamic with two evils inhering in the historical emphasis. One is the evil of fanaticism, the consequence of giving ultimate significance to historically contingent goals and values. The other is the creative, but also confusing, Messianism, the hope for a heaven on earth, for a kingdom of universal peace and righteousness. I have sought to interpret modern Communism as a secularized version of the persistent Messianism characteristic of both Hebraic and Christian thought. I still think that this is the context in which we must understand modern Communism.

I placed a special emphasis on the eschatology of the New Testament with its special symbols of the Christ and anti-Christ, taking them as symbols of the fact that both good and evil grow in history, and that evil has no separate history, but that a greater evil is always a corruption of a greater good. I believe that the perils of a nuclear age substantiate this interpretation much more vividly than I expected when I presented the thesis. But I am not now so sure that the historic symbols will contribute much to the understanding by modern man of his tragic and ironic history with its refutation of the messianic and utopian hopes of the Renaissance and Enlightenment.

Thus it is apparent that old men are incapable of changing their essential emphases and must in any case stand by the record, hoping that the moving drama of history may validate a part of the truth they sought to discern. We will say nothing about the insights which have been refuted and cast into the dustpan of history.

REINHOLD NIEBUHR

1963

CONTENTS

Preface   vii

THE NATURE AND DESTINY OF MAN
II. HUMAN DESTINY

I. *HUMAN DESTINY AND HISTORY*   1

WHERE A CHRIST IS NOT EXPECTED   6
1. *History Reduced to Nature*   7
2. *History Swallowed Up in Eternity*   11
WHERE A CHRIST IS EXPECTED   15
1. *Types of Messianism*   16
2. *Prophetic Messianism*   23
    a. THE RELATION OF PROPHETISM TO MESSIANISM   26
    b. THE FAILURE OF MESSIANISM TO ANSWER THE
      PROPHETIC PROBLEM   31

II. *THE DISCLOSURE AND THE FULFILLMENT
OF THE MEANING OF LIFE AND HISTORY*   35

JESUS' OWN REINTERPRETATION OF PROPHETIC MESSIA-
NISM   38
1. *Jesus' Rejection of Hebraic Legalism*   39
2. *Jesus' Rejection of Nationalistic Particularism*   41
3. *Jesus' Rejection of the Answer of Hebraic Mes-
   sianism for the Problem Presented by Prophet-
   ism*   42
4. *Jesus' Reinterpretation of the Eschata*   47

xi

THE ACCEPTANCE BY CHRISTIAN FAITH OF THE EX-
PECTED AND THE REJECTED MESSIAH   52

   1. *Christ Crucified as the "Wisdom of God and
The Power of God"*   54
   2. *The Relation of the "Wisdom of God" to the
"Power of God"*   57
      a. THE IDENTITY OF WISDOM AND POWER   57
      b. THE DIFFERENCE BETWEEN WISDOM AND POWER   61
   3. *The Foolishness of God and the Wisdom of Men* 62

III. *THE POSSIBILITIES AND LIMITS OF HISTORY*   68

  SACRIFICIAL LOVE AND THE SINLESSNESS OF CHRIST   70
  THE RELATION OF CHRIST'S PERFECTION TO HISTORY   76
    1. *The Perfection of Christ and Innocency*   76
    2. *The Perfection of Christ and Possibilities of His-
tory*   81
  THE RELATION OF CHRIST'S PERFECTION TO ETERNITY   90
  SUMMARY   95

IV. *WISDOM, GRACE AND POWER (THE FULFILL-
MENT OF HISTORY)*   98

  THE BIBLICAL DOCTRINE OF GRACE   100
  GRACE AS POWER IN, AND AS MERCY TOWARDS, MAN   107
    1. *"I am Crucified with Christ"*   108
    2. *"Nevertheless I Live"*   110
    3. *"Yet not I: but Christ Liveth in Me"*   114
      a. GRACE AS THE POWER NOT OUR OWN   115
      b. GRACE AS THE FORGIVENESS OF OUR SINS   119

V. *THE CONFLICT BETWEEN GRACE AND
PRIDE*   127

  PRE-AUGUSTINIAN CONCEPTIONS OF GRACE   129
  THE CATHOLIC CONCEPTION OF GRACE   134
  THE DESTRUCTION OF THE CATHOLIC SYNTHESIS   148

VI. *THE DEBATE ON HUMAN DESTINY IN MODERN CULTURE: THE RENAISSANCE* 157

    THE MEANING OF THE RENAISSANCE 160

    SECTARIAN PROTESTANTISM AND THE RENAISSANCE 169

    THE TRIUMPH OF THE RENAISSANCE 181

VII. *THE DEBATE ON HUMAN DESTINY IN MODERN CULTURE: THE REFORMATION* 184

    THE LUTHERAN REFORMATION 185

    THE CALVINISTIC REFORMATION 198

    A SYNTHESIS OF REFORMATION AND RENAISSANCE 204

VIII. *HAVING, AND NOT HAVING, THE TRUTH* 213

    THE PROBLEM OF THE TRUTH 214

    THE TEST OF TOLERANCE 220

        1. *Catholicism and Toleration* 221

        2. *The Reformation and Toleration* 226

        3. *The Renaissance and Toleration* 231

IX. *THE KINGDOM OF GOD AND THE STRUGGLE FOR JUSTICE* 244

    THE RELATION OF JUSTICE TO LOVE 246

    LAWS AND PRINCIPLES OF JUSTICE 247

    STRUCTURES OF JUSTICE 256

        1. *The Unity of Vitality and Reason* 258

        2. *Types of Power in Social Life* 260

        3. *The Organization and Balance of Power* 265

    THE CHRISTIAN ATTITUDE TO GOVERNMENT 269

    JUSTICE AND WORLD COMMUNITY 284

X. *THE END OF HISTORY* 287

    THE NEW TESTAMENT IDEA OF THE END 289

        1. *The Parousia* 290

        2. *The Last Judgment* 291

        3. *The Resurrection* 294

Contents

The End and the Meaning of History   299

The Diversity and Unity of History   301

    1. *The Rise and Fall of Cultures and Civilizations*   302

    2. *The Individual and History*   308

    3. *The Unity of History*   313

INDEX OF SCRIPTURAL PASSAGES   323

INDEX OF PROPER NAMES   323

INDEX OF SUBJECTS   325

THE NATURE AND DESTINY OF MAN
VOLUME II. HUMAN DESTINY

CHAPTER I

HUMAN DESTINY AND HISTORY

MAN IS, and yet is not, involved in the flux of nature and time. He is a creature, subject to nature's necessities and limitations; but he is also a free spirit who knows of the brevity of his years and by this knowledge transcends the temporal by some capacity within himself. Man "brings his years to an end as a tale that is told," having an even shorter life span than some dumb creatures. But the sense of melancholy which the anticipation of death induces in the human spirit is not known in the animal world. To brood either anxiously or with studied and learned serenity upon the fact that man is as "the grass which flourisheth in the morning and in the evening is cut down and withereth" is to reveal the whole dimension of existence which distinguishes man from the animal world.

Man's ability to transcend the flux of nature gives him the capacity to make history. Human history is rooted in the natural process but it is something more than either the determined sequences of natural causation or the capricious variations and occurrences of the natural world. It is compounded of natural necessity and human freedom. Man's freedom to transcend the natural flux gives him the possibility of grasping a span of time in his consciousness and thereby of knowing history. It also enables him to change, reorder and transmute the causal sequences of nature and thereby to *make* history. The very ambiguity of the word "history" (as something that occurs and as something that is remembered and recorded) reveals the common source of both human actions and human knowledge in human freedom.[1]

There is no point in human history in which the human spirit is freed of natural necessity. But there is also no point at which the mind cannot transcend the given circumstances to imagine a more ultimate possibility. Thus the conflicts of history need not be accepted as normative, but man looks towards a reality where these conflicts are overcome in a reign of universal order and peace. History thus moves between the limits of nature and eternity. All human actions are conditioned on the one hand by nature's necessities and limitations, and determined on the other hand by an explicit or implicit loyalty to man's conception of the changeless principles which underlie the change. His loyalty to these principles prompts him to seek the elimination of contingent, irrelevant and contradictory elements in the flux, for the sake of realizing the real essence of his life, as defined by the unchanging and eternal power which governs it.

A basic distinction may be made between various interpretations of the meaning of life by noting their attitude towards history. Those which include history in the realm of meaning see it as a process which points and moves towards a fuller disclosure and realization of life's essential meaning. Those which exclude it, do so because they regard history as no more than natural finiteness, from which the human spirit must be freed. They consider man's involvement in nature as the very cause of evil, and define the ultimate redemption of life as emancipation from finiteness. In the one case history is regarded as potentially meaningful, waiting for the ultimate disclosure and realization of its meaning. In the other case it is believed to be essentially meaningless. It may be regarded as a realm of order; but the order is only the subordinate one of natural necessity which affects the meaning of life negatively. It is a mortal coil which must be shuffled off.

[1] *Cf.* Paul Tillich, *The Interpretation of History,* Part IV, Ch. 2.

The difference in the attitude of various cultures towards history is determined by contradictory estimates of man's transcendence over historical process, including his final transcendence over himself. In the one case it is assumed that since this capacity for self-transcendence represents the highest capacity of the human spirit, the fulfillment of life must naturally consist in man's emancipation from the ambiguities of history. His partial immersion in and partial transcendence over nature must be transmuted into a total transcendence. Some sort of *eternity* is therefore the goal of human striving in non-historical religions and philosophies; and the eternity which is man's end is the fulfillment of history to the point of being its negation. In this eternity there is "no separation of thing from thing, no part standing in isolated existence estranged from the rest and therefore nowhere is there any wronging of another."[2]

In religions which regard history as contributing to the meaning of life the attitude towards man's partial involvement in, and partial transcendence over, the process of nature and the flux of time, is totally different. This ambiguous situation is not regarded as the evil from which man must be redeemed. The evil in the human situation arises, rather, from the fact that men seek to deny or to escape prematurely from the uncertainties of history and to claim a freedom, a transcendence and an eternal and universal perspective which is not possible for finite creatures. The problem of sin rather than finiteness is, in other words, either implicitly or explicitly the basic problem of life. Yet the problem of finiteness is not eliminated. It is recognized that a man who stands in an historical process is too limited in vision to discern the full meaning of that process, and too limited in power to fulfill the meaning, however much the freedom of his knowledge and his power is one element in the stuff of history. Hence the temporal problem of human history and destiny in historical religions is: how the transcendent meaning of history is to be disclosed and fulfilled, since man can discern only

[2] Plotinus. *Enneads,* III, ii:1.

partial meanings and can only partially realize the meanings he discerns. In modern corruptions of historical religions this problem is solved very simply by the belief that the cumulative effects of history will endow weak man with both the wisdom and the power to discern and to fulfill life's meaning.

In the more profound versions of historical religion it is recognized, however, that there is no point in history, whatever the cumulations of wisdom and power, in which the finiteness of man is overcome so that he could complete his own life, or in which history as such does not retain the ambiguity of being rooted in nature-necessity on the one hand while pointing towards transcendent, "eternal" and trans-historical ends on the other hand.

Historical religions are therefore by their very nature prophetic-Messianic. They look forward at first to a point in history and finally towards an *eschaton* (end) which is also the end of history, where the full meaning of life and history will be disclosed and fulfilled. Significantly, as in the optimistic expectations of a "day of the Lord" which the first great literary prophet, Amos, found at hand and criticized, these Messianic expectations begin as expressions of national hope and expectations of national triumph. Only gradually it is realized that man's effort to deny and to escape his finiteness in imperial ambitions and power add an element of corruption to the fabric of history and that this corruption becomes a basic characteristic of history and a perennial problem from the standpoint of the fulfillment of human history and destiny. It is recognized that history must be purged as well as completed; and that the final completion of history must include God's destruction of man's abortive and premature efforts to bring history to its culmination.

The basic distinction between historical and non-historical religions and cultures may thus be succinctly defined as the difference between those which expect and those which do not expect a Christ. A Christ is expected wherever history is regarded as potentially meaningful but as still awaiting the full disclosure and fulfillment of its meaning. A Christ is not expected wherever the meaning of life is explained from the standpoint of either nature or supernature in such a way that a transcendent revelation of history's meaning is not regarded as either possible or necessary. It is not regarded as possible when, as in various forms of naturalism, the visions and ambitions of historical existence which point beyond nature are regarded as illusory; and nature-history is believed to be incapable of receiving disclosures of meaning which point beyond itself. It is not regarded as necessary when man's capacity for freedom and self-transcendence is believed to be infinitely extensible until the ambiguities of history are left behind and pure eternity is achieved. The significance of a Christ is that he is a disclosure of the divine purpose, governing history within history. Wherever it is believed that man's capacity to transcend self and history can be disassociated from his finiteness, the meaning of salvation is conceived as essentially redemption from history, obviating any necessity of, or desire for, the fulfillment of man in history, or for the disclosure of history's ultimate meaning.

A Christ is expected wherever history is thought of as a realm of fragmentary revelations of a purpose and power transcending history, pointing to a fuller disclosure of that purpose and power. He is expected because this disclosure is regarded as both possible and necessary. It is regarded as possible because history is known to be something more than the nature-necessity in which it has its roots. It is regarded as necessary because the potential meaningfulness of history is recognized as fragmentary and corrupted. It must be completed and clarified.

The interpretation of the cultures of the world in this fashion according to their possession, or lack, of Messianic expectations, draws upon insights which are possible only after the logic of Messianic expectations has reached its culmination in the Christian belief that these expectations have been fulfilled in Christ. It is not possible to interpret cultures according to their expectation or want of expectations of *a* Christ without drawing upon the faith that *the* Christ has been revealed; for there can be no interpretation of the meaning of life and history without implicitly or explicitly drawing into the interpretation the faith which claims to have found the end of these expectations. This is to say, merely, that there can be no interpretation of history without specific presuppositions and that the interpretation which is being attempted in these pages is based upon Christian presuppositions. The Christian answer to the problem of life is assumed in the discussion of the problem. In that sense our interpretation is, as every interpretation must be in the final analysis, "dogmatic" or confessional. Yet it is not purely dogmatic or confessional; for it seeks to analyze the question and expectations for which a particular epic of history is regarded as the answer, and also to determine why these questions and expectations are not universal in history. Such an analysis must begin with a further inquiry into the character of non-historical forms of culture which regard Christ "as foolishness" because they have no questions for which Christ is the answer and no expectations and hopes for which his Cross is the fulfillment.

II

WHERE A CHRIST IS NOT EXPECTED

Nothing is so incredible as an answer to an unasked question. One half of the world has regarded the Christian answer to the problem of life and history as "foolishness" because it had no questions for which the Christian revelation was the answer and no longings and hopes which that revelation fulfilled. The cultures of this half of the world were non-Messianic because they were non-historical. Their failure to regard history as basic to the meaning of life may be attributed to two primary methods of looking at life which stand in contradiction to each other. The one is the method of regarding the system of nature as the final reality to which man must adjust himself. The other regards nature from the human perspective as either chaos or a meaningless order from which man will be freed either by his reason or by some unity and power within him higher than reason. There are systems of thought, of which Stoicism is the classic example, which combine both methods or which reveal a certain degree of ambivalence between the two; but the two most consistent methods of denying the meaningfulness of history are to reduce it to the proportions of nature or to regard it as a corruption of eternity.

1. *History Reduced to Nature*

The history of classical materialism from Democritus to Lucretius gives us a much more consistent view of life as seen from the perspective of nature than any modern form of naturalism; because there are few forms of modern naturalism which have not surreptitiously insinuated something of a Hebraic-Biblical view of life into their naturalism, thereby making nature the bearer and even the artificer of a meaningful history (as for instance when the fact of evolution in biology is made to bear the idea of progress in history). Only in classical thought, and in a few exceptional modern reversions to consistent classicism,[1] is the effort made to reduce history to the exact proportions of nature.

The attempt to deny the reality of history, by reducing it to the dimension of a meaningless natural sequence, is most perfectly expressed in classical thought in its meditations upon death and its protestations against the fear of death. The fact that man dies is indubitable proof of his organic relation to the world of nature and would seem to prove "that a man hath no preeminence above a beast"[2] for "all go unto one place; all are of the dust, and all turn to dust again."[3] Moreover, death is not only a revelation of human finiteness; but the endless sequence of life and death proves history, in one of its aspects at least, to be no more than a series of meaning-

---

[1] Modern forms of naturalism in which the moral values of history are conceived as standing in tragic defiance of the "trampling march of unconscious power" (Bertrand Russell) represent a significant departure from the more consistent naturalism of classicism.

[2] Ecclesiastes 3:19.   [3] *Ibid.*, 3:20.

less recurrences of the natural world. Classical naturalism seeks to reduce history to this simple dimension. "Consider," declares Lucretius, "how utterly unimportant to us was the past antiquity of infinite time, that elapsed before we were born. This then nature exhibits to us as a specimen of the time which will again be after our death. For what does appear terrible in it? Does anything seem gloomy? Is not all more free from any trouble than sleep?" [4]

Yet however inexorable death may be as law of nature, the fear of death is just as inevitable an expression of that in man, which transcends nature. It proves that he does have "preeminence above a beast"; because the fear of death springs from the capacity not only to anticipate death but to imagine and to be anxious about some dimension of reality on the other side of death. Both forms of fear prove man's transcendence over nature. His mind comprehends the point in nature at which his own existence in nature ends; and thereby proves that nature does not fully contain him. The fact that he fears extinction is a negative indication of a dimension in the human spirit, transcending nature. The fact that he is anxious about a possible realm of meaning on the other side of death, and speculates, in the words of Hamlet's soliloquy that "to die, to sleep" may mean "perchance to dream," is the positive indication of man's freedom transcending nature. The fear of death is thus the clearest embryonic expression of man's capacity as a creator of history.

Classical naturalism seeks to beguile man from this fear of death by attempting to persuade him that it is illusory and unwarranted. The argument contains two points. One is that there is nothing in history which man need to fear, since there is in fact no history, but only natural sequence and natural recurrence. "If universal nature," declares Lucretius, "should suddenly utter voice and thus upbraid

---

[4] *De rerum natura,* Book III, 955–80.
The thought of Lucretius contains inconsistent strains in which a minimal meaning is assigned to history either by regarding it as a process of degeneration (Book II) or as revealing progress (Book V).

any of us: 'What cause have you O Mortal thus excessively to indulge in bitter grief? Why do you groan and weep at the thought of
death? . . . Why do you not, O unreasonable man, retire like a guest
satisfied with life and take your undisturbed rest with resignation.
. . . . *Everything is always the same.* . . . All things remain the
same even if you should outlast all the ages in living; and still more
would you see them the same if you should never come to die.' " [5]

The other point in the argument is that there is no more to fear
in a possible super-history than in history itself, because man does
not transcend his temporal life and hence need not anticipate
judgment beyond death. Thus Epicurus writes: "There is nothing
terrible in living to a man who rightly comprehends that there is
nothing terrible in ceasing to live; so that it was a silly man who said
that he feared death not because it would grieve him when it was
present but because it did grieve him when it was future. . . . The
most formidable of all evils, death, is nothing to us, since, when we
exist, death is not present to us; and when death is present we have
no existence. It is no concern then to either the living or the dead;
since to the one it has no existence and the other class has no
existence itself." [6]

The fact that classical naturalism must seek to beguile men from
the fear of death not only by reducing history to the dimension of
natural sequence but also by denying the reality of any possible realm
of life and meaning beyond history is doubly significant. It proves
that there can be no sense of history at all (as embodied embryoni-
cally in the fear of death) without a further sense of an eternity
transcending history. The "partial simultaneity" of man by which
he comprehends the sequences of time into his consciousness inevitably carries with it, by way of implication, a sense of a divine "total
simultaneity" which comprehends the sequence of time beyond

---

[5] Book III, 925–55.
[6] Letter of Epicurus to Menæceus in Diogenes Laertius, *Lives and
Opinions of Eminent Philosophers,* Yonge's translation, p. 468.

man's own capacity of comprehension. A suprahistorical eternity is implied in history because the capacity by which man transcends temporal sequence, while yet being involved in it, implies a capacity of transcendence which is not limited by the sequence.

The fear of death also proves that the moral dimension of history, the distinction between good and evil is not annulled by the fact that the grave claims the righteous and the unrighteous; and the earth

> ". . . visits still
> With equalest apportionment of ill
> Both good and bad alike, and brings to one same dust
> The just and the unjust." [7]

The fear of death includes the fear of a possible punishment of evil; and consideration of the impartiality of death does not annul this fear. Nor is it destroyed by the argument that there is no reality beyond the fact of death, since the very fear which this argument is meant to quiet is an indication of height and depth in the human spirit which nature as such cannot contain. [8]

[7] Arthur Hugh Clough, "Easter."

[8] Virgil frequently testifies to the fear of punishment as a natural element in the fear of death as for instance in the words:

> "When at last the life has fled,
> And left the body cold and dead,
> E'en then there passes not away
> The painful heritage of clay;
> Full many a long contracted stain
> Perforce must linger deep in grain.
> So penal sufferings they endure
> For ancient crime to make them pure:
> Some hang aloft in open view
> For winds to pierce them through and through,
> While others purge their guilt deep-eyed
> In burning fire of whelming tide.
> Each for himself we all sustain
> The durance of our ghostly pain.
> > *Aeneid,* Book VI.

The effort of classical naturalism to reduce history to the proportion of nature is, in short, abortive. It annuls the very meaning of life by its disavowal of history.

2. *History Swallowed Up in Eternity*

"Christ," declares St. Paul, is "to the Greeks foolishness" because "they seek after wisdom." This is to say that the expectation of the disclosure and fulfillment of the meaning of history at a point in history or at the end of history, has no meaning for the Greek world. It seeks after wisdom and therefore does not expect a Christ. It has no need of Christ because it finds a Christ in every man: the *logos* principle. If classical materialism reduces history to the proportions of natural sequence and temporal process, classical idealism and mysticism seek to flee the world of history precisely because they find no more meaning in history than classical naturalism finds. But they find something in man which classical naturalism does not find; and by that something man is to be emancipated from history. That something is either the intellectual principle of his soul, or something even more transcendent than his mind. Classical idealism and mysticism in short understand the transcendent freedom of the human spirit; but they do not understand it in its organic relation to the temporal process. The natural and temporal process is merely something from which man must be emancipated. That emancipation is the very fulfillment of the meaning of life. There is no yearning for fulfillment in history; there is only a desire to be freed from history.

In Platonism the intellectual principle, the *logisticon,* is the organ of this emancipation. "The true lover of knowledge," declares Plato, "is always striving after being . . . that is his nature; he will not rest at those *multitudinous particular phenomena* whose existence is appearance only, but will go on . . . the keen edge will not be blunted nor the force of his passion abate until he have attained the true knowledge of every essence by a sympathetic and kindred power in the soul and by that power drawing near and *becoming in-*

corporate with very being, have begotten mind and truth, he will
know and truly live and increase; and then and not till then, will he
cease from travail." [9]

The important point in Platonism is that the "brightest and best
of being, in other words the Good" belongs to the world of "being"
and not to the world of "becoming," [10] and that a "power resides in
each of us" which enables us to reach that world. This is to say that
history is either an inferior or an illusory world: "the prison house
is the world of sight," the "Absolute Good" is the world of changeless essence underlying the changing world; and "the light of
reason only without the assistance of the senses" [11] is the power in
man which makes it possible for him to rise to this world of pure
being.

Since the human mind transcends itself in infinite regression,
and human reason is able to contemplate the fact of human reason,[12]
rational and intellectual methods of transcending, and escaping
from, history always finally give way to more mystical techniques in
which the effort is made to unite the soul with the Absolute, the

---

[9] *Republic*, 490–505.
There are many similar intellectualistic denials of the reality of the
"multitudinous particular phenomena" which are the very stuff of
history in Plato, though the general purpose of the *Republic* represents a
contradictory impulse towards historical concretion. There is not in Plato,
and there is not in any philosophy or religion, an absolutely consistent
denial of history. In Hinduism the Brahmin caste uses the prestige of its
superior ability to transcend history and transmutes it into a form of
social-political power with which to dominate historical society. The
prestige of its priestly skill in fleeing history becomes the basis of its
power to dominate society.

[10] *Republic*, 518.

[11] *Republic*, 532 B. All these quotations are taken from the *Republic,*
because the *Republic* reveals a dominant impulse towards historical concretion already referred to. The fact that the dominant note in Platonism
is not obscured in a book which departs somewhat from the Platonic
logic is therefore significant.

[12] See the discussion of the relation of "spirit" to "reason" in Vol. I,
Ch. V.

human with the divine, by isolating and cultivating a power of the
soul, even higher and purer than reason. This is to say that Platonism finally culminates in neo-Platonism in the history and logic of
otherworldly and non-historical cultures.

In the thought of Plotinus *nous* is not so much the rational principle in the soul as the power of self-consciousness. The *nous* does
not contemplate the world, nor even the rational principle underlying the phenomenal reality. It contemplates itself until it is united
and becomes identified with the "Authentic Being" of the final
"Good" about which one must "not even say that it has intellection,"
for that "would be dividing it." [13]

The eternity to which the soul rises is an undifferentiated unity
which finally swallows up all particularity. Plotinus is very precise
in asserting that the eternity of the "Intellectual World" negates,
rather than fulfills, history. "There can be no memory in the Intellectual World," he declares. "There will not even be memory of the
personality, no thought that the contemplator is the self. In contemplative vision, especially when it is vivid, we are not at the same
time aware of our own personality; the activity is toward the
object of vision with which the thinker becomes identified." [14]
Thus the end of life is the annulment of history and of the
self in history. Whatever is involved in "process" never "possesses
Being." [15]

It is hardly necessary to trace the logic of non-historical cultures
in the oriental world; for Taoism, Hinduism, and Buddhism distinguish themselves from the non-historical tradition in Western
classicism, chiefly by a more consistently mystical and less rationalistic disavowal of the meaningfulness of history. [16]

[13] *Enneads,* Book III, 10.
[14] *Ibid.,* Book II, 4.
[15] *Ibid.,* Book IV, 8.
[16] Even in Buddhism, though it is the most consistent of all a-historical
religions, there are elements which are inconsistent with the dominant
idea of redemption from history. The impulse towards history is particu-

The fact that there is a preliminary, rationalistic technique in Western non-historical cultures and that this technique should always result in tangents of thought which affirm rather than annul history (as in Plato's *Republic*) are indicative of a basic ambivalence towards history in the Western world, which culminates in the contrast and kinship of Hellenic and Hebraic culture. Reason is quite obviously a principle of order in history, though history-in-nature never fully conforms to rational principles. Reason is furthermore both a symbol of the freedom of man over nature and of his involvement in it. On this account only mystical forms of other-worldliness are completely consistent in denying the meaningfulness of history.

The conflict between materialism and idealism, between naturalism and supernaturalism in Greek classicism is partly bridged in Stoic thought, at the price, of course, of complete consistency. For Stoicism is never quite certain whether the *logos* principle, to which man is to conform, is an order imbedded in nature as such or whether it is a principle of human freedom; whether man is to conform to *physis* or to a principle unique to human nature, because the latter is peculiarly endowed with *logos*. "The end of life," declares Seneca, "is to act in conformity with nature, that is at once with the nature which is in us and with the nature of the universe." Since the "nature of the universe" includes both the determined order of *physis* and the peculiar freedom of man, this basic idea of Stoic ethics contains a fundamental confusion. The general tendency of Stoicism is, however, in the direction of the naturalistic side of the classical debate.

In that debate the *logos* principle is imbedded in nature for the naturalists and transcends nature in the unique freedom of the mind for the idealists. "The result [of the triumph of idealism in this

---

larly apparent in Mahayana Buddhism in which the Bodhisattvas renounce the final redemption from history in order to mediate redemption in history.

debate] was to vindicate the possibility of freedom, but at the cost of rehabilitating 'chance' or 'necessity' which thus once more emerged as the function of the (more or less) independent matter." [17]

There is in short no expectation of a Christ, no Messianic hope, in classical culture because the sovereignty to which man must be subordinated is not of the kind which is partly hidden and may be expected to be more fully revealed. In the one case Nature is god and obedience to that god requires the disavowal of all the unique fears, hopes, ambitions and evils which are the stuff of history. In the other case Reason is god; and the necessities and contingencies of history are, from the perspective of reason, reduced to pure "chance" or to a mechanistic necessity, which means that the history is essentially meaningless because it is partly imbedded in nature. There is no necessity or possibility in either case of a fuller revelation of the ultimate sovereignty of life in history and therefore of a fuller disclosure of the meaning of life. The only alternatives are either to reduce the meaning of life to the comparative meaninglessness of the natural order, or to emancipate life from this meaninglessness by translating it into the dimension of pure reason, which is to say, pure eternity.

III

WHERE A CHRIST IS EXPECTED

No Christ could validate himself as the disclosure of a hidden divine sovereignty over history or as a vindication of the meaningfulness of history, if a Christ were not expected. This is to say that if history is not regarded as potentially meaningful, the claim that potential meaning has been realized and that obscurities and ambiguities in

[17] The quotation is from *Christianity and Classical Culture* by Charles Norris Cochrane, p. 167. This work is a profound analysis of the inadequacies of the classical mind in coming to terms with the unique realities of history, in contrast to nature or reason.

history have been clarified would not be credible. Any Christ must be "foolishness to the Greeks," both ancient and modern. Christ may also be a "stumblingblock to the Jews"; but he is not "foolishness" to them. He may be a stumblingblock because, though expected, he proves not to be the kind of a Messiah who was expected. In fact one can assert dogmatically that the true Christ *must* be a stumblingblock in the sense that he must disappoint, as well as fulfill, expectations. He must disappoint some expectations because Messianic expectations invariably contain egoistic elements, which could not be fulfilled without falsifying the meaning of history. Every Messianic expectation contains an explicit or implicit assumption that history will be fulfilled from the particular locus of the civilization and culture which has the expectation.

The fact that there can be no Christ without an expectation of Christ relates Christianity as founded in a unique revelation to the whole history of culture; the fact that the true Christ cannot be the Messiah who is expected separates Christianity from the history of culture. In order to validate this view of the matter it is necessary to examine the history of Messianic expectations more fully.

I. *Types of Messianism*

The prophetic-Messianic interpretation of history culminates in Hebraic religion, and more particularly in the prophetic-apocalyptic, as against the legalistic tradition, of Hebraism. But Hebraic Messianism is not *sui generis* just as Greek classicism is only the most profound, and not the only elaboration, of a non-historical view of life. One can find some degree of Messianism in every culture in which history is taken seriously. The most explicit expressions of it are to be found in the cultures of the great early empires of Egypt, Mesopotamia and Persia. But even Roman imperialism is not without Messianic notes. The history of the Roman Empire is comprehended as a meaningful whole, and efforts are made to interpret universal history in relation to the history of the Roman Empire.

The idea in both Greek and Roman mythology of a "golden age," representing either a period of natural goodness and simplicity from which subsequent history has departed or a period of primitive crudeness from which subsequent ages have gradually risen to the achievements of civilization, lays a foundation for Roman Messianism. The Messianic age is regarded as a restoration of the primitive goodness. The idea that the fulfillment of history is, in some sense, a restoration of its early virtue is thus of very early origin.[1]

[1] The most significant Messianic note in Roman literature is the well known passage in Virgil's Fourth *Eclogue*:

> Bless him, the infant with whom
>   discontinues the era of iron;
> Bless him with whom will arise
>   the new race that is gloriously golden,
> Bless, chaste Lucina, the boy:
>   now reigneth thy brother Apollo.

This Virgilian Messianic vision includes the hope of a transformed nature:

> Goats will return by themselves
>   to our homesteads, with udders distended
> Nor any longer our cattle
>   shall fear huge terrible lions.
> Then will the serpent die out
>   and herbs disappear that bear poison.

The conception of a God-like Caesar who will rule the world is similar to the Egyptian hopes for the rule of a divine shepherd-King:

> But that boy will partake of the life of the Gods;
>   he will meet them,
> Meet all the heroes; and he
>   will in turn by the gods be beholden.
> Over a pacified world will he rule
>   patriarchic in virtue.

For a full discussion of the relation of Roman Messianism and its indebtedness to other Messianic literature, see Eduard Norden, *Die Geburt des Kindes, Geschichte einer Religioesen Idee*.

To understand the logic of Messianism and its integral relation to the cultures for which history is included in the meaning of life it is necessary to include three elements or levels of Messianism, (*a*) the egoistic-nationalistic element, (*b*) the ethical-universalistic element and (*c*) a supra-ethical religious element as expressed in Prophetism. Of these three elements the first and second are expressed in pre-prophetic Messianism, while all three are present in the Messianism of the Hebrew prophets.

a. On the egoistic-nationalistic level Messianism looks forward to the triumph of the nation, empire or culture in which the Messianic hope is expressed. This means that history is regarded as obscure and that life is threatened with meaninglessness primarily because the collective life of nation or empire, which is the primary source of meaning, is known to be more finite than it pretends to be. The symbol of its insecurity is the power of its foes. The fulfillment of life's meaning is thus contained in the triumph of *our* nation or civilization over its foes. While this simple conception of the problem of life and history represents historical culture on its lowest level, it is an element which is not eliminated from even the highest level of prophetic Messianism. Even on that level the Messiah is expected to vindicate Israel against its enemies. Nor is this element ever completely eliminated from Christian conceptions of history in which the egoistic-nationalistic element is refuted in principle. In them it is understood that Christ does not vindicate a race or a nation. It is the sovereignty of God which is vindicated. But it is difficult to believe this without surreptitiously including the vindication of the righteous or of the believers, as against the unbelievers, in the divine vindication. This is a subtler form of egoistic corruption in the interpretation of history which we must analyse further presently. It must be added that it is not only impossible for the highest forms of Christian prophetism to remain free of egoistic corruptions; it is also impossible for the most advanced civilization to be safe against reversions to very primitive egoistic-nationalistic interpretations of history, as for instance in contemporary Nazism.

b. The ethical-universalistic level of Messianism

On the second level of Messianism the problem of history is not the impotence of *our* race, empire or nation, and the answer to the problem of history, therefore, cannot be the triumph of *our* people over our foes. The problem of history is the impotence of the good against the evil forces in history. The momentary triumph of evil in history is seen as a threat to the meaningfulness of history and this threat is overcome by the hope of the coming of a Messianic king who will combine power and goodness. This is the significance of the figure of the Messianic "shepherd king," an important symbol not only in Hebraic but in Babylonian and Egyptian Messianism.[2]

The shepherd king is gentle despite his power. As a judge he rises to the heights of imaginative justice in which justice and mercy become one, for "he shall not judge after the sight of his eyes, neither reprove after the hearing of his ears; but with righteousness shall he judge the poor, and reprove with equity for the meek of the earth." [3]

It is sometimes assumed that it was the primary contribution of the Hebrew prophets to lift Messianism from the egoistic-nationalis-

[2] *Cf.* Isaiah 40:11: "He shall feed his flock like a shepherd: he shall gather the lambs with his arm, and carry them in his bosom, and shall gently lead those that are with young." Also Ezekiel 37:24: "And my servant David shall be king over them; and they all shall have one shepherd."

In the Egyptian Messianic tract "Admonitions of Ipuwer" the ideal king is described as follows: "He brings cooling to the flame. It is said he is shepherd of all men. There is no evil in his heart. When his herds are few he passes the day to gather them together, their hearts being fevered." J. H. Breasted, *The Dawn of Conscience*, p. 198.

In the Messianism of the early empires, that of Persia comes nearest to transcending this egoistic-imperialistic element and achieving a genuine universalism in its interpretation of history. But since the fully formed Persian Messianism is Zoroastrianism, and Zoroastrianism is a prophetic reform movement in Parseeism, this universalism must be regarded as prophetic rather than pre-prophetic; the only prophetic Messianism, outside of Hebraism.

[3] Isaiah 11:3-4.

tic to the universalistic level, upon which the ethical meaning of history becomes the primary concern; and the seeming power of evil, and the seeming impotence of virtue in history is regarded as the greatest problem. It is true that prophetic Messianism moves, on the whole, on this level; and the first great prophet, Amos, undoubtedly challenges nationalistic elements in the current expectations of the "day of Yahweh." It is nevertheless erroneous to identify the universalistic element with prophetism, not only because that element was present in an undeveloped form in pre-prophetic Messianism (as we have noted in Egypt and Babylon as well as in Israel) but also, as will become apparent subsequently, because prophetic Messianism contains an even profounder element than the triumph of universalism over nationalism.

It is significant that the ethical Messianism, which overcomes the moral obscurities of history by the hope of an ultimately perfect conformity of power and goodness, contains by implication all the important and characteristic insights of cultures which take history seriously, as against those which do not.

The hope of an ideal king implies that the meaningfulness of history is obscured not primarily by the irrationalities, necessities and contingencies of nature; but by a uniquely historical phenomenon, the factor of "power." The injustices which threaten the moral meaning of history are derived from the power of will over will, of which nature as such knows very little. There are, indeed, slight forms of power in nature, as for instance the leadership of the oldest or strongest male in the herd; a form of power which is incidentally a nexus between animal and human social organization. But, in general, nature knows only competing impulses of survival and not competing wills to power.

Power is the product of spirit. It never exists without an alloy of physical force but it is always more than physical compulsion. This fact is symbolized by the importance of the priest, as distinguished from the soldier, as agent of social organization in all early societies. The implied recognition of ethical Messianism, that the evils of history arise, not primarily from the contingencies of nature but from a uniquely historical phenomenon, the power of will over will, is thus to discover the moral enigma of history in history itself, and not primarily in history's relation to nature or in its corruption by natural contingencies.

But there is an even profounder understanding of history in ethical Messianism. Its strictures are directed particularly against unjust "rulers" and "elders." It recognizes that injustice flows from the same source from which justice comes, from the historical organization of life. The profoundest social tract of Egypt, "The Eloquent Peasant," pictures a peasant indicting the Grand Visier in the words: "Thou art set for a dam for the poor man to save him from drowning, but behold thou art his moving flood." [4] This indictment may be regarded not only as a shrewd expression of the moral ambiguity of all government, as both an instrument of, and a peril to justice; it is, more profoundly considered, a recognition of the basic paradox of history. It recognizes that the creative and destructive possibilities of human history are inextricably intermingled. The very power which organizes human society and establishes justice, also generates injustice by its preponderance of power.

The hope that the injustice of power may be overcome in a Messianic shepherd king might seem, at first blush, to be no more than the pious expectation of a "good Caesar" to which Christian political thought has occasionally degenerated.[5] But ethical Messianism is saved from this superficiality by the transcendent element in its Messianic expectations. The Messianic king who will combine power and goodness, strength and gentleness, justice and mercy, is never a purely historical figure. He is a god become earthly king. In Egyptian Messianism Re himself comes to earth to establish justice. This transcendent element is present in Babylonian and Hebraic Messianism as well.

[4] Breasted, *op. cit.,* p. 189.
[5] Most recently in the pietistic movement known as "Buchmanism."

To recognize that only God can perfectly combine power and goodness is to understand that power is not evil of itself; but that all power in history is in peril of becoming an instrument of injustice because it is itself one of the competing powers in human society, even while it seeks to become (as is the case of the power of government) a transcendent power through which subordinate conflicts are harmonized. A Messianism which recognizes that the inevitable egoistic corruption in all historical creativity cannot be eliminated if God Himself does not become the wielder of historical power, uses mythical symbols to express an insight into the character of human history which all modern utopian creeds have obscured.

On the other hand the hope of a shepherd king distinguishes Messianism as sharply from non-historical religions as from false interpretations of history. To look forward to an ideal harmony of life with life in human society, through the intervention of divine power, means that the fulfillment of life is sought in history and not in eternity. History is not regarded as evil by reason of being a realm of vitality; and perfection is not defined as some realm of devitalized forms, some eternal calm from which the vitalities of life have been abstracted.

The hope of the shepherd king is thus a very profound expression of the ethos of historical cultures. Its weakness lies in the fact that it hopes for an impossible combination of the divine and the historical. The God who is both powerful and good by reason of being the source of all power, and not some particular power in history, cannot remain good if he becomes a particular power in human society. Perfect goodness in history can be symbolized only by the disavowal of power. But this did not become clear until the One appeared who rejected all concepts of Messianic dominion and became a "suffering servant."

Prophetic Messianism did not arrive at this answer. But the great contribution of prophetic Messianism consists in the fact that it interpreted history too profoundly to allow the solution of the Messianic king to remain tenable. It saw history involved in the inevitable tragedy of tempting the rulers and the nations, who performed a special mission in history, to the sins of pride and injustice.

c. Thus a new religio-ethical dimension is introduced into the interpretation of history, which must be considered in terms of the relation of prophetism to Messianism.

2. *Prophetic Messianism*

Hebraic prophetism enters the history of culture with a strong criticism of current Messianism by the first of the literary prophets, Amos.[6] This criticism is sometimes interpreted as a rejection of the nationalistic implications of Messianism in favor of a more universalistic conception. This interpretation is correct as far as it goes; for Amos undoubtedly regarded the "Holy One of Israel" as a God who transcended the interests of Israel. Amos prophesied judgment upon other nations as well as upon Israel [7] and declares in Yahweh's name, that his sovereignty is manifested in the destiny of other peoples as well as in the history of Israel. Thus Amos' words: "Are ye not as children of the Ethiopians unto me, O children of Israel? saith Yahweh. Have not I brought up Israel out of the land of Egypt? and the Philistine from Caphtor, and the Syrians from Kir?" [8] have rightly been regarded as the first comprehension of universal history in human culture. Here history is seen not from the perspective of a nation but as a universal whole. And God is regarded as the sovereign of all peoples.

The anti-nationalistic emphasis in the oracles of Amos is heightened by his specific judgment of the destruction of Israel by the God of Israel, who is not dependent upon the triumph of his chosen

---

[6] Amos' strictures against current Messianism are contained in the words: "Woe unto you that desire the day of Yahweh! to what end is it for you? The day of Yahweh is darkness, and not light." Amos 5:18.

[7] Upon Damascus 1:3–5, upon Philistia 1:6–8, upon Ammon 1:13–15 and upon Moab 2:1–3.

[8] Amos 9:7.

nation for his glory.[9] Moreover the nationalistic priesthood regards his message as a threat to Israel. Amaziah, the priest, suggests that his prophesies of judgment upon the northern kingdom may be prompted by prejudices as a member of the southern kingdom.[10] Thus Amos' insights become the fountain source of the ethical-universalistic note in Hebraic prophecy. Viewed merely from the perspective of the history of ethics it is therefore not wrong to think of the prophetic movement as the consummation of the universalistic tendencies in the Hebraic interpretation of life and history, even if one recognizes, as one must, that prophetism is never completely purged of the nationalistic imperialistic interpretation of the meaning of history.

Nevertheless such an ethical interpretation of prophetism obscures its real profundity. Amos' predictions of judgment upon Israel are really only incidental to a more far-reaching criticism of all forms of optimistic Messianism. We cannot even be certain that the current Messianic ideas which Amos criticizes were purely nationalistic. They may have contained elements of universalism. The "day of Yahweh" may have been regarded as a triumph of God over the "dragon" or "serpent," symbol of the power of evil in history.[11] At any rate it is not so much the particularism as the optimism of the Messianic conceptions which comes under the prophet's strictures; and his criticisms make no concessions to the Messianic hope of the fulfillment of history in either nationalistic or universal terms.[12] For Amos' history is primarily a series of judgments, first upon

[9] Amos 3:2: "You only have I known of all the families of the earth: therefore I will punish you for all your iniquities."

[10] Amos 7:12: "Also Amaziah said unto Amos, O thou seer, go, flee thee away into the land of Judah, and there eat bread and prophesy there. But prophesy not again any more at Bethel; for it is the king's chapel and it is the king's court."

[11] Cf. *inter alia* W. O. E. Oesterley, *The Evolution of the Messianic Idea*, Ch. 16.

[12] If we assume, as most Old Testament critics do, that the hopeful words of Amos 9:11–15 are interpolated.

Israel and then upon all the nations. The judgment falls with particular severity upon Israel, precisely because it has been singled out
for a special mission in history and has failed to perform it. Israel's
special mission gives it no special security in history. On the contrary it is the assumption that it has a special security and can count
upon a special divine favour, which represents the corruption of
pride which must be punished.

If the implications of this conception of God's relation to history
are fully analysed it will become apparent that Hebraic prophetism
is not so much the triumph of universalism in the history of ethics
as the beginning of revelation in the history of religion. It is the
beginning of revelation because here, for the first time, in the history
of culture the eternal and divine is not regarded as the extension
and fulfillment of the highest human possibilities, whether conceived
in particularistic or universalistic terms. God's word is spoken *against*
both his favoured nation and against all nations. This means that
prophetism has the first understanding of the fact that the real
problem of history is not the finiteness of all human endeavors,
which must wait for their completion by divine power. The real
problem of history is the proud pretension of all human endeavors,
which seeks to obscure their finite and partial character and thereby
involves history in evil and sin.

When a word of God is spoken not only against a nation, but
against all nations, because they are all involved in pride and injustice, human culture as an enterprise which seeks to comprehend the
meaning of life and history from any or all human perspectives is
transcended. Here revelation, with its correlate of faith, begins. The
correlate is faith, because prophetism, unlike mysticism, does not
make the effort to find the eternal and divine, which has eluded
it in history, in some deeper level of human consciousness. It
apprehends a divine word of judgment, spoken against the whole
human enterprise, by faith. It can only be by faith because man
can transcend himself sufficiently to know that an ultimate word

may be spoken against him; but he cannot himself speak that word.[13]

a. The relation of prophetism to Messianism

The subsequent history of Hebraic prophetism and Messianism contains the two elements of nationalistic and universalistic Messianism in various compounds, together with the new dimension in the interpretation of history which was added by prophetism and for which Messianism never finds an adequate answer.

Contrary to evolutionary interpretations of prophetic thought, the conflict between the nationalistic and universalistic motifs in prophetism are not resolved by a gradual triumph of the latter over the former. The universalistic note is present, as we have seen, in the

[13] There is of course no absolute beginning for anything in history, including the beginning of "revelation." However sharply defined the idea of divine transcendence may be in Hebraic prophetism, Martin Buber plausibly maintains in his *Koenigtum Gottes* that this prophetic idea of divine transcendence is involved in the monotheism of Israel from the beginning. According to Buber the highly developed concept of transcendent majesty in Isaiah 45:5–10 is no different than the idea implied in the decalogue when God declares: "I am the Lord thy God, which brought thee out of the land of Egypt, from the house of bondage; thou shalt have none other gods before me" (Deuteronomy 5:6–7). "Nothing has been added or subtracted," writes Buber, "an unconditioned character implicit at first, now expresses itself explicitly" (p. 89).

There is of course no possibility of determining to what degree prophetic conceptions have been read back into Israel's history. But on the other hand Buber is right in seeing that something of the prophetic conception was implicit from the beginning, or the fully developed idea could not have gained credence.

This whole question is important because it reveals the very dialectical relation between "natural" and "revealed" religion. The whole relation is determined by the very character of human self-transcendence. Man transcends himself sufficiently to know that he cannot be the centre of his own existence and that his nation, culture or civilization cannot be the end of history. This is the "natural" ground for revelation. But he does not transcend himself in such a way as to be able to state the end of existence, except as, by faith, he apprehends the voice of God who speaks to him and "against" him.

first of the great prophets, Amos. It wins no gradual ascendancy over the nationalistic one. In the prophet Joel the nationalistic inter-pretation of history reaches extravagant proportions while the book of Jonah must be regarded as primarily a refutation of such national-ism. In Isaiah there are inconsistent elements of both nationalism and universalism.[14] In the apocalyptic books, which bring Hebraic Messianism to a consummation, history sometimes culminates in a general resurrection [15] while other apocalypses anticipate only the resurrection of Israel.[16] Purely nationalistic versions of Messianism were still powerful in Jesus' own day and his second temptation in the wilderness is presumably an account of his rejection of the political-nationalistic conception of the Messianic task.[17]

But this conflict is not the primary problem of prophetic Mes-sianism. The real issue is between the highest form of Messianism (according to which history culminates in an age which resolves the problem of justice by combining power and goodness in the person of a Messianic king), and the insight of prophetism according to which all nations and peoples are involved in rebellion against God. The problem of the meaning of history according to prophetism is how history can be anything more than judgment, which is to say, whether the promise of history can be fulfilled at all.

This higher problem becomes the unsolved question of prophetic Messianism. For it is hardly too much to say that insofar as proph-etism expresses itself in Messianic hopes it does not do very much more than refine and elaborate the ethical note which was present in preprophetic Messianism. It condemns the "rulers," the "judges"

---

[14] Isaiah predicts both a final judgment upon the Gentiles and the wicked in Israel (Isaiah 17:9–14) and a judgment upon the Gentiles and a vindication of Israel (Isaiah 13:9 to 14:2). The same ambiguity is to be found in Malachi (3:18 and 4:3) and in Zechariah (Ch. 12).

[15] As in the Book of Enoch, the Testament of the Twelve Patriarchs, the Apocalypse of Baruch and the Fourth Ezra.

[16] As in II Maccabees, Assumption of Moses and in portions of the Book of Enoch.

[17] Luke 4:5.

and the "princes" of Israel who "turn aside the poor in the gate from their right"[18] and who "swallow up the needy even to make the poor of the land to fail."[19] This is the note in Hebraic prophetism and Messianism which is the fountain and source of radical ethico-political criticism upon the pride of rulers and the injustice of the powerful.[20] The Messianic hope which corresponds to this prophetic criticism is the hope of the ideal Davidic, shepherd king in whose reign injustice and conflict will be overcome and justice and peace will be established. The hope is expressed in more or less transcendent terms. In the apocalyptic literature the transcendent note is heightened. The Davidic king is supplanted by the "son of man," who is a transcendent and heavenly figure; and the fulfillment of history becomes also the end of history; for the finite and natural basis of history is superseded.[21] There is, in other words, a consistent recognition of the sources of conflict and injustice and a realization of the fact that the ethical ideals of history transcend the limitations of nature and finiteness; but this realization becomes more pronounced and explicit in the apocalypses as compared with the Messianic hope of the prophets.

Yet this development in which the Messianic reign is conceived in more and more consistently transcendental terms does nothing to solve the problem which prophetism had introduced into Messianic thought. For the real problem of prophetism is not the finite char-

[18] Amos 5:12.
[19] *Ibid.*, 8:4.
[20] Cf. *inter alia,* Isaiah 3:16, Isaiah 5:8, Micah 2:1-2, Hosea 10:13, Isaiah 61:8 and many other passages too numerous to mention.
[21] The Messianic reign transcends the limitations of nature even in as early a version as that of Isaiah, according to which "the wolf also shall dwell with the lamb, and the leopard shall lie down with the kid" (Isaiah 11:6). In the vision of Ezekiel the hope of peace and justice carries with it the expectation of a change in nature: "Therefore will I save my flock, and they shall no more be a prey; and I will judge between cattle and cattle. And I will set up one shepherd over them . . . And I will make with them a covenant of peace, and will cause the evil beasts to cease out of the land" (Ezekiel 34:22-25).

acter of all historical achievement, though that remains one of the subordinate problems. The real problem is presented by the prophetic recognition that all history is involved in a perennial defiance of the law of God.

The prophets believe that Israel is especially guilty before God precisely because it is uniquely commissioned by God and seeks falsely to derive a special security from this mission. According to Micah, Israel declares: "Is not the Lord among us? None evil can come upon us." And this presumption leads to a terrible judgment: "Therefore shall Zion for your sake be plowed as a field." [22] This sin rises higher than the injustices which flow from power, and the wars which issue from competing will-to-power. It is the more primal sin of pride.[23]

The failure of Israel to fulfill its special historical destiny is regarded by the prophets as an ineluctable fate, though they do not for that reason excuse it. Here the prophetic interpretation of history approaches the Christian doctrine of original sin.[24]

If taken seriously, the consummation of history cannot be a Messianic reign which helps the righteous to triumph over the unrighteous, or which resolves the conflicts of history in a reign of peace, or which abases the mighty and exalts the poor and the meek. The consummation of history can only be in a divine mercy which makes something more of history than merely recurring judgment. The problem of history, according to prophetism, is not that God should be revealed as strong enough to overcome the defiance of

---

[22] Micah 3:11–12.

[23] See Chs. V and VII in Vol. I.

[24] Jeremiah expresses his pessimism in the words: "Can the Ethiopian change his skin, or the leopard his spots? Then may ye also do good, that are accustomed to do evil" (Jeremiah 13:23). And Isaiah has an even more deeply pessimistic conception of the effect of the divine word upon Israel. The consequence of the divine word is to "make the heart of this people fat, and make their ears heavy and shut their eyes"; and this spiritual obtuseness will not yield to anything but a judgment in which the "cities be wasted without an inhabitant" (Isaiah 6:9 ff.).

the evil against His will; but as having resources of mercy great enough to redeem as well as to judge all men.

It is significant that, though the prophets begin by the realization of the sin of pride in the life of Israel, the idea is gradually expanded to become a principle of interpretation for the whole of history. All the nations are regarded as being in rebellion against God. Each in its turn receives some special mission from God or enjoys some special privilege and makes its momentary eminence or security the basis of a pride which must finally destroy it.[25]

It is this level of prophetic insight for which prophetic Messianism has no answer. The prophets do of course affirm the mercy of God as well as the awfulness of His wrath and the certainty of His judgments. But there is no certainty about the relation of mercy to judgment. On the whole the prophetic recognition of this ultimate problem is most perfectly expressed in the longing for mercy recorded in Isaiah 64: "Oh that thou wouldest rend the heavens, that thou wouldest come down, that the mountains might flow down at thy presence. . . . When thou didst terrible things which we looked not for, thou camest down, the mountains flowed down at thy presence. . . . But we are all as an unclean thing, and all our righteousnesses are as filthy rags. . . . For thou hast hid thy face from us, and hast consumed us, because of our iniquities. . . . Be not wroth very sore, O Lord, neither remember iniquity for ever."[26] The distinction between the righteous and the unrighteous disappears in the discovery that "all our righteousnesses are as filthy rags" and that "we are all as an unclean thing." The assurance that God will complete history by overcoming the ambiguity of the momentary triumph of evil yields to the question of how God will complete history by overcoming the perennial evil in every human good. The "hidden" sovereignty of God, which demands a fuller disclosure in the Messianic reign, is hidden, not because the divine power is not

[25] See particularly Ezekiel's series of judgments upon the nations. Ezekiel 26–34.
[26] Isaiah 64:1–9.

fully disclosed but because the relation of divine mercy to divine wrath remains a mystery.

b. The failure of Messianism to answer the prophetic problem

If we are to understand why the true Christ was a "stumbling-block" to the Jews, that is to those who expected a Christ, as well as foolishness to the Gentiles who did not expect him, and why Christian faith regards him as the true Christ both because he was expected and because he was not the Christ who was expected, it is necessary to see why Hebraic Messianism (though able to rise from particularism to universalism, and from an inchoate to an explicit recognition of the fact that the fulfillment of history transcended the finite and natural basis of history), was never able to come to terms fully with the issue which prophetism had raised. There were two reasons for this failure.

The first reason was that the misery of Israel during and after the exile made it difficult and well-nigh impossible to face the ultimate issue of history before the pressing perplexities of the penultimate issue. The people of Israel had been judged by God for their sins, and history had executed His terrible wrath. But when they reflected upon their fate they were overwhelmed by the incongruity of the fact that the jailers and executors of divine judgment were worse than they. The prophets might well insist that the nemesis of each proud nation would come in turn; but that did not change the immediate impression of a very unjust history which obscured the justice of God. This is to say that a "vertical" interpretation of history in which all men and nations are judged for falling short of the divine demands still leaves the problem of the relative good and evil of any short span of history unsolved, and more particularly the seeming triumph of the relatively evil over the relatively good.[27]

[27] Our own generation would have faced this same perplexity in the event of the triumph of tyranny over the forces of democratic civilization. Such a triumph would undoubtedly reveal all the weaknesses and vices of the democratic civilization and in that sense would have been

Inevitably, the Messianic hope, which holds out the prospect of a triumph of the good over evil in history, will gain the ascendancy over a more ultimate hope in any catastrophic period in which the momentary triumph of the relative evil over the relative good threatens history with meaninglessness. The questions, "Why do the righteous suffer?" and "Why do the wicked triumph?" were bound to pre-occupy the mind of Israel in the exilic and post-exilic period.

But there is an even profounder reason why the more ultimate issue raised by prophetism could not be answered in prophetic Messianism. It is an affront to human self-righteousness. We shall see to what degree the Christian faith, though explicitly accepting the ultimate issue, is subject to covert denials of it.[28] It is comparatively easy for man to recognize his weakness and to know that he is too inextricably involved in history as process and flux to be able to complete it. But it is not so easy to recognize that his premature and pretentious efforts to fulfill what he cannot fulfill involve human history in tragic realities of sin, which only a divine mercy can purge. For this reason the most plausible culmination of Messianism is one which substitutes the "righteous" for a particular race or nation and then looks forward to the culmination of history and the vindication of God through the triumph and the vindication of the righteous of all nations.

Furthermore, it is a question whether it is possible to interpret life and history consistently in terms of a problem for which the answer is not known. The final problem of prophetism is one for which Messianism had no answer. It is natural, therefore, that it should justified as a divine judgment upon the sins of civilization. But the question would still remain: Why should the tyrants triumph? Why should those who are more evil than ourselves be the executors of judgment? Under the pressure of that perplexity every vital religion will deal with proximate as well as with ultimate problems of history. It will hope for the destruction of tyranny as a mediate goal of history, whatever may be its insights into the ultimate problem of life and history.

[28] Chs. V–VII.

revert to the problem for which it had the answer. It was certain that the hidden sovereignty of God would guarantee the ultimate triumph of good over evil in history. But it was not certain how the divine mercy is related to the divine wrath and how the perplexity of a total history standing in defiance of God would be resolved.

It is particularly interesting to note how the apocalyptic writings (in which Hebraic Messianism culminates and in which, despite a fantastic imagery, the logic implied in this Messianism is really driven to its final conclusion) [29] deal with this issue. The apocalyptic books generally look forward to the final disclosure of the "hidden" Messiah, which is to say that the Messianic reign is regarded as the final revelation of the obscured sovereignty of God and the confused meaning of history.[30] This final disclosure is conceived, on the whole, as a vindication of God and the righteous. The unrighteous will be destroyed; and some of the apocalyptic books imaginatively and proleptically indulge in a veritable orgy of vindictive triumph. Yet the more ultimate problem appears again and again as an afterthought.[31] The most remarkable relation between the ultimate and penultimate problem of history is to be found in one of the latest and certainly one of the profoundest books of apocalyptic literature:

---

[29] The idea that Hebraic apocalypse is a corruption rather than a logical culmination of the Messianic hope has gained currency in secularized schools of criticism which do not understand the basic significance of the problem of time and eternity, of history and super-history with which the apocalyptic writings are concerned.

[30] In the Similitudes of Enoch the hidden Messiah is described as follows: "Before the suns and the signs were created and before the stars of the heavens were made his name was uttered before the Lord of spirits. . . . He hath been chosen and *hidden,* before him before world was created."

[31] In the Book of Enoch there are interpolations which dwell upon the necessity of mercy as well as of judgment. Both in the Psalms of Solomon and the Similitudes of Enoch the final problem of the relation of judgment to mercy is alluded to. *Cf.* J. Wicks, *The Doctrine of God in Jewish Apocryphal and Apocalyptic Literature.*

the Ezra Apocalypse. In the so-called Salathiel vision of this late apocalypse the questions of the "seer" are always put in terms of the ultimate problem, while God's answers always reassure the seer by assurances taken from the conventional Messianic hope. He is told that the righteous will triumph and the unrighteous will perish and that it is not his business to worry about the fate of the latter. But this answer does not resolve his perplexities; for his problem is whether there are any righteous who deserve to triumph.[32]

This apocalyptic book, actually written, or at least compiled, in the Christian era, leaves a profound impression with its invariably right questions and its usually wrong answers. Here is the perfect symbol of how Hebraic prophetism overreaches itself with an ultimate question for which it has no answer, and which it seeks to suppress because it lacks the answer.

This must be understood, if the Christian answer to the Messianic question is to be appreciated; and if we are to realize how the Christ validates himself as the true Christ both by fulfilling and by disappointing Messianic expectations.

[32] *Cf.* iv Ezra 7:45: "And now I see that the coming age shall bring delight to the few but torment to the many. For the evil heart has grown up in us which has estranged us from God, and brought us to destruction, . . . *and not a few only but well nigh all that have been created.*"

iv Ezra 7:118–120: "O thou Adam what hast thou done? For though it wast thou that hast sinned, the fall was not thine alone but also ours who are thy descendants. For how does it profit us that the eternal age is promised us whereas we have done the works that bring death? And that there is foretold us an imperishable hope whereas we are so miserably brought to futility."

CHAPTER II

THE DISCLOSURE AND THE FULFILLMENT OF THE MEANING OF LIFE AND HISTORY

CHRISTIANITY ENTERS the world with the stupendous claim that in Christ (that is in both the character of Christ and the epic of his life) the expectations of the ages have been fulfilled. The specific form of this claim was the belief that the Kingdom of God had come, or in the words of Jesus, "This day is this scripture fulfilled in your ears." [1] The claim was that in the life, death and resurrection of Christ, the expected disclosure of God's sovereignty over history, and the expected establishment of that sovereignty had taken place. In this disclosure of the power and will which governs history, both life and history had found their previously partly hidden and partly revealed meaning, though it is not denied that God remains, despite this revelation, partly *Deus absconditus.*

Before analysing the import of this "absurd" claim further,[2] it is necessary to explore the relation of the meaning of life, the meaning of history, and the sovereignty of God. The prophetic-Messianic hope anticipates the disclosure and fulfillment of the meaning of history through the revelation and establishment of God's sov-

[1] Luke 4:21.
[2] St. Paul admits the absurdity of the claim. It is "foolishness" to the Greeks, a "stumblingblock" to the Jews: it is the "foolishness of God" which is "wiser than men." 1 Cor. 1:25.

ereignty. This expectation is explicit in including the meaning of history in the meaning of life. Implicitly it assumes that the meaning of life transcends the meaning of history. If history cannot find its meaning except in the disclosure of a divine sovereignty, which both governs and transcends it, it is implicitly, though not explicitly, assumed that history, however meaningful, cannot give life its full meaning. Each individual transcends and is involved in the historical process. In so far as he is involved in history, the disclosure of life's meaning must come to him in history. In so far as he transcends history the source of life's meaning must transcend history.

This is covertly or implicitly recognized in prophetic Messianism because of the element of transcendence in its expectations. It is always looking toward the fuller disclosure of a God who transcends and is yet immanent in the historical process. Furthermore the ultimate level of prophetic Messianism states the problem of human existence in terms which history cannot solve. Each life and each portion of history are found to stand in proud and rebellious contradiction to the divine and eternal purpose; which means that only a transcendent mercy can overcome this contradiction.

The fact that the meaning of life transcends the meaning of history is only implicitly recognized in prophetic Messianism, for the "Kingdom of God" is expected on earth, however much it is a transmuted and sublimated "earth" or nature which becomes the scene of the Kingdom. This lack of explicitness is partly overcome in the apocalyptic culmination of the prophetic movement, in which it is literally a "new heaven" and a "new earth" which become the scene of the Messianic kingdom. It is particularly significant that in this expected fulfillment of the Messianic kingdom, the individuals of previous ages are resurrected to participate in the culmination of history. This is symbolic of the fact that each individual is believed to stand in a direct relation to the eternal by reason of transcending the historical process; and are also known to stand in an indirect relation to it, by reason of being involved in the historical process. The Christian belief that the meaning of both life and history is disclosed and fulfilled in Christ and his Cross, is in a sense a combination of Hellenic and Hebraic interpretations of life. It conforms to the Hellenic interpretations of life because in these there is an understanding of the fact that the meaning of life transcends history; but in them history tends to be excluded from the realm of meaning, and life is fulfilled by escaping from the historical process. In Christianity it is fulfilled, though not wholly, within the historical process. New Testament faith conforms to the Hebraic interpretations of life because in them life is fulfilled in history, though in Christianity the implicit difference between "life" and "history" is made explicit. That is why Christianity is preached to both "Jews and Greeks" though it develops on the ground of Hebraism and not on the ground of Hellenism. It is a greater "foolishness" to the Greeks who do not expect a Christ at all, than it is a "stumblingblock" to the Jews, who expect a different kind of Christ.[3]

To the Greeks the Christ is foolishness because he represents a disclosure of the eternal in history. In so far as history participates in flux and in "becoming" it is not able, according to Greek opinion, to anticipate or entertain a disclosure of the eternal will which underlies it. In so far as man has within himself some element of the eternal "being" which transcends flux and finiteness, no disclosure of the eternal will is necessary. To declare, as Christian faith does,

---

[3] There is of course no completely consistent merging of Hellenic and Hebraic, of mystic and apocalyptic viewpoints in the New Testament, nor a consistent dominance of the latter over the former. Broadly speaking the synoptic gospels are consistently apocalyptic and the conception of the Kingdom of God, which dominates synoptic thought, is one which expresses the historical-apocalyptic approach to life. In the thought of St. Paul apocalyptic and mystic viewpoints stand in uneasy tension to each other, but the apocalyptic predominates. The Fourth Gospel on the other hand represents a tension of the two viewpoints under the dominance of the mystic. The Johannine conception of "eternal life" is a slightly Hellenized version of the synoptic "Kingdom of God." But it is significant that the Fourth Gospel is not consistently Greek in its presuppositions. Its retention of the idea of the resurrection is indicative of its organic relation to the synoptic-Hebraic viewpoint.

that a disclosure of the eternal will and purpose is both possible and necessary is to accept the paradox of man and history fundamentally. It is to understand that man is, even in the highest reaches of his transcendent freedom, too finite to comprehend the eternal by his own resources. But it is also understood that man is, even in the deepest involvement of process and nature, too free of nature to be blind to the possibilities of a disclosure of the Eternal which transcends him.

II

JESUS' OWN REINTERPRETATION OF PROPHETIC MESSIANISM

The Christian community came into being by the faith that Jesus was the Christ who had fulfilled the expectations of the ages. But this belief runs counter to the actual expectations of the prophetic movement in the period of its culmination. The Christ whom Christian faith accepts is the same Christ whom Messianism rejects, as not conforming to its expectations. The acceptance would not have been possible if Jesus had not himself transformed the Messianic expectation in the process of negating and fulfilling it.[1]

In tracing how Jesus himself reinterpreted prophetic Messianism, it is necessary to begin with an aspect of his teaching which concerns not the reinterpretation but the acceptance of the prophetic-Messianic tradition.

[1] The final truth about life is always an absurdity but it cannot be an absolute absurdity. It is an absurdity inasfar as it must transcend the "system" of meaning which the human mind always prematurely constructs with itself as the centre. But it cannot be a complete absurdity or it could not achieve any credence. In this sense Kierkegaard goes too far in his statement: "Anything that is almost probable or probable, or extremely and emphatically probable, is something he [man] can almost know, or as good as know, or extremely and emphatically almost know —but it is impossible to believe. For the absurd is the object of faith, and the only object that can be believed." *Concluding Unscientific Postscript*, translated by D. F. Swenson and W. Lowrie, p. 189. The relation between Kierkegaard's view and Barth's theory of the relation of revelation to culture is obvious. *Cf.* Karl Barth, *The Doctrine of the Word of God*, pp. 226 ff.

1. *Jesus' Rejection of Hebraic Legalism*

The most obvious conflict in the gospels is not between types of Messianism but between the Messianism in terms of which Jesus interprets his life and ministry, and the official legalism of his day. His conflict with the Pharisees is, in a sense, a final conflict in the heart of Hebraism between two facets of Hebraic spirituality: legalism and Messianism. They existed side by side, partly contra-dicting and partly supplementing each other from the very begin-ning of known Hebraic history. The Deuteronomic code was an effort to place legalism in the service of prophetism and to give to prophetic insights the permanence of legal codes. Beginning with the restoration of the second temple and ending with its destruction in 70 A.D. legalism gained a gradual ascendancy over prophetism, so that in Jesus' own day the apocalyptic movement, which informed his thought, was borne by unofficial rather than official Judaism. There was, of course, no absolute distinction between them, since Phariseeism had its own apocalyptic tendencies.

Legalism is a kind of arrested and atrophied religion of history. In Hebraism it rests upon the idea that the God, who delivered Israel out of the land of Egypt, made the decalogue a part of the covenant between Himself and the nation. This legalism is there-fore type and symbol of every form of legalistic religious conscious-ness which binds the counsels of God prematurely to a law which is contingent to time and place. The Talmudic reinterpretations, applications and extensions of the Torah seek to do justice to the endless variety of problems and occasions for which the original law seems to be inadequate. But the policy of adding law to law cannot solve the essential weakness of law as the disclosure of the divine purpose in history. Jesus observed that the glosses, footnotes and reinterpretations of the elders actually had the effect of diluting the original force of the law.[2]

The criticisms of legalism in both the gospels and epistles give

[2] Mt. 15:6. "Thus have ye made the commandment of God of none effect by your tradition."

an indirect insight into a prophetic rather than legalistic interpretation of life. The criticisms take the following forms:

(*a*) No law can do justice to the freedom of man in history. It cannot state the final good for him, since in his transcendence and self-transcendence no order of nature and no rule of history can finally determine the norm of his life. This may be the import of Jesus' statement: "Except your righteousness shall exceed the righteousness of the scribes and Pharisees, ye shall in no case enter the kingdom of heaven." [3] In the Pauline epistles this emphasis upon the transcendence of the human spirit over any particular law is expressed in the Pauline word: "Stand fast therefore in the liberty wherewith Christ hath made us free, and be not entangled again with the yoke of bondage," [4] which is to say that no proximate law, but only an ultimate law, represented by a disclosure of God's own nature can be normative for man.

(*b*) No law can do justice to the complexities of motive which express themselves in the labyrinthine depths of man's interior life. This is the burden of Jesus' paradoxical extension of the law to the point of its abrogation in the Sermon on the Mount [5] in which the demands of the law are extended so that hate as well as murder, lust as well as divorce are prohibited. But this means in effect that law is relativized as social law, since the demands exceed anything which could be enforced by society upon the individual. Law becomes a matter between God and the individual.

(*c*) Law cannot restrain evil; for the freedom of man is such that he can make the keeping of the law the instrument of evil. He can screen evil motives by outward conformity to the law: "For ye make clean the outside of the cup and of the platter, but within they are full of extortion and excess." [6] He can also use observance of the law as the vehicle of sinful pride. [7] These criticisms, whether indicating the law's inability to define the ultimate good or to restrain

[3] Mt. 5:20.   [5] Mt. 5:27–48.
[4] Gal. 5:1.   [6] Mt. 23:25.
[7] The parable of the Pharisee and Publican, Lk. 18:9 ff.

the ultimate evil, namely, man's use of virtue as the vehicle of pride, all reveal Christ's understanding of life and history in terms of the heights of its freedom.[8] They are criticisms which are possible only from a perspective which assumes the dimension of Eternity in human history, knows the height and depth of good and evil in each moment of existence and realizes the futility of capturing the vitalities of human existence in any system or of fixing the infinite possibilities of life upon any particular level.

The conflict between Jesus and the Pharisees is thus a final conflict between the prophetic-Messianic and the legalistic facets in Hebraism. In modern Judaism there are both legalistic and mystical tendencies but no strong forward-looking historical tendencies. The sense of history expresses itself retrospectively. In modern Jewish life Messianic and apocalyptic tendencies, still surviving in the ethos of Hebraism, have been forced to find expression in secularized versions of Messianism, such as the liberal idea of progress and Marxism or in slightly heterodox movements such as Hassidism. Christianity appropriated the prophetic Messianic tradition, though, of course, not in such a way as to render the Christian tradition immune to recurring fallacies of legalism. The tendency to find a premature security, a premature righteousness and a superficial sense of meaning in law, is a recurring tendency in all life and culture.

2. *Jesus' Rejection of Nationalistic Particularism*

While it is wrong to assume, as is sometimes done, that Jesus' rejection of the nationalistic element in prophetic Messianism represents his primary emphasis in the reinterpretation of prophetic Messianism, it is obviously true that the Messianic interpretations which verge on nationalistic idolatry are rejected, despite such remnants of nationalistic interpretations as are found in his encounter with the

[8] The Pauline attitude towards the law includes most of these criticisms but adds the significant idea that the law is powerless. It states a norm without giving power to fulfill it.

Syrophenician woman. There the assertion that "I am sent but to the lost sheep of the house of Israel" may be regarded as a tentative and testing remark which is refuted by Jesus' own assurance to the alien woman: "O woman, great is thy faith: be it unto thee even as thou wilt." [9]

The story of the Good Samaritan obviously implies the rejection of nationalistic Messianism and the account of the temptation in the wilderness includes the rejection of the idea of a national triumph as a legitimate Messianic hope.[10] One of the most perfect disavowals of nationalism in the gospels is to be found in a word of John the Baptist: "And think not to say within yourselves, We have Abraham to our father; for I say unto you, that God is able of these stones to raise up children unto Abraham." [11] Here the freedom of God over the instruments of his will, very specially over the one chosen instrument, the nation of Israel, is asserted according to highest insights of prophetic universalism, as against the lower level of nationalistic Messianism. It is significant, however, that Christianity does not finally purge itself of nationalistic particularism until St. Paul asserts the right to preach the gospel to the Gentiles, rejects the validity of the Jewish law for Christians, and substitutes the church for the nation as the "Israel of God." However important it may be to recognize the rejection of nationalism in Jesus' interpretation of prophecy, it is quite wrong to imagine that this represents the final achievement of Jesus' Messianism, though modern interpretations of Christianity, which see no more in Jesus' life and ministry than the culmination of a certain moral development, frequently confine Jesus' Messianism to these proportions.

3. *Jesus' Rejection of the Answer of Hebraic Messianism for the Problem Presented by Prophetism*

We have previously noted that prophetism presents a problem for which Messianism has no adequate answer; and that this problem

[9] Mt. 15:21 ff.; Mk. 7:24 ff.   [10] Mt. 4:1 ff.   [11] Mt. 3:9.

became obscured again and again, partly because the vicissitudes of Israel's history accentuated the necessity of the vindication of the righteous over the unrighteous to the exclusion of the more ultimate problem; partly because the ultimate problem of prophetism is an affront to human self-esteem; and partly because it is a problem for which there is no answer within the limits of Messianism. This ultimate problem is given by the fact that human history stands in contradiction to the divine will on any level of its moral and religious achievements in such a way that in any "final" judgment the righteous are proved not to be righteous. The final enigma of history is therefore not how the righteous will gain victory over the unrighteous, but how the evil in every good and the unrighteousness of the righteous is to be overcome.

This enigma is involved in the prophetic interpretation of history, beginning with Amos' rigorous analysis of the pride of nations and running through the whole of prophetic literature. But it remains a mystery only partly disclosed and not at all solved until Jesus makes it the basis for his reinterpretation of Messianism. Jesus' parable of the Last Judgment [12] reveals the logic of this reinterpretation most perfectly. The symbolism of the parable, the picture of the Messianic judge separating the sheep from the goats, the righteous from the unrighteous, is a recurring motif of apocalyptic literature. Jesus accepts it and on one level of his own interpretation it would appear that history culminates in the Messianic vindication of the righteous and the destruction of the wicked. But a significant new note is added. The righteous are humble and do not believe themselves to be righteous. They accept the judge's commendation with the confession, "Lord, when saw we thee an hungred, and fed thee? or thirsty, and gave thee drink? When saw we thee a stranger, and took thee in? or naked, and clothed thee? or when saw we thee sick, or in prison, and came unto thee?" [13] While the righteous are contritely aware of their unworthiness of this vindication, the unrighteous are equally unconscious of their guilt. The distinction

[12] Mt. 25: 31–46.   [13] Mt. 25:37–39.

between the righteous and the unrighteous is significantly not obscured. There are those who serve their fellowmen and there are those who do not. But the ones who do are conscious of the fact that in any final judgment they are discovered not to have fulfilled the law of life; while the ones who do not are too self-centred to know of their sin. Thus the final judgment, as Jesus sees it, actually includes both levels of prophetic Messianism, the more purely moral and the supra-moral. The distinction between good and evil in history is not destroyed; yet it is asserted that in the final judgment there are no righteous, i.e., in their own eyes. Jesus' conflict with Pharisaic self-righteousness is governed by the same conviction. It is the contrite publican who is "justified" before the righteous Pharisee, for "whosoever shall exalt himself shall be abased; and he that shall humble himself shall be exalted." [14]

 Here then is the first reason why Jesus' Messianism was an offense and was bound to be rejected. The fact that it affronted the egotism of a nation was insignificant beside the greater offense of outraging the pride of man as man. The second reason for the "offensive" character of Jesus' Messianism was in the answer which he gave to the problem emphasized by this reinterpretation of life and history. This answer is most succinctly stated in his own words, "The Son of man must suffer." [15] The answer introduces the outrageous idea of a suffering Messiah into the Messianic thought, which had not entertained any other conception than that of a triumphant Messiah. The idea that the "Son of man must suffer" represents a combination of the "son of man" idea taken from the apocalypses of Daniel and Enoch and the idea of the "suffering servant" taken from Isaiah 53. The figure of the "son of man" is that of a heavenly conqueror and judge, through whom history is brought to culmination. The suffering servant figure is not a Messianic symbol; or, if so, only in a very secondary sense. Most probably it was meant to designate the nation rather than any individual. If so, it represented a profound effort to give the sufferings of Israel a higher meaning by the

[14] Mt. 23:12.   [15] Mk. 8:31.

suggestion that its mission and triumph in the world would not be achieved by the usual triumph over others but by its vicarious suffering for the sins of others. To declare, as Jesus does, that the Messiah, the representative of God, must suffer, is to make vicarious suffering the final revelation of meaning in history. But it is the vicarious suffering of the representative of God, and not of some force in history, which finally clarifies the obscurities of history and discloses the sovereignty of God over history.

This synthesis of the suffering servant idea in Isaiah and the son of man figure in apocalyptic literature, as Rudolf Otto rightly observes, "was not made bit by bit in the gradual growth of post-humous apologetics in some unknown church but . . . was due to an incomparably original conception on the part of one who could also conceive that the Kingdom was actually coming as he himself has conquered Satan."[16]

The synthesis represents something more than the collation of two hitherto unrelated concepts, the one Messianic and the other quasi-Messianic. It represents a profound reinterpretation of the meaning of history. If the revelation of history's meaning is given through vicarious suffering of a guiltless individual or nation this means one of two things. It may mean that vicarious love is a force in history which gradually gains the triumph over evil and therefore ceases to be tragic. This is the optimistic interpretation which liberal Christianity has given the Cross of Christ. According to this interpretation the power of love in history, as symbolized by the Cross, begins tragically but ends triumphantly. It overcomes evil. But the idea of the suffering servant in history may also mean that vicarious love remains defeated and tragic in history; but has its triumph in the knowledge that it is ultimately right and true. Such a tragic conception still leaves the problem of the evil in history unresolved. How is the evil of history overcome? Does the power of the guilty, under which the guiltless suffer, go on indefinitely? Is history a constant repetition of the triumph of evil on the plane

---

[16] *The Kingdom of God and the Son of Man,* p. 255.

of the obvious and is the triumph of the good merely the inner triumph of its own assurance of being right?

The synthesis of Jesus, according to which the suffering servant is not merely a character of history, but is the representative of the divine, transcends both the simple optimism of the first interpretation and the purely tragic implication of the second conception. It is God Who suffers for man's iniquity. He takes the sins of the world upon and into Himself. This is to say that the contradictions of history are not resolved in history; but they are only ultimately resolved on the level of the eternal and the divine. However, the eternal and the divine which destroys evil is not some undifferentiated eternity which effaces both the good and evil of history by destroying history itself. God's mercy must make itself known in history, so that man in history may become fully conscious of his guilt and his redemption. The Messiah must give his life "a ransom for many."[17]

Thus Jesus' own reinterpretation of Messianism contains the two offensive ideas that the righteous are unrighteous in the final judgment and that God's sovereignty over history is established and his triumph over evil is effected not by the destruction of the evil-doers but by his own bearing of the evil. It must be noted that the second, as well as the first, idea is implied in prophetism, however offensive it may be in its explicit form. Just as the idea that the distinction between the righteous and the unrighteous disappears in the final judgment, is implicit in the most radical prophetic analyses of history, so also the idea that God suffers in history is implicit in the whole Hebraic-prophetic idea that God is engaged and involved in history, and is not some unmoved mover, dwelling in eternal equanimity.[18]

[17] Rudolf Otto calls attention to the fact that *lutron* (ransom) had a unique religious connotation before it had a commercial-juridical meaning. It was a sacrifice by which religious guilt was covered or removed. *Ibid.,* p. 259.

[18] Though implicit in Old Testament theology the idea never became explicit in Judaism. C. G. Montefiore writes: "Rabbinic Judaism, as all

The absurd and offensive nature of Jesus' reinterpretation of Messianism not only prompted his rejection by the Jews. It aroused baffled incredulity in the small circle of his disciples. Peter's reaction to Jesus' prediction of his suffering: "Be it far from thee, Lord: this shall not be unto thee" [19] may be regarded as symbolic of the resistance to the truth of Christianity which develops not only outside, but inside of, the Christian faith. The eschatological fellowship surrounding Jesus could not understand the idea until it had been transmuted into a fact of history. Yet even when transmuted into a fact, the final truth of Christianity is not easily accepted. Nor can it be accepted once and for all. The history of Christianity is the history of the truth of Christ contending constantly against the truth as men see it.

4. *Jesus' Reinterpretation of the Eschata*

Prophetic and apocalyptic hopes anticipated an end which would both disclose and establish the sovereignty of God; which would both reveal the meaning of life and fulfill it. In Jesus' own reinterpretation, these two facets of history's culmination are, at least partially, separated. The indication of this separation is given in the double affirmation that on the one hand the "Kingdom of God has come" and on the other hand that "the Kingdom of God will come." On the one hand, history has reached its culmination in the disclosure of the hidden sovereignty of God and the revelation of the meaning of life and history. On the other hand history is still waiting for its culmination in the second coming of the triumphant

subsequent Judaism, denied in its fullness the doctrine of a 'suffering God.' Perhaps this denial may be the reason why Rabbinic Judaism had little to say upon the subject of suffering which supplements or enlarges or goes beyond the Old Testament. The Rabbis went willingly to martyrdom and they extolled it. But the perception of a certain splendor in suffering or in the endurance of suffering, which most of us would now acknowledge, is wanting in them." Introduction to *A Rabbinic Anthology*, p. xli.

[19] Mt. 16:22.

Messiah. In combining the conceptions of the "suffering servant" and the "Son of man," Jesus, in effect, attributed the qualities of the suffering servant to his first coming and the qualities of the triumphant Son of man to a second coming,[20] either his own or another.

This separation of two aspects of Messianic fulfillment was not altogether new in the thought of Jesus. In later apocalyptic literature the coming of the Messiah and the final judgment, resurrection and culmination of history are not synchronous.[21] In Jesus' own interpretation there was indeed a victory over Satan and the power of evil in the first coming as a suffering servant. Yet ultimate victory was postponed until "The Son of man shall come in the glory of his Father with his angels; and then he shall reward every man according to his works." [22] "The modern theory of 'realized eschatology' according to which the coming of Christ effectively fulfills Messianic prophecies and reduces the promises of a second coming in the New Testament to insignificance, must be challenged. The strain of thought embodied in the New Testament hope of a 'second coming' is indispensable for the Christian interpretation of history and for a true understanding of New Testament thought."[23]

The full implication of the double idea that the "Kingdom of God has come" and that it is "coming" is that history is an interim. Whatever may be the meaning of Jesus' parables of the leaven and the mustard seed, he certainly does not present the "Kingdom"

[20] In a profound analysis of this problem F. D. V. Narborough declares: "Just as our Lord accepted the rôle of the Servant . . . in the present age, so he seems to have accepted the 'Son of man' as, to some extent, an indication of his rôle in the age to come." Narborough's essay in Ch. 2 of *Essays on the Trinity and Incarnation* edited by A. E. J. Rawlinson.

[21] W. O. E. Oesterley declares: "In the Old Testament and Apocalyptic writings the 'last times' by no means always or necessarily imply the end of all things. Although when the last times are to come about is never stated definitely, they are always presented as a process upon which shall follow the inauguration of a new age." *Doctrine of Last Things,* p. 195.

[22] Mt. 16:27.

[23] For exposition of idea of "realized eschatology," see C. H. Dodd, *The Gospel and History.*

which has entered into history through his suffering and death as a force which will gradually transmute history into something quite different from what it is. In obvious contradiction to modern liberal interpretations of the power of love in history, Jesus discourages the hope that the preaching of the gospel will banish evil from history. "In this rejoice not," he warns his disciples, "that the spirits are subject unto you; but rather rejoice, because your names are written in heaven."[24] The love which enters history as suffering love, must remain suffering love in history. Since this love is the very law of history it may have its tentative triumphs even in history; for human history cannot stand in complete contradiction to itself. Yet history does stand in actual contradiction to the law of love; and Jesus anticipates the growth of evil as well as the growth of good in history. Among the signs of the end will be "wars and rumours of wars" and the appearance of false Christs.[25]

In thus conceiving history after Christ as an interim between the disclosure of its true meaning and the fulfillment of that meaning, between the revelation of divine sovereignty and the full establishment of that sovereignty, a continued element of inner contradiction in history is accepted as its perennial characteristic. Sin is overcome in principle but not in fact. Love must continue to be suffering love rather than triumphant love. This distinction becomes a basic category of interpreting history in all profound versions of the Christian faith, and has only recently been eliminated in modern sentimentalized versions of that faith.

One seemingly serious, but actually superficial, change in Jesus' own interpretation must be made. He expected the historic interim between the first and second establishment of the Kingdom to be

---

[24] Lk. 10:20.

[25] Mt. 24:6. This element in Jesus' own eschatology finally achieves its definitive expression in the figure of the "Anti-Christ" in the Johannine epistles, who appears at the end of history. Taken seriously, as it should be, this symbol refutes every modern liberal interpretation of history which identifies "progress" with the Kingdom of God. We shall deal with this issue more fully in Chapter X.

short.[26] In this error he was followed both by St. Paul and the early church, with the consequent false and disappointed hope of the *parousia* in the lifetime of the early disciples. This error was due to an almost inevitable illusion of thought which deals with the problem of the relation of time and eternity. The *eschata* which represent the fulfillment and the end of time in eternity are conceived literally and thereby made a point in time. The sense that the final fulfillment impinges on the present moment, the feeling of urgency in regard to anticipating this fulfillment, expresses itself in chronological terms and thereby becomes transmuted into a "proximate futurism," into the feeling that the fulfillment of history is chronologically imminent.

In reinterpreting the New Testament idea of the *parousia* (and, as we shall see later, all other ideas dealing with the relation of history and super-history, such as resurrection and judgment) it is important to take Biblical symbols seriously but not literally. If they are taken literally the Biblical conception of a dialectical relation between history and superhistory is imperiled; for in that case the fulfillment of history becomes merely another kind of time-history. If the symbols are not taken seriously the Biblical dialectic is destroyed, because in that case concepts of an eternity are connoted in which history is destroyed and not fulfilled.

This single adjustment in the New Testament view is defined as superficial rather than serious to distinguish the idea of "interim" as here used from that of Albert Schweitzer.[27] According to his conception the whole ethic and religion of Jesus is based upon his illusion of his proximate return. The absolute character of his ethic is due, in the opinion of Schweitzer, to the belief that the "time is short." The real fact is that the absolute character of the ethic of Jesus conforms to the actual constitution of man and history, that

[26] Mt. 10:23: "Ye shall not have gone over the cities of Israel till the Son of man be come." Mt. 16:28: "Verily I say unto you, There be some standing here, which shall not taste of death, till they see the Son of man coming in his kingdom."

[27] Cf. *The Quest of the Historical Jesus.*

is, to the transcendent freedom of man over the contingencies of nature and the necessities of time, so that only a final harmony of life with life in love can be the ultimate norm of his existence. Yet man's actual history is subject to contingency and necessity and is corrupted by his sinful efforts to escape and to deny his dependence and his involvement in finiteness. The idea that the time is short expresses Christianity's understanding that these limitations and corruptions of history are not finally normative for man.

Thus reconstructed, the idea that history is an "interim" between the first and the second coming of Christ has a meaning which illumines all the facts of human existence. History, after Christ's first coming, has the quality of partly knowing its true meaning. In so far as man can never be completely in contradiction to his own true nature, history also reveals significant realizations of that meaning. Nevertheless history continues to stand in real contradiction to its true meaning, so that pure love in history must always be suffering love. But the contradictions of history cannot become man's norms, if history is viewed from the perspective of Christ. For the Christian, the anticipation of a final judgment and fulfillment means an emancipation from the proximations of good and the concretions of evil which represent the "standards" of history. Thus the absolute ethical and religious demands of the gospel are not irrelevant, though the expectation of Christ's imminent return has only occasionally been a living hope within the church since the second century. Even the idea of a proximate second coming is not irrelevant when understood symbolically; for it expresses the idea that every moment of time makes not only for the fulfillment of life, but hastens man towards the dissolution of death. This fact of death threatens life with meaninglessness unless man is "saved by hope" and understands life in such a way that neither his involvement in history nor his transcendence over it destroys the meaning of life. To understand life and history according to the meaning given it by Christ is to be able to survey the chaos of any present or the peril of any future, without sinking into despair. It is to have a vantage point from which one may realize that momentary securities are perennially destroyed both by the vicissitudes of history and by the fact of death which stands over all history.

This faith is perfectly expressed in the Pauline confession: "Who shall separate us from the love of Christ? Shall tribulation, or distress, or persecution, or famine, or nakedness, or peril, or sword? . . . Nay in all these things we are more than conquerors through him that loved us. For I am persuaded, that neither death nor life, nor angels, nor principalities, nor powers, nor things present, nor things to come, nor height, nor depth, nor any other creature, shall be able to separate us from the love of God, which is in Christ Jesus our Lord." [28]

III

THE ACCEPTANCE BY CHRISTIAN FAITH OF THE EXPECTED
AND THE REJECTED MESSIAH

The correlate of revelation is faith. The mutual relation between the two is so close that revelation cannot be completed without faith. The revelation of God in Christ, the disclosure of God's sovereignty over life and history, the clarification of the meaning of life and history, is not completed until man is able, by faith, to apprehend the truth which is beyond his apprehension without faith. The truth is not completely beyond his apprehension; otherwise Christ could not have been expected. It is nevertheless beyond his apprehension, or Christ would not have been rejected. It is a truth capable of apprehension by faith; but when so apprehended there is a consciousness in the heart of the believer that he has been helped to this apprehension. This consciousness is summed up in the confession: "No man can say that Jesus is the Lord, but by the Holy Spirit" [1] and is suggested in Christ's acknowledgment of Peter's

[28] Romans 8:35, 37, 38.   [1] I Cor. 12:3.

confession: "Flesh and blood hath not revealed it unto thee, but my Father which is in heaven."[2]

The revelation of Christ is not completed until the little Christian community surveys the whole Christian epic, which includes the life and the teachings of Christ, but also and supremely the sacrificial death upon the Cross, understood by Christ as a necessary "ransom for many." Included in this history is not merely the immediate epic but also the history of expectation. Christ could not be the Christ, if he had not been expected; which is why the gospels (particularly St. Matthew) make a great deal of the fulfillment of prophecy, though the correlations between expectation and fulfillment are sometimes conceived in a mechanical and literalistic fashion. It is by the contemplation of the whole of this history in terms of expectation and fulfillment that Christian faith arrives at the confession, "Surely this was the Son of God." If the revelation in Christ had been merely the record of a high form of "God consciousness," or merely the culmination of man's search after God, or the portrayal of a high type of virtue, if Christ had merely revealed God to us by symbolizing divine goodness in his own goodness (which are the interpretations of Christian revelation in liberal Christianity), the revelation would have stood complete in itself. It would have been an historic fact or a form of historic striving which man comprehends and apprehends by his reason and appropriates for the sake of his growing wisdom and his developing culture. But such interpretations of life and faith do not proceed from a radical or profound analysis of the problem of life. They assume that the problem of life is to discover the highest form of goodness; to learn what is "worthy of man's highest devotion." They do not understand life in its twofold character of involvement in finiteness and transcendence over it; or the further complication of the corruption of sin which is the consequence of premature and self-sufficient efforts to escape from the weakness, dependence and insufficiency of the human situation.

[2] Mt. 16:17.

Wherever history is understood as solving its own problems by the cumulation of knowledge and wisdom and the consequent increase of virtue; whenever the complexities of history's relation to eternity are not known to be characteristic of history on every level of its development, the Christian claim that God has been revealed in Christ cannot be taken seriously. This is why liberal Christianity can give no satisfactory answer to the question why Christ, rather than some other "good" character of history, should be revered as divine, or how we can have the assurance that an evolutionary development may not produce a higher form of "goodness" more worthy of our "highest devotion."

1. *Christ Crucified as the "Wisdom of God and the Power of God"*

The faith of the Christian community, that the expectations of the ages have been fulfilled in Christ, that the hidden sovereignty of God has been fully revealed, and the meaning of life disclosed and fulfilled, is most accurately expressed in the succinct phrase of St. Paul, that this Christ who was not expected by the Greeks ("unto the Greeks foolishness"), and who was not the Christ the Jews expected ("unto the Jews a stumblingblock") is nevertheless "unto them which are called both Jews and Greeks, the power of God and the wisdom of God." [3] The Johannine assertion that "the law was given by Moses but *grace* and *truth* came by Jesus Christ" [4] makes the same affirmation, correlating two slightly different, but almost identical definitions of the significance of Christ.

The *wisdom* and the *truth* in Christ is the purpose and the will of the divine sovereign of life and history, which had been partially revealed and partially obscured in life and history. The Christian affirmation is that it is now fully disclosed. The *power* and *grace* in Christ is the dynamic authority of the divine sovereign of life and history, which had been partly revealed by the actualization of good in history and partly obscured by the defiance of sin. The Christian

[3] 1 Cor. 1:23-24.   [4] John 1:17.

affirmation is that this divine power is now established and disclosed in such a way that there can be no question about any other power being able to overcome it.

From the perspective of human history, which cannot be fully comprehended from its own perspective or fulfilled by its own power, the *wisdom* and the *power* in Christ is what gives life its meaning and guarantees the fulfillment of that meaning.

But what is it in this revelation of Christ which gives the final answer to the problem of man, who is both free and bound, both involved in finiteness and transcending it; and betrayed into sin by this situation? It can certainly not be the simple assurance that God is merciful rather than vindictive, to which some modern sentimental versions of the Christian faith have reduced the Christian revelation. This simple and sentimental contrast between the Old and the New Testament answers no significant or ultimate question. In the New Testament the Atonement is the significant content of the Incarnation. To say that Christ is the "express image of his person"[5] is to assert that in the epic of this life and death the final mystery of the divine power which bears history is clarified; and, with that clarification, life and history are given their true meaning.

It will be remembered that the prophets were certain about the wrath and the justice of God. They were less certain about His mercy. They knew that there was mercy; for history in its processes disclosed God's "longsuffering" as well as His wrath. But they could not be certain about mercy for it seemed to stand in contradiction to the divine justice. Did the one abrogate the other? The *wisdom* apprehended in Christ finally clarifies the character of God. He has a resource of mercy beyond His law and judgment but He can make it effective only as He takes the consequences of His wrath and judgment, upon and into Himself.

Thus the insistence of Christ that the Son of man must suffer is, quite accurately, elaborated and completed in the faith of the church, that the sufferings of this Son of man are the disclosure of God's

[5] Heb. 1:3.

suffering. The suffering of God is on the one hand the inevitable consequence of sin's rebellion against goodness; and on the other hand the voluntary acceptance by divine love of the consequence of sin. The classical Christian idea of Atonement emphasizes that God is both the propitiator and the propitiated.[6] The Father sends the Son into the world to become a sacrifice for sin. But it is also the wrath of the Father which must be propitiated. There can be no simple abrogation of the wrath of God by the mercy of God. The wrath of God is the world in its essential structure reacting against the sinful corruptions of that structure; it is the law of life as love, which the egotism of man defies, a defiance which leads to the destruction of life. The mercy of God represents the ultimate freedom of God above His own law; but not the freedom to abrogate the law. All the various efforts of theology to rationalize the mystery of the Atonement in commercial and juridical theories of God's justice or even the absurd patristic theory which had credence before Anselm (according to which God played a trick upon the devil by confronting him with the divine in the shape of a man) are efforts to state the paradox of the divine mercy in relation to the divine wrath. Implausible as many of the theories are and much as they may obscure rather than clarify the ultimate mystery, none of them completely effaces the central truth embodied in the doctrine of the Atonement. The justice and the forgiveness of God are one, just as Father and Son are equally God. For the highest justice of God is the holiness of His love. It is love as law which man affronts and defies. Yet forgiveness and justice are not one, just as Father and Son are two. The fact that God cannot overcome evil without displaying in history His purpose to take the effects of evil upon and into Himself, means that the divine mercy cannot be effective until the seriousness of sin is fully known. The knowledge that sin causes suffering to God is an indication of the seriousness of sin. It is by that knowledge that man is brought to despair. Without this despair there is no possibility of the contrition which appropriates the divine

6 *Cf.* G. Aulen, *Christus Victor.*

forgiveness. It is in this contrition and in this appropriation of divine mercy and forgiveness that the human situation is fully understood and overcome. In this experience man understands himself in his finiteness, realizes the guilt of his efforts to escape his insufficiency and dependence and lays hold upon a power beyond himself which both completes his incompleteness and purges him of his false and vain efforts at self-completion.

It must be emphasized that this final revelation of the divine sovereignty over life and this final disclosure of the meaning of life in terms of its dependence upon the divine judgment and mercy is not simply some truth of history which is comprehended by reason, to be added to the sum total of human knowledge. It must be constantly apprehended inwardly by faith, because it is a truth which transcends the human situation in each individual just as it transcended the total cultural situation historically. "Forgiveness," declares Kierkegaard quite rightly, "is a paradox in the Socratic sense insofar as it involves a relationship between the eternal truth and the existing individual. . . . The individual existing human being must feel himself a sinner; not *objectively* which is nonsense but *subjectively* which is the most profound suffering. . . . He must try to understand the forgiveness of sins and then despair of understanding. With the understanding directly opposed to it, the inwardness of faith must lay hold of this paradox." [7]

2. *The Relation of the "Wisdom of God" to the "Power of God"*
a. The identity of Wisdom and Power

The assertion of Christian faith is that the knowledge of God through the crucified Christ is both "wisdom" and "power," both "grace" and "truth"; which is to say that not only are life and history now fully known by having found their true end and meaning beyond themselves but they are also completed and fulfilled. Christ as "power" and as "grace" can be mediated to the individual only if the truth of the Atonement is appropriated inwardly. In that case

[7] Søren Kierkegaard, *Concluding Unscientific Postscript*, p. 201.

the alternate moods of despair and false hope are overcome and the individual is actually freed to live a life of serenity and creativity.

The understanding of the intimate relation between wisdom and power is constantly imperiled by Christian interpretations of the doctrine of the Atonement which seek to make it merely a disclosure of wisdom. This is particularly true on the Hellenic side of Christian faith. It will be remembered that Christ was not expected among the Greeks either because it was thought impossible for God to reveal Himself in history (since history was regarded as no more than temporal succession and natural sequence); or because it was thought unnecessary (since each man's reason was each man's Christ). When the gospel is finally preached to the Gentiles the general tendency is to appropriate its truth only in so far as it conforms to their problem. Their problem is the problem of finiteness and eternity and their conviction is that the chasm between the two is unbridgeable. What they appropriate from the gospel therefore is the affirmation that this chasm can be bridged. Thus Clement declares that, "The word of God became man in order that thou mayst learn from man how man becomes God." [8] Origen, the greatest of the Alexandrian theologians, thought of Christ primarily as the mediator between the "uncreated One and the created many" and Prophyry passed the judgment upon him that "though his outward life was that of a Christian . . . he thought like the Greeks." [9]

[8] *Protrepticus* I, 8.

[9] A. Harnack, *History of Dogma*, Vol. II, p. 341. Such a judgment does not do justice to the Scriptural content in Origen's thought, particularly his emphasis upon grace as a power which philosophy could not give, upon the necessity of the forgiveness of sins and upon the hope of the resurrection as against the Greek idea of immortality.

Nevertheless Origen, and the Greek Fathers generally, were inclined to regard Christ, not so much as an answer to the problem of sin as the Bible defined it, but as an answer to the problem of death. Sometimes Christ seemed no more than a supplement to the answer which Plato and the philosophers had already given. Sometimes he was regarded as

The obsession of the Greek mind with the problem of finiteness and eternity had two consequences, as Greek thought sought to appropriate the "foolishness" of the gospel. One was that it exhausted itself in accepting an un-Greek answer to a Greek problem. It did accept the Christian affirmation that the eternal had made itself known in history. But it regarded that fact, of itself, as the answer to the final problem of life. It did not fully understand that the particular content of the divine disclosure was the knowledge of the mercy and the justice of God in their paradoxical relationship, in other words, the Atonement. The specific theological formulation of this error lies in the emphasis upon the Incarnation, to the exclusion of the doctrine of the Atonement or, at least, its relegation to a subordinate position. This error persists in certain types of Catholic and Anglican thought, sometimes more particularly in the latter because of its great dependence upon patristic theology.

Hastings Rashdall, a typical Anglican rationalist, takes satisfaction in the fact that the doctrine of the Atonement was "never heartily accepted" in the church before St. Augustine and that it was "sometimes wholly ignored." [10] One might add that one possible reason why Christian thought before Anselm had nothing but an implausible theory of the Atonement when it did give the doctrine attention (the theory that God played a trick upon the devil and caught the

a more adequate bridge between the historical and the eternal than Greek philosophy afforded.

Irenæus, though no pure Hellenist, described salvation through Christ as a way of attaining "incorruptibility and immortality" which could not have been attained in any other way than by man's becoming united in Christ with incorruptibility and immortality" (*Against Heresies,* III, xix, 1).

Gregory of Nyssa's entire "Great Catechism" is essentially devoted to the refutation of the two typically Hellenic objections to the gospel, namely that philosophy made the coming of Christ unnecessary and that the revelation of the eternal in the finite was impossible.

[10] *The Idea of the Atonement,* p. 206. For Rashdall the final idea in Christian revelation is truly a "stumblingblock."

devil by "baiting the hook with Christ"), is because the doctrine was of no sufficient importance really to engage its mind. In typical Hellenistic Christianity doctrines of the Atonement are essentially irrelevant because the disclosure of God in history does not require a specific content. It is sufficient that God should make Himself known against the scepticism of the Greek mind that this is not possible. He need not make known His wrath and mercy, since it is not sin but finiteness which troubles man.

Greek thought tends to develop another error when the Christian idea of the relation of "power" to "wisdom" is stated in Greek terms. When Greek thought seeks to express the idea that "God was in Christ" and made Himself known in history in the Incarnation, it tries to state this truth in metaphysical terms. This means in effect that an ultimate truth, transcending all human wisdom and apprehended by faith, is transmuted into a truth of human wisdom and incorporated into a metaphysical system.

The effect of this procedure is clearly seen in the Christological controversies of the early Christian ages. These controversies end in the formula of Chalcedon and the Nicene creed in which the affirmation of Christian faith is made in defiance of Greek thought but within the limitations of Greek terms. The Greek idea that there is an absolute gulf between the "passible" and the "impassible," between the temporal and the eternal is refuted and transcended. But the Christian affirmation that God makes Himself known in history through Christ is partly obscured by the terms used to affirm it. The indication of this tendency is the theory of the two natures of Christ, in terms of which early Christian thought is forced to state its conviction about Jesus' historical and human character on the one hand, and his significance as the revelation of the divine on the other. By stating this double facet of Christ in ontic terms, a truth of faith, which can be expressed only symbolically, is transmuted into a truth of speculative reason. Christ is, according to these statements of faith, both God and man. It is asserted that his humanity does not derogate from his divinity or his divinity from his humanity. All definitions of Christ which affirm both his divinity and humanity in the sense that they ascribe both finite and historically conditioned and eternal and unconditioned qualities to his nature must verge on logical nonsense. It is possible for a character, event or fact of history to point symbolically beyond history and to become a source of disclosure of an eternal meaning, purpose and power which bears history. But it is not possible for any person to be historical and unconditioned at the same time. But the logical nonsense is not as serious a defect as the fact that the statement tends to reduce Christian faith to metaphysical truths which need not be apprehended inwardly by faith. The relation between "power" and "wisdom" is thereby destroyed because the final truth about life is not apprehended in such a way that the "existing individual" (Kierkegaard) is shattered in his self-esteem at the very center of his being; his insecurity as a finite individual in the flux of time is not robbed of all false securities of power or pride; his anxiety is not heightened until it reaches despair. Out of such despair contrition is born; and of contrition faith is conceived; and in that faith there is "newness of life," which is to say "power."

b. The difference between Wisdom and Power

Despite the intimate relation between the "wisdom of God" and the "power of God" which, according to Christian faith, is revealed in Christ, despite the confidence that a full understanding of the meaning of life also leads to the fulfillment of life, and that a full disclosure of the mercy of God also means the effective accretion of "grace" in the life of the believer, it must be emphasized that Christian faith has a more unambiguous confidence in Christ's full disclosure of life, history and God, than in the fulfillment of life's meaning. The idea of "power" and "grace" in Christian thought is ambiguous. On the one hand the believer is regarded as capable of fulfilling life as it has been disclosed to him. On the other hand he remains in both the finiteness of history and in the corruption of sin. The "grace" of God is on the one hand a power of God in man which completes his incompleteness. It is on the other hand the merciful power of God over man, whereby sin is overcome by God's mercy, but not by human goodness. The fulfillment of history, according to Christian faith, has two facets. According to the one there is fulfillment in every moment in which man establishes relation to God in contrition and faith. According to the other, life waits for its fulfillment and "we are saved by hope." These two aspects of fulfillment are in conformity with Christ's own interpretation of the Kingdom as having come and as coming.[11]

3. *The Foolishness of God and the Wisdom of Men*

St. Paul defines the truth revealed in "Christ crucified" as the "foolishness of God which is wiser than men" as the "hidden wisdom" which "none of the princes of this world knew, for had they known it they would not have crucified the Lord of glory." Yet this foolishness, this wisdom which could not be anticipated by human wisdom, becomes to "them which are called" the "power of God and the wisdom of God."[12] In these Pauline paradoxes we have a very exact and succinct definition of the relation of revelation to human culture. The truth which is revealed in the Cross is not a truth which could have been anticipated in human culture and it is not the culmination of human wisdom. The true Christ is not expected. All human wisdom seeks to complete itself from the basis of its partial perspective. The pride of nations and of national and imperial cultures is only a primitive form of the pride of man as man, who will seek to complete the meaning of life from the standpoint of some human virtue or achievement and who will confuse and corrupt life's meaning by that very attempt.

But on the other hand when the Christ is accepted, the truth embodied in him becomes the basis of a new wisdom. This is to say that while *Heilsgeschichte* is not merely an aspect of general history, nor its natural culmination, neither is it a completely sepa-

[11] We shall deal with this problem more fully in Chapters IV and V.
[12] 1 Cor. 1 and 2.

rate history. Its revelations are what give history meaning. It is not
true that life would be meaningless but for the revelations embodied
in *Heilsgeschichte*. Life and history are filled with suggestions of
meaning which point beyond themselves; and with corruptions of
meaning due to premature solutions.

The truth as apprehended by faith is not something which simple
men believe upon authority and wiser men deduce from experience.
For there is an element in the truth of faith which defies the wisdom of both wise and foolish, more particularly of the wise. But
on the other hand a truth of faith is not something which stands
perpetually in contradiction to experience. On the contrary it illumines experience and is in turn validated by experience. The finiteness of the human mind does not completely exclude the truth of
faith for the reason that the finite mind is sufficiently free to transcend itself and to know something of its own finiteness. It is this
capacity of self-transcendence which gives rise to both the yearning
after God and to the idolatrous worship of false gods. It leads both
to the expectation of Christ and to the expectation of the false
Christ, who will vindicate us, but not our neighbour. Neither the
finiteness of the human mind nor the sinful corruption of the mind
or the "ideological taint" in all human culture can completely efface
the human capacity for the apprehension of the true wisdom. Since
there can be no total corruption of truth or virtue [13] there is always
a residual desire for the true wisdom, and the real God and the
final revelation of the meaning of life, below and above the sinful
tendency to build a world of meaning around ourselves as the
center. It is this residual virtue which emerges in true contrition.
Faith and contrition are so closely correlated because it is the apprehension of the truth beyond ourselves in faith which makes us
contritely conscious of our previous effort to complete the structure
of truth from within ourselves; and this contrition in turn validates
the truth of faith. It becomes "the power of God and the wisdom
of God" to "them that are called." This circular relation between

[13] *Cf.* Vol. I, Ch. X.

contrition and faith in the interior complexities of the soul gives partial justification to both the theologies which regard "grace" as a completion of "nature" and those which set "grace" in contradiction to nature. Protestant theology is right in setting grace in contradiction to nature in the sense that the vicious circle of false truth, apprehended from the standpoint of the self, must be broken and the self cannot break it. In that sense the apprehension of the truth in Christ is always a miracle; and "flesh and blood have not revealed it unto us." But Protestant theology, more particularly radical Protestant theology (Barth), is wrong in denying the "point of contact" (*Anknuepfungspunkt*) which always exists in man by virtue of the residual element of *justitia originalis* in his being.[14]

The relation between the truth, apprehended in God's self-disclosure, and the truth about life which men deduce through a rational organization of their experience, might best be clarified through the analogy of our knowledge of other persons. We know what we know about other persons, partly through an observation of their behaviour. But human personality, unlike animal life, has a depth and uniqueness which cannot be understood purely in terms of external behaviour. The depth is partly comprehended by assuming that the depths of self-consciousness within ourselves correspond to that in the other person. The uniqueness of the other person is partly falsified, however, by our effort to understand him in terms which we have drawn from the knowledge of ourselves. This represents the sinful corruption in human intercourse, the projection of ourselves into the life of the other, our effort to understand the uniqueness of the other by a false assumption that our

---

[14] See Emil Brunner's *Nature and Grace* and Karl Barth's answer, *Nein*. In this debate Brunner seems to me to be right and Barth wrong; but Barth seems to win the debate because Brunner accepts too many of Barth's presuppositions in his fundamental premises to be able to present his own position with plausibility and consistency. Barth is able to prove Brunner inconsistent, but that does not necessarily prove him to be wrong.

own desires, hopes and ambitions are identical with those of the other.

The other self cannot be understood until he speaks to us. Only the "word" of the other self, coming out of the depth or height of his self-transcendence can finally disclose the other "I" as subject and not merely as object of our knowledge. Only this communication can give the final clue to the peculiar behaviour of the other. This behaviour always contains contradictory elements which make the real meaning of the behaviour something of a mystery. When the other self finally speaks, the self-disclosure of his words partly clarifies obscurities in his previously observed behaviour and partly negates false conclusions which the self has made by trying to understand the other self in terms of its own characteristic prejudices and passions. The knowledge gained from this self-disclosure of the other self does not stand in complete contradiction to the knowledge gained from the observation of his behaviour. It could stand in such contradiction only if the depths of self-transcendence of the other self were in complete contradiction to the life of the self as involved in its physical organism. There is contradiction between the knowledge gained from the observation of the behaviour and the knowledge gained from the self-disclosure of the other person only in so far as the self has interpreted the other falsely. Finally, the knowledge gained by such self-disclosure completes incomplete knowledge, previously known through the study of behaviour. The word of self-disclosure is thus partly a completion of incomplete knowledge, partly a clarification of obscurities and contradictions and partly a correction of falsifications.

This is exactly the relation of the self-disclosure of God as received by faith to such other knowledge as man has about the "hidden" God. When prophetic Messianism affirms that life and history are under the sovereignty of a hidden God it declares, not that life and history are meaningless, but that they can be understood only in terms of a dimension deeper and higher than the system of nature, that there are obscurities and contradictions in the "behaviour" of history which can be clarified only if the unique purpose of God is more fully disclosed; and that human explanations of this behaviour must be corrected since they contain sinful elements. These sinful elements in the knowledge of God are more pronounced than in the knowledge of the other self because they involve the pride of the finite self seeking to understand, not merely another self, but the eternal ground and source of existence in terms of itself.

This whole analogy implies the concept of divine "personality" which is indeed an invariable implication of prophetic and Christian interpretations of life and history, in contrast to more rationalistic and pantheistic philosophies. While the concept of personality cannot be cleansed completely of anthropomorphic elements, inasmuch as all human personality implies limitations of the senses and a tension between freedom and finiteness which are not applicable to the divine,[15] it is nevertheless a serviceable analogical concept because it connotes precisely that height of freedom on the one hand and that relation to organic process on the other which prophetic and Christian faith assumes in understanding God's transcendence over, and his immanent relation to, the world.[16]

[15] See Francis H. Bradley's rigorous analysis of these anthropomorphic elements in the concept of personality, leading him to the rejection of the concept in his definition of the Absolute. *Appearance and Reality*, particularly pages 413 ff. and 531 ff.

[16] Though Karl Barth protests against all forms of analogical reasoning when dealing with the "wholly other," he nevertheless avails himself of the analogy of the concept of personality when defining the character of the divine. He seeks to hide his analogic logic by inverting it. He declares that concepts of human personality are derived from the concept of divine personality. "Personalness," he writes, "means being the subject not only in the logical but in the ethical sense, being a free subject, free even in respect of the periodical limitations which are given with its individuality as such, able to dispose of its own existence and nature. If we represent to ourselves what this means, it will not occur to us to see in this personalizing of the word of God a case of anthropomorphism. The problem is not whether God is a person but whether we are. Or shall we find among us one who in the full and real sense of this concept

The self-disclosure of God in Christ is significantly regarded by Christian faith as the final "word" which God has spoken to man. The revelation of the Atonement is precisely a "final" word because it discloses a transcendent divine mercy which represents the "freedom" of God in quintessential terms: namely God's freedom over His own law. Yet this freedom is not capricious. It is paradoxically related to God's law, to the structure of the world. This is the paradox of the Atonement, of the revelation of the mercy of God in its relation to the justice of God.

When this word of revelation is spoken it completes incomplete knowledge, in so far as human history is a realm of reality having its final basis in eternity. There are elements in the "behaviour" of history which point to this "hidden" source of its life. It is in that sense that history is meaningful but pointing beyond itself. Secondly, the word of revelation clarifies obscurities and contradictions in history. In that sense history is meaningful but its meaning is threatened by meaninglessness. Finally the "word" of God corrects falsifications which have been introduced into the human interpretations of life's meaning by reason of man's effort to explain history from the standpoint of himself as its center. In that sense the word of revelation stands in contradiction to human culture and is "foolishness" to the wise.

But precisely because it is such foolishness, transcending human wisdom, it becomes, once accepted, the basis for a satisfactory total explanation of life. It becomes truly wisdom. Revelation does not remain in contradiction to human culture and human knowledge. By completing the incompleteness, clarifying the obscurities and correcting the falsifications of human knowledge it becomes true wisdom to "them that are called."

----

we can call a person. But God is really a person, really a free subject." *Doctrine of the Word of God,* p. 157. Barth's logic cannot hide the fact that, however imperfect human personality is in contrast to divine personality, he has taken the very concept of personality from human life and has applied it to the divine. From what other source could he have derived it?

Revelation of God in Christ's sacrificial death clarifies the meaning of history or the final perfection of man

CHAPTER III

THE POSSIBILITIES AND LIMITS OF HISTORY

THE CHRISTIAN faith affirms that the same Christ who discloses the sovereignty of God over history is also the perfect norm of human nature. He is the "second Adam" as well as the "Son of God." As the revelation of the paradoxical relation of the divine justice and mercy He discloses the ultimate mystery of the relation of the divine to history. This revelation clarifies the meaning of history; for the judgment of God preserves the distinction of good and evil in history; and the mercy of God finally overcomes the sinful corruption in which man is involved on every level of moral achievement by reason of his false and abortive efforts to complete his own life and history.

Christ as the norm of human nature defines the final perfection of man in history. This perfection is not so much a sum total of various virtues or an absence of transgression of various laws; it is the perfection of sacrificial love. The same Cross which symbolizes the love of God and reveals the divine perfection to be not incompatible with a suffering involvement in historical tragedy, also indicates that the perfection of man is not attainable in history. Sacrificial love transcends history. It does not transcend history as a thought transcends an act. It is an act in history; but it cannot justify itself in history. From the standpoint of history mutual love

68

is the highest good. Only in mutual love, in which the concern of one person for the interests of another prompts and elicits a reciprocal affection, are the social demands of historical existence satisfied. The highest good of history must conform to standards of coherence and consistency in the whole realm of historical vitality.[1] All claims within the general field of interests must be proportionately satisfied and related to each other harmoniously. The sacrifice of the self for others is therefore a violation of natural standards of morals, as limited by historical existence.

Furthermore the sacrifice of the interests of the self for others is psychologically impossible when life is conceived only in terms of nature-history. If the self identifies its life with physical existence the basic ethical paradox of the gospel ethic: "Whosoever loseth his life shall find it" can have no meaning. This paradox can have meaning only if the dimension of life is known to transcend historical existence. The rewards which Jesus promises to those who follow him are therefore identified with "the resurrection." Sacrificial love thus represents a tangent towards "eternity" in the field of historical ethics. It is nevertheless the support of all historical ethics; for the self cannot achieve relations of mutual and reciprocal affection with others if its actions are dominated by the fear that they may not be reciprocated. Mutuality is not a possible achievement if it is made the intention and goal of any action. Sacrificial love is thus paradoxically related to mutual love; and this relation is an ethical counterpart of the general relation of super-history to history.

The relation of sacrificial to mutual love cannot be defined as a truth of revealed religion of which nothing is known apart from the revelation of God in Christ. Any rigorous analysis of the ethical problem of history discloses that history transcends itself in such a way that the highest good transcends historical canons and possibilities. For this reason the popular imagination fastens upon the Cross as the symbol of the highest ethical norm, even when and if

[1] *Cf.* L. T. Hobhouse, *The Rational Good.*

the full profundity of the religious meaning of the Cross is not understood. Human experience constantly yields some knowledge of the fact that concern for the other rather than the self leads inevitably to consequences which cannot be justified in purely historical and this-worldly terms. Nevertheless the ethical truth embodied in the Cross is clarified by the religious revelation contained in the Cross. For without the latter's disclosure of the relation of God to history ethical life tends to degenerate either into an egoistic utilitarianism which makes self-regarding motives ethically normative; or into a mystical ethics which flees from the tensions and incomplete harmonies of history to an undifferentiated unity of life in eternity.

II

SACRIFICIAL LOVE AND THE SINLESSNESS OF CHRIST

The paradoxical relation of sacrificial to mutual love clarifies the Christian doctrine of the sinlessness of Christ. Furthermore it makes the doctrine that Jesus was both human and divine religiously and morally meaningful and dispenses with the necessity of making the doctrine metaphysically plausible. The impossibility of doing the latter is fully attested by the ages of Christological controversy in which Christian thought sought futilely to express the idea that Christ was fully human and yet transcended the human. This controversy produced a long series of heresies in which either the human or the divine quality of the life of Christ was denied or obscured. The heresies were refuted by orthodox affirmations which were forced to commit themselves to metaphysical absurdities. Since the essence of the divine consists in its unconditioned character, and since the essence of the human lies in its conditioned and contingent nature, it is not logically possible to assert both qualities of the same person. It is even more impossible to affirm that the divine nature of Christ does not qualify the human qualities, or that the conditioned character of human existence is not in contradiction to the

The meaning of the idea that God is revealed in Christ

unconditioned character of the divine. The chasm between the human and the divine, between the historical and the eternal cannot be bridged by metaphysical speculations which begin with absolute distinctions between them.

The significance of the affirmation that God is revealed in Christ, and more particularly in his Cross, is that the love (*agape*) of God is conceived in terms which make the divine involvement in history a consequence of precisely the divine transcendence over the structures of history. The final majesty of God is contained not so much in His power within the structures as in the power of His freedom over the structures, that is, over the *logos* aspects of reality. This freedom is the power of mercy beyond judgment. By this freedom He involves Himself in the guilt and suffering of free men who have, in their freedom, come in conflict with the structural character of reality.[1] The *agape* of God is thus at once the expression of both the final majesty of God and of His relation to history.

The love of Christ, His disinterested and sacrificial *agape,* as the highest possibility of human existence, stands in paradoxical, rather than contradictory, relation to the majesty of God, so conceived. The assertion that Christ is both human and divine is contradictory when defined in terms which Christian orthodoxy used to refute the heresies which denied, from one side or the other, that there could be a relation between the historical and the eternal. These contradictions were asserted, nevertheless, because they expressed, though inadequately, what Christian faith has always apprehended beyond all metaphysical speculations, about the paradoxical relation of a divine *agape,* which stoops to conquer, and the human *agape,* which rises above history in a sacrificial act.

[1] Professor Charles Hartshorne's *The Vision of God* gives a very profound analysis of this problem and presents the thesis that God's perfection must be defined primarily in terms of His capacity for self-transcendence, or in his phrase in His "self-surpassing" character rather than in the traditional concepts of omnipotence, if the Christian doctrine of His ability to enter into loving relationship with suffering men is to have any meaning.

Though the relation between the divine and human in Christ is not contradictory, it is paradoxical. The final majesty, the ultimate freedom, and the perfect disinterestedness of the divine love can have a counterpart in history only in a life which ends tragically, because it refuses to participate in the claims and counterclaims of historical existence. It portrays a love "which seeketh not its own." But a love which seeketh not its own is not able to maintain itself in historical society. Not only may it fall victim to excessive forms of the self-assertion of others; but even the most perfectly balanced system of justice in history is a balance of competing wills and interests, and must therefore worst anyone who does not participate in the balance.

The significant contrast between the divine and the human in Christ is not, as Greek thought assumed, the contrast between the "impassible and the passible." It is a contrast between the perfect coincidence of power and goodness in the divine. It is impossible to symbolize the divine goodness in history in any other way than by complete powerlessness, or rather by a consistent refusal to use power in the rivalries of history. For there is no self in history or society, no matter how impartial its perspective upon the competitions of life, which can rise to the position of a disinterested participation in those rivalries and competitions. It can symbolize disinterested love only by a refusal to participate in the rivalries.[2] Any participation in them means the assertion of one ego interest against another.

In apprehending the Cross as the symbol of this ultimate perfection Christian faith has always been profounder than the theologies

---

[2] For this reason the ethics of nonresistance as taught in the Sermon on the Mount is in perfectly consistent relation with the love symbolized in the Cross. Modern Christianity is wrong, however, in presenting this ethic as one which might, if generally practiced, become successful in history. It is even more mistaken if it declares that a non-violent participation in all the claims and counterclaims of historical social life preserves the essentials of the gospel ethic of nonresistance. *Cf.* Richard B. Gregg, *The Power of Non-Violence.*

which sought to rationalize it. For faith has consistently regarded the Cross as the point in history where the sinful rivalries of ego with ego are transcended; and it has not tried with too much consistency to fit every action of the historical Jesus into the symbol of this perfection. The theologians on the other hand have attempted to give either metaphysical or legalistic interpretations of this perfection. If they attempted the former they leaned heavily upon the doctrine of the Virgin birth to prove that the divine perfection was not tainted by ordinary human nature. The flaw in the logic of the Virgin birth apologetics is amply revealed by the need of the corollary Catholic doctrine of the immaculate conception of the Virgin Mary. The son of a human mother, even though born without a human father, is still organically related to the whole human situation; and the doctrine of the immaculate conception of his mother is a mere gesture in overcoming the dilemma; for even an infinite regression of immaculate conceptions would hardly serve to remove the taint.

How Christ was sinless

The more moralistic liberal Protestant interpretations of the sinlessness of Christ are probably most perfectly expressed in Schleiermacher's conception of the perfection of Christ's "God-consciousness." But Schleiermacher is forced by his conception into a very unscriptural denial that Christ was "in all points tempted like as we are" yet without sin.[3] Schleiermacher is quite right of course in suggesting that to be tempted means in a sense to have sinned; for temptation is a state of anxiety from which sin flows inevitably. And this anxiety is a concomitant of finite and insecure existence.[4] It is not possible for this reason to assert the sinlessness of every individual act of any actually historical character. It is possible to assert that in Jesus there is a remarkable coincidence and consistency of doctrine, of purpose and of act. His ethical doctrine contains an uncompromising insistence upon conformity to God's will without reference to the relativities and contingencies of historical situations.

BUT

[3] Friedrich Schleiermacher, *The Christian Faith*, pp. 415 ff.
[4] *Cf*. Vol. I, Ch. VII.

The animating purpose of his life is to conform to the *agape* of God. His life culminates in an act of self-abnegation in which the individual will ceases to be a protagonist of the individual life; and the life ends upon the Cross. The Cross could not have the symbolic significance for Christian faith if the life and the doctrine were not consistent with it. But on the other hand the Cross symbolizes the perfection of love more consistently than any cumulation of individual acts. The moralistic conception of sinlessness is inevitably betrayed into a legalistic interpretation of life. Perfection or sinlessness is interpreted as conformity to a given code of conduct. But how is the ultimacy of that code determined?

The Cross symbolizes the perfection of *agape* which transcends all particular norms of justice and mutuality in history. It rises above history and seeks conformity to the Divine love rather than harmony with other human interests and vitalities. This harmony is a desirable end of historical striving; but it can never be a final norm. For sinful egoism makes all historical harmonies of interest partial and incomplete; and a life which accepts these harmonies as final is bound to introduce sinful self-assertion into the ethical norm.

The interpretations which define the sinlessness and perfection of Christ in either metaphysical or legalistic terms can have no real illumination for human conduct. If only a God-man, who transcends the conditions of finiteness absolutely, can define and delineate the norm of human existence, the contrition which contemplation of such a norm may prompt is quickly transmuted into complacency. For we must live our life under the conditions of finiteness; and may therefore dismiss any ideal or norm as irrelevant which does not have to meet our conditions.

But the actual situation is that, though we are subject to the conditions and limitations of nature, we are not absolutely conditioned or limited. The human spirit rises in indefinite transcendence over the natural conditions of life; and there is no particular point at which conscience can be made easy by the assurance that an action beyond this point would mean loss of life or sacrifice of our interests. There is always the possibility of sacrificing our life and in-

the perfection of Christ be dis- cerned only by faith can

terest; and this possibility always has the corresponding assurance that to lose our life thus is to gain it. But such a gain cannot be measured in terms of the history which is bound to nature. The gain can only be an integrity of spirit which has validity in "eternity." It can have meaning only when life is measured in a dimension which includes the fulfillment of life beyond the present conditions of history. But life can be measured in that dimension only "by faith," just as the perfection of Christ can be discerned only "by faith." The effort to reduce that perfection to a simple historical fact, which can be measured in terms of historical norms and standards, is to reduce paradox to absurdity. The perfection of *agape* as symbolized in the Cross can neither be simply reduced to the limits of history, nor yet dismissed as irrelevant because it transcends history. It transcends history as history transcends itself. It is the final norm of a human nature which has no final norm in history because it is not completely contained in history.

All this has been understood by the wisdom of faith, though it has been withheld from the wise. Theologies continue to elaborate systems which either claim the authority of the Cross for the relative norms of history or which raise the perfection of the Cross and the sinlessness of Christ to a position of irrelevance. But meanwhile Christian faith has always understood, beyond all canons of common sense and all metaphysical speculations, that the perfection of the Cross represents the fulfillment—and the end—of historical ethics.

The ethical implications of the Cross illumine the actual character of human history. This insight is possible only after the religious implications of the Cross have given the answer to the problem which is presented by the character of history. There are ultimate problems of life which cannot be fully stated until the answer to them is known. Without the answer to them, men will not allow themselves to contemplate the full depth of the problem, lest they be driven to despair. The Christian doctrine of Christ as the "second Adam," as normative man, is thus a doctrine which hovers between natural and revealed religion. It belongs to natural religion in the sense that any rigorous analysis of the moral life of man will, par-w/o faith

tially disclose the tangents towards the eternal in all morality. It belongs to revealed religion because it is not possible, without faith, to follow these implications through to their final logical conclusion. Without faith the ethical life of man is always haunted by the sceptical reflection that "a living dog is better than a dead lion," [5] which is to say that all moral imperatives are limited by the survival impulse which lies at the foundation of historical existence.

III

THE RELATION OF CHRIST'S PERFECTION TO HISTORY

A complete analysis of the relation of Christ's perfection to history would result in a comprehensive statement of the Christian interpretation of history. Some aspects of this interpretation have already been considered and others remain to be discussed. It is nevertheless advisable and necessary to consider the most important characteristics of this interpretation in the present connection. Upon the basis of the Christian conviction that the *agape* of Christ is the disclosure of both the divine love which bears history and the human love which is history's "impossible possibility," one may define the main principles of the Christian interpretation of history. This can be done most simply by considering (*a*) The perfection of Christ in relation to innocency, or to the beginning of history; (*b*) The perfection of Christ in relation to mutual love or to the substance of history; and (*c*) The perfection of Christ in relation to eternal fulfillment, or the end of history

1. *The Perfection of Christ and Innocency*

The idea that Christ is the "essential" man, the perfect norm of human character, is expressed scripturally in the Pauline phrase that Christ is the "second Adam." [6] Christ's perfection reestablishes the

---

[5] Ecclesiastes 9:4.

[6] *Cf.* 1 Cor. 15:22 and Romans 5:12 ff. The actual phrase is used sparingly. But the whole New Testament consistently regards Christ as the final norm of human character. The Johannine prologue regards

virtue which Adam had before the fall. We have previously noted that Christian theology has difficulty in defining the perfection before the fall and that its definitions frequently border on the fantastic.[7] But the doctrine of the second Adam, when taken seriously, is a protection against these confusions and fantasies. Christian thought understands (even though it does not always realize the full implications of the doctrine) that it is not possible to define the lost perfection of Adam, the ideal possibilities of human life, except in terms drawn from the perfection of Christ. It is significant, however, that whenever it states this conviction it is forced into the corollary belief that the perfection of Christ not only reestablishes but exceeds the primitive perfection.[8]

To say that the innocency of Adam before the fall can be restored only in terms of the perfection of Christ is to assert that life *can approach its original innocency only by aspiring to its unlimited end.*

Christ as the historical manifestation of the divine *logos* which is the pattern of the whole creation.

[7] Vol. I, Ch. X.

[8] Irenæus is very fond of the idea that Christ "recapitulates Adam in Himself." He believed that the "plasm of the first man never lost the image of God," that Christ restored this image, that he is the "first man" walking once more upon the earth "at the end of a long line which was from the beginning," but that He exceeds the goodness of Adam before the Fall as perfection transcends innocence (*Against Heresies,* Book III, xix and xxiv).

Gregory of Nyssa describes salvation as being "restored to the fashion of the pure Adam, man attains the stature of the last, and becomes even higher than he was because he becomes deified." *The Great Catechism,* par. 37.

Thomas Aquinas asks the question whether if man had not sinned God would have become incarnate and answers in the affirmative, giving as the reason that in Christ "the last creature, *viz.,* man, is joined to the first principle: *viz.,* God." It belongs to God, he declares, "to manifest Himself by some infinite effect." If man had not sinned, he might have been united to God "in a natural manner as to an end"; but to be united to God in person exceeds the limits of the perfection of nature." (*Summa Theologica,* Part III, Q. 1, Art. 3.) The argument is somewhat artificial; but the underlying conception of unlimited possibilities for human nature is important.

no historical state of man which could rightly be called innocency

The paradoxical character of the interpretation of history involved in this affirmation is already implied in the tentative confusion of defining Adam's state before the fall as both "perfection" and "innocency." Primeval goodness represents innocency in so far as it is a harmony of life with life which has not yet been disturbed or disrupted by freedom. This is why there is some justification for the thought which runs from Irenæus to Hegel, according to which the primeval goodness is a kind of prehistoric state from which both historic virtue and evil finally emerge. In Hegel's thought, the fall is a necessary prerequisite of virtue; for in it the individual comes to self-consciousness; and sinful self-assertion is a necessary prelude to the harmonious and loving relationship of life with life in terms of freedom. Innocency is thus the harmony of life with life without freedom. Mutual love is the harmony of life with life within terms of freedom; and sacrificial love is harmony of the soul with God beyond the limitations of sinful and finite history.

But it is impossible to use the symbol of primeval or prehistoric innocency exactly for the reason that the uniqueness of man consists in his freedom and self-transcendence; and there is therefore no possible historical state of man, however primitive the society, or however undeveloped the child, in which there is harmony without freedom. An inchoate freedom has already disturbed the harmony of nature. This is one reason why it is not possible to assign a historical locus to the perfection before the fall; [9] and also why the ideal possibility of life, symbolized in the first Adam, cannot be defined consistently as "innocency" but must always contain some connotation of "perfection."

In terms of social history there are no primitive societies in which life is related to life in the frictionless harmony of the ant-hill. We do know something about the character of primitive societies; a great deal more, at least, than the eighteenth century philosophers who used the idea of a "state of nature" as a foil for their interpretation of historical society. We know that on the one hand primitive

[9] *Cf.* Vol. I, Ch. X.

societies were held together by natural impulses of gregariousness
and consanguinity and that in them the individual is never completely emancipated from the "primeval we" consciousness.[10] In this
characteristic, primitive society is organically related to animal herds
and families. Its history must be regarded as prehistory. But on the
other hand we know of no primitive society which does not adopt
various stratagems to achieve the unity which the animal herd has
by nature. Political artifice supplies some cement of its social cohesion.[11] The very strictness with which primitive custom binds the
individual to the group and prohibits individual deviations from
established norms (however capricious the origin of such norms may
be) is the mark of the primitive community's fear of anarchy. The
primitive community has no freedom in its social structure, not
because the individual lacks an embryonic sense of freedom but
precisely because he does have such a sense; and the community is
not imaginative enough to deal with this freedom without suppressing it. This means that the brotherhood of even the most primitive
community cannot be a completely "innocent" mutual relation of
life to life. In so far as freedom has arisen to destroy the harmony of
nature, the community seeks to suppress it for the sake of preserving
the social unity. There are thus elements of tyranny in the social
cohesion of the primitive community. Furthermore the relation of
the primitive community to other communities are minimal at first;
and when they develop they begin as conflict relations. The innocency of primitive life thus embodies the twin evils of the tyrannical

[10] *Cf.* Fritz Kunkel, *Charakter, Einzelmensch und Gruppe.*
[11] Henri Bergson regards the "static religion" of the primitive community as the "defensive reaction of nature against the dissolvent power
of intelligence." But this religion is obviously not purely a stratagem of
"nature." It represents a partly conscious and partly unconscious reaction
to the situation created by human freedom and the religion is itself a
product of that freedom. It is because there are conscious elements in the
strategy of primitive religion that some interpreters are able to regard
the priest as a conscious imperialist who manipulates religion for the
purpose of gaining social power in the primitive community. See Bergson, *Two Sources of Morality and Religion,* p. 112.

subordination of life to life and the anarchic conflict of life with life.

Where there is history at all there is freedom; and where there is freedom there is sin. Yet the mutualities of the primitive community are inexact symbols of the loving relation of life to life. There is a certain validity in the perennial inclination of men to focus upon the past, whether in terms of the prehistory of the human race, or in terms of some imagined innocency and simplicity in the life of their own nation, as symbol of the brotherhood which they intend to achieve in history.

The same symbolic inexactness becomes apparent in analysing the innocency of a child. A child does not enter the world with a developed self-consciousness. It is held within the "primeval we" consciousness of the family. As its self-consciousness develops it reveals a self-centeredness which is akin to the self-sufficiency of the primitive community. But as it relates itself to other lives it also betrays impulses to dominate them, tendencies toward jealousy and envy which reveal its developing freedom, the anxieties which are concomitants of that freedom, and the usual abortive strategies intended to overcome these anxieties. A child is thus never completely innocent; and yet its innocency is an inexact symbol of the goodness towards which all life should move. This ambiguity of childlike innocency gives a certain plausibility to the contradictory approaches to the symbol of the child in Christian thought. Jesus consistently uses the symbol of childlike goodness for the perfection to be achieved in the Kingdom of God; while orthodox theologians, beginning with Augustine, regard childhood as involved in sinful corruption and as therefore in need of redemption.

The whole character of human history is thus implicitly defined in the Christian symbolism of the "first" and "second" Adam. To define the norm of history provisionally in terms of prehistoric innocency is to recognize that a part of the norm of man's historic existence lies in the harmonious relation of life to life in nature. To define it ultimately in terms of a sacrificial love which transcends history is to recognize the freedom of man over his own history without which historical creativity would be impossible. The actual historic achievements of man in history, his creation of larger and larger units of "brotherhood," the building of city-states, nations and empires, are always corrupted by the twin evils of the tyrannical subordination of life to life and the anarchic conflict of life with life. There is therefore no pure ethical norm in history; nor any hope of history gradually purifying itself so that it will achieve this norm. The "essential," the normative man, is thus a "God-man" whose sacrificial love seeks conformity with, and finds justification in, the divine and eternal *agape,* the ultimate and final harmony of life with life. Yet this eternal norm is not presented without a provisional glance at the primitive harmony of life in nature. The Christian faith appreciates what is valid in romantic primitivism as a part of the Christian affirmation of the goodness of creation. But the Christian interpretation of life and history has a too lively sense of the freedom which reaches into eternity to interpret life merely in terms of primitive innocency. To this innocency it relates the tragic perfection of the Cross.

2. *The Perfection of Christ and Possibilities of History*

We have previously noted [12] that the disclosure of the character of God and the meaning of history in Christ has a threefold relation to the conceptions of the meaningfulness of history as established in historic cultures and their Messianic hopes. It (*a*) completes what is incomplete in their apprehensions of meaning; (*b*) it clarifies obscurities which threaten the sense of meaning; and (*c*) it finally corrects falsifications of meaning which human egoism introduces into the sense of meaning by reason of its effort to comprehend the whole of life from an inadequate centre of comprehension.

The perfection of Christ, the transcendent *agape* symbolized in the Cross, has exactly this same threefold relation to the ethical realities of history. The ethical norm of history as comprehended by the "natural" resources of man, by his sober examination of the facts and requirements of life in human society, is mutual love. Man

[12] Vol. II, Ch. II.

knows both by experience and by the demand for coherence in his rational nature, that life ought not to be lived at cross purposes, that conflict within the self, and between the self and others, is an evil. In that sense love is the law of life according to the insights of natural religion and morality. It is normative, at any rate, in any religion or culture which takes socio-historic existence seriously and does not seek immediate flight into a non-historical unity of life.

The sacrificial love of the Cross has a threefold relation of transcendence to these accepted norms of mutuality in history.

a. Sacrificial love (*agape*) completes the incompleteness of mutual love (*eros*), for the latter is always arrested by reason of the fact that it seeks to relate life to life from the standpoint of the self and for the sake of the self's own happiness. But a self which seeks to measure the possible reciprocity which its love towards another may elicit is obviously not sufficiently free of preoccupation with self to lose itself in the life of the other. Considerations of prudence thus inevitably arrest the impulse towards, and concern for, the life of the other. Aristotle's chapters on friendship [13] reveal these difficulties in the logic of mutuality very clearly, though it is only fair to say that Aristotle has his own tangent towards transcendence; for in the final instance the friend in Aristotle's Ethics affirms the interests of the other for the sake not of some obvious advantage to the self but for the sake of the "happiness" of the self, in its transcendent integrity of spirit.

David Hume's discussion of the same problem [14] brings out the issue very clearly. He begins by envisaging a possible mutual love in history which would obviate all the defenses against, and restrictions upon, human egoism which systems of justice establish. "Suppose," he declares, "that the necessities of the human race continue as at present, yet the mind is so enlarged and so replete with friendship and generosity, that every man has the utmost tenderness for every man, and feels no more concern for his own interest than for

[13] In *Nicomachean Ethics,* Chs. VIII and IX.
[14] In *An Inquiry Concerning the Principle of Morals.* Sec. III, Part I.

that of his fellows; it seems evident that the use of justice would, in that case, be suspended by an extensive benevolence; nor would the divisions and barriers of property and obligation have been thought of. Why should I find another by deed or promise to do me a good office when I know that he is already prompted by the strongest inclination to seek my happiness; and would of himself perform the desired service, except the hurt he thereby receives be greater than the benefit accruing me? . . . Why raise landmarks between my neighbor's field and mine, when my heart has made no division between our interests; but shares his joys and sorrows with the same force and vivacity as if originally my own? . . . And the whole human race would form only one family where all would live in common and everything be used freely without regard to property."

Here we have a vision of the perfect love of the Kingdom of God; and it is significant that Hume defines it partly in terms of actual achievements in family life. "We may observe," he declares, "that the case of families approaches to it; and the stronger the mutual benevolence is among individuals, the nearer it approaches, till distinctions of property be lost and confounded among them." But Hume does not understand the paradoxical relation between sacrificial and mutual love at all. He is certain that love can justify itself only "from its necessary use to the intercourse and social state of mankind." Therefore if it should not be able to validate itself by consequences of perfect mutuality; if the "returning or disguised selfishness of men" proved the "inconvenience" of a social state in which the self had no protection against the selfishness of others, even "imprudent fanatics" would be persuaded to return "anew to ideas of justice and of separate property."

Hume is quite right, of course, in insisting that social morality must seek the best possible harmony of life with life, given the egoism of man, and that men do, in fact, elaborate systems and restraints of justice to protect themselves and each other against human egoism. Even the "imprudent fanatics" of our own day, the Christian perfectionists, who think that *agape* is a simple possibility of history, avail themselves of such schemes of justice. But Hume does not understand that whatever achievements of mutuality actually exist in history have never been established by the cool calculations of social usefulness which he suggests. For such calculations would inevitably be too impressed by the peril of the "disguised selfishness" of men to encourage any venture of real brotherhood towards them.

History does contain an indefinite series of achievements in the organization of larger realms of brotherhood. The Biblical warning "if ye love them which love you, what reward have ye" [15] is certainly relevant to historic realities; for the failure of pure love to calculate possible reciprocal responses to it is the force which makes new ventures in brotherhood possible. The consequence of mutuality must, however, be the unintended rather than purposed consequence of the action. For it is too uncertain a consequence to encourage the venture towards the life of the other. According to the ethic of Jesus the actual motive of *agape* is always conformity to the will of God: "that ye may be children of your Father in heaven." Thus the harmonies which are actually achieved in history always are partly borrowed from the Eternal. [16]

[15] Mt. 5:46.

[16] Professor Anders Nygren's profound analysis of this problem in his *Agape and Eros* (S. P. C. K., London) has the virtue of revealing the contrast between the pure and disinterested love which the New Testament regards as normative and the egoistic element which is connoted in all love doctrines (*eros*) of classical thought. But he makes the contrast too absolute. Non-Christian conceptions of love do indeed seek to justify love from the standpoint of the happiness of the agent; but the freedom of man is such that he is not without some idea of the virtue of love which does not justify itself in terms of his own happiness. It is significant that Jesus does not regard the contrast between natural human love and the divine *agape* as absolute. He declares: "If ye then, being evil, know how to give good gifts unto your children, how much more shall your Father which is in heaven give good things to them that ask him" (Mt. 7:11).

Rudolf Bultmann makes the contrast between the demands of the Kingdom of God and the ethical possibilities of history even more absolute. He denies that the rigorous demands of the Sermon on the Mount

There are no limits to be set in history for the achievement of more universal brotherhood, for the development of more perfect and more inclusive mutual relations. All the characteristic hopes and aspirations of Renaissance and Enlightenment, of both secular and Christian liberalism are right at least in this, that they understand that side of the Christian doctrine which regards the *agape* of the Kingdom of God as a resource for infinite developments towards a more perfect brotherhood in history. The uneasy conscience of man over various forms of social injustice, over slavery and war, is an expression of the Christian feeling that history must move from the innocency of Adam to the perfection of Christ, from the harmony of life with life in unfree nature to the perfect love of the Kingdom of God. The vision of universal love expressed by St. Paul in the words: "There is neither Jew nor Greek, there is neither bond nor free, there is neither male nor female, for ye are all one in Christ Jesus," [17] is meant primarily for the church. But it cannot be denied that it is relevant to all social relationships. For the freedom of man makes it impossible to set any limits of race, sex, or social condition upon the brotherhood which may be achieved in history.

Even the purest form of *agape,* the love of the enemy and forgiveness towards the evil-doer, do not stand in contradiction to historical possibilities. Penal justice can achieve more and more imaginative forms; and these more imaginative and generous treatments of the evil-doer can be historically justified by the reclamation of the criminal. But they cannot be initiated purely by considerations of

---

have any relation to " 'the highest good' in the ethical sense." He declares that the "Kingdom of God is something miraculous, in fact absolute miracle, opposed to all the here and now; it is 'wholly other.'" (*Jesus and the Word,* pp. 35–37.) His insistence that the ethical injunctions of the New Testament have no relation to the observable ethical good of human experience but must be merely accepted in faith, may be regarded as excessive Hebraism and deficient in the Greek sense of the relation between God and the structural aspects of historic reality. His position is nicely refuted in the Johannine prologue in which Christ is regarded as the very foundation of the structures of history.

[17] Gal. 3:28.

their social value; for a considerable risk is always involved in such treatment. Furthermore every society will mix concern for the safety of society and sinful elements of vindictive passion with whatever elements of forgiving *agape* may be insinuated into its penological procedures. But there is no limit to the possible admixture of forgiving love in criminal justice, except of course the absolute limit that no society will ever deal with criminals in terms of pure forgiveness or achieve a perfect relation between justice and forgiveness.[18]

b. The Cross represents a transcendent perfection which clarifies obscurities of history and defines the limits of what is possible in historic development.

Every interpretation of human history which has some understanding of the transcendent norm of historical ethics is inclined to fall into the error of regarding the transcendent norm as a simple possibility. This error runs through the thought of most sectarian versions of Christianity and through the secularized forms of Christianity in the Renaissance and the Enlightenment. It is an error to which American liberal Protestantism has been particularly prone because sectarian and secular perfectionism have been compounded in this form of the Christian faith. Marxist apocalypticism also shares in this error. Whether by sanctifying grace (as in sectarian interpretations) or by the cumulative force of universal education (as in secular liberalism) or by a catastrophic reorganization of society (as in Marxism), it is believed possible to lift historic life to the plane upon which all distinctions between mutual love and disinterested and sacrificing love vanish. The Marxist version of this perfection, in which all rules of justice are transcended, is vividly

[18] W. Wiesner in his chapter in the Oxford Conference Report, *The Christian Faith and the Common Life,* presents a radical Lutheran version of the relation of forgiveness to the necessities of retributive justice and declares that they stand in contradiction to each other. There is as much truth, and as little, in this position as in the Tolstoyan perfectionism which imagines that there is a possibility of eliminating judge, jailor, and executioner from the historic schemes of retributive justice.

expressed by Lenin: "Every right," he declares, "is an application of the same measure to different people who are not the same and not equal to each other. This is why 'equal right' is really a violation of equality and an injustice. . . . Different people are not alike. One is strong and another weak. One is married and another not. . . . The first phase of communism can therefore still not produce justice and equality. Unjust differences in wealth will still exist; but the unjust exploitation of man by man will become impossible. . . . Immediately upon attainment of formal equality for all members of society . . . there will inevitably arise before humanity the question of going further from formal equality to real equality, *i.e.*, to realizing the rule: 'From each according to his ability and to each according to his need.' " [19]

This is a significant secular vision of the "Kingdom of God," where even the highest form of equal justice is transcended in an uncoerced and perfect mutuality. The Marxist finds such a vision plausible because he imagines that sinful egoism is derived merely from the class organization of society. The secular liberal finds similar visions plausible, primarily because he thinks that universal education will progressively universalize the mind until each person will be able (and willing?) to affirm the interests of others as much as his own. The sectarian and perfectionist Christian finds it plausible because he believes that sanctifying grace can destroy sin in fact as well as in principle. We shall have to deal with these errors more fully in subsequent chapters. In this context we need only to call attention to the fact that the Christian faith in its profoundest versions has never believed that the Cross would so change the very nature of historical existence that a more and more universal achievement of sacrificial love would finally transmute sacrificial love into successful mutual love, perfectly validated and by historical social consequences.

The New Testament never guarantees the historical success of the "strategy" of the Cross. Jesus warns his disciples against a too

[19] N. Lenin, *The State and Revolution*, Ch. 5, Par. iii and iv.

sanguine historical hope: "In this rejoice not, that the spirits are subject unto you; but rather rejoice because your names are written in heaven." [20] In that warning we have a telling refutation of the utopian corruptions of Christianity. Whatever the possibilities of success for *agape* in history (and there are possibilities of success because history cannot be at complete variance with its foundation) the final justification for the way of *agape* in the New Testament is never found in history. The motive to which Christ appeals is always the emulation of God or gratitude for the *agape* of God.

Thus the Cross clarifies the possibilities and limits of history and perennially refutes the pathetic illusions of those who usually deny the dimension of history which reaches into Eternity in one moment, and in the next dream of achieving an unconditioned perfection in history.

Since this possibility does not exist, it is not even right to insist that every action of the Christian must conform to *agape*, rather than to the norms of relative justice and mutual love by which life is maintained and conflicting interests are arbitrated in history. For as soon as the life and interest of others than the agent are involved in an action or policy, the sacrifice of those interests ceases to be "self-sacrifice." It may actually become an unjust betrayal of their interests. Failure to understand this simple fact and this paradoxical relation between individual and collective action has resulted in the unholy alliance between Christian perfectionism and cowardly counsels of political expediency in dealing with tyrants in our own day.

The preservation of cultures and civilizations is frequently possible only as individuals disregard their own success and failure and refuse to inquire too scrupulously into the possibilities or probabilities of maintaining their own life in a given course of action. Thus effective collective historical action depends to a considerable degree upon the individual's contempt for, or indifference to, his own fate; an indifference which is possible only if the individual possesses an

[20] Luke 10:20.

implicit or explicit faith in a dimension of existence which is deeper and higher than physical life and which makes it possible for him to confess: "Whether we live, we live unto the Lord; and whether we die, we die unto the Lord: whether we live therefore, or die, we are the Lord's." [21]

c. The Cross represents a perfection which contradicts the false pretensions of virtue in history and which reveals the contrast between man's sinful self-assertion and the divine *agape.*

Just as the Cross symbolizes the meaning of life which stands in contradiction to all conceptions of the "truth," seeking to complete the meaning of history from the inadequate centre of the hopes and ambitions of a particular nation or culture, so also it symbolizes the final goodness which stands in contradiction to all forms of human goodness in which self-assertion and love are compounded.

There are no forms of historical reality which do not contain this sinful admixture. There are no forms of remedial justice from which the egoistic element of vindictiveness has been completely purged. The coming decades of post-war reconstruction will offer us ample proof of this tragic fact. There are no political strategies for extending the realms of mutuality in the human community which remain immune to the egoistic corruption of imperialism. Every human community must be organized from a given centre of power; and that centre of power must try to be an impartial adjudicator of the interests of others even while it remains an interested and partial social force, individual or collective, international or intranational, among the many social forces which must be brought into an equilibrium. We cannot be complacent about this imperial corruption in all forms of political justice and social organization. The Cross is a constant source of contrition in regard to the corruption. But neither does history, even on its highest levels, achieve a purity which removes the contradiction between the divine *agape* and the egoistic element in the human community. That tragic aspect of history will be illumined anew when the world powers which have

[21] Romans 14:8.

defeated tyranny seek to organize the community of nations.[22] This is an aspect of historical reality which has been almost completely obscured by modern interpretations of history. Radical Reformation thought frequently emphasizes it to the exclusion of the other aspects we have considered. Recognition of this aspect of history has the distinction of being a unique Christian insight; for practically all other forms of interpreting history, whether classical or modern, whether mystical or legalistic, find some way of destroying the ultimate contradiction between the self-assertion of the human life and the divine *agape*.

IV

THE RELATION OF CHRIST'S PERFECTION TO ETERNITY

If the Christian doctrine of Christ as the "second Adam" refutes both the romantics, who think a return to primeval innocency possible, and the evolutionary optimists who think that history moves towards a perfection in which nature-history is transcended without ceasing to be grounded in nature, it also refutes the mystics who seek perfection by contemplation of, and final incorporation into, an eternity from which all vitalities and particularities of history have been subtracted. In Meister Eckhardt's heretical Christian mysticism, the goal of life is significantly unrelated to the innocency of Adam but is like the state of unity which preceded creation itself. "The poor man," he declares, "is not he who wants to do the will of God but he who lives in such a way as to be free of his own will and from the will of God, *even as he was when he was not*."[1] In the slightly less heretical and more Christian mysticism of Jacob Boehme the unity, defined as perfection, is not placed in an eternity preceding creation. But the perfection of Adam in the created world

---

[22] The Christian answer to the problem of the perennial and inevitable character of this corruption will be considered in Chapters VIII and IX.

[1] *Meister Eckhardt* by Franz Peiffer, translated by D. de B. Evans, Vol. I, p. 220.

is defined as an androgynic unity which is free of the tension and disunity of sexual differentiation. In common with Platonism and Hellenic Christianity, Boehme believes that bisexuality is a consequence of sin. Furthermore he thinks that Adam's perfection must have meant that he had a body which was "without intestines and without stomach," a rather vivid symbol of the mystic aversion to the physical basis of life.[2]

There is a tendency in all forms of rationalism and mysticism, including Christian rationalism and mysticism, to define perfection in history as the contemplation of the Eternal, rather than as a love which co-ordinates will to will under the will of God; and to define the perfection which transcends history as absorption into an Eternal Logos or an eternal unity, purer than *Logos* and form itself. Even the naturalistic Aristotle defines the ultimate good as the contemplation of eternal perfection,[3] and the Aristotelian and Platonic influence in medieval Christianity has frequently prompted it to define the perfection towards which life must move as contemplation rather than loving action; that is, to make *gnosis* rather than *agape* the final norm.

It is important to realize that the Christian doctrine of an incarnated *Logos* who becomes the "second Adam" is as rigorously opposed to dualistic doctrines which seek escape from history, as to romantic and naturalistic ones, in which history fulfills itself too simply. Man is neither a unity without freedom, nor freedom without vitality. Rooted in the necessities and limitations of nature he has a freedom which can only find its final security in God. Significantly St. Paul distinguishes love as sharply from *gnosis* as from law. To distinguish it from law is to emphasize the freedom of man, for which no law can be the final norm. To distinguish it from *gnosis* is to emphasize the difference between a contemplation of the eternal

[2] *Cf.* Ernst Benz, *Der Vollkommene Mensch nach Jacob Boehme,* pp. 51–70. Benz calls attention to the fact that the mystic aversion towards biological function rather justifies Nietzsche's remark that man's abdomen might well dissuade him from thinking himself a God.

[3] *Nicomachean Ethics,* Bk. X, vii, 7 and 9.

and a vital emulation of the divine love in which all the emotions and volitions of life are included.[4] The God whom Christians worship reveals his majesty and holiness not in eternal disinterestedness but in suffering love. And the moral perfection, which the New Testament regards as normative, transcends history not as thought transcends action but as suffering love transcends mutual love. It is an act rather than a thought which sets the Christ above history, and being an act, it is more indubitably in history than a mere thought.

In the Pauline conception there is a legitimate *gnosis,* a knowledge of God "in part," which is transcended in the consummation when "I shall know even as I am known."[5] But the elements in the historical which really abide are "faith, hope, and love, and the greatest of these is love."

While the Christian conception of love has had too great an authority in the church to allow any but heretical mystics, such as Eckhardt, to transmute the idea of ultimate perfection into one of pure contemplation, Christianity nevertheless has difficulty in preserving the Biblical conception of love against mystical and rationalistic tendencies to interpret this love in such a way that it becomes purely the love towards God and ceases to be related to brotherhood and community in history. If sectarian and liberal versions of Christianity are inclined to forget that the perfection of Christ transcends history, the mystical tradition in medieval Christianity forgets that the perfection of love revealed in Christ is relevant to history.

"There is nothing in the world to be compared with God," de-

---

[4] The *locus classicus* of the Pauline rejection of *gnosis* is in 1 Cor. 13. "Though I speak with the tongues of men and of angels and . . . though I have the gift of prophecy and understand all mysteries and all knowledge . . . and have not love, it profiteth me nothing." The argument is probably directed particularly against the *gnosis* promised in the mystery cults; but it is equally valid against gnosticism in the broader sense, which would include emancipations from evil promised in all forms of rationalism and mysticism.

[5] 1 Cor. 13:12.

clares St. John of the Cross, "and he who loves any other thing together with Him wrongs Him." [6] This sentiment clearly contradicts
Christ's own interpretation of the love commandment, with its
affirmation that the "second" commandment, enjoining the love of
the neighbour, is "like unto" the first, which enjoins love of God.
This medieval mystic in whom the mystical version of Christianity
is expressed in the most classic form, goes so far as to exclude the
love of the neighbour specifically from the ultimate perfection. He
writes: "As long as the soul has not attained unto the state of union
of which I speak, it is good that it should exercise itself in love, in
the active as well as the contemplative life. But once it is established
there it is no longer suitable that it should occupy itself with other
works or with exterior exercises which might raise the slightest
possible obstacle to its life of love with God, and I do not even
except those works most relevant to God's service." [7]

Significantly this logic drives the great mystic into a virtual dualism in which the innocency of Adam, the essential goodness of the
created world, is completely obscured as a relevant truth, and the
final perfection of man becomes identical with a final absorption
into the divine. St. John of the Cross declares: "For since the soul
has been made one thing with God it is after a certain manner God
by participation; for though this is not so as perfectly as in the next
life, the soul is, as it were, the shadow of God. And since the soul
by means of this substantial transformation is the shadow of God, it
does in and through God that which He does through Himself in
the soul, *in the same way as he does it.*" [8]

Though Catholic mysticism exceeds the limits usually maintained
by a Catholic rationalism in this emphasis, the renowned modern
neo-Thomist, Jacques Maritain, is probably not wrong in declaring
that there is no contradiction between anything implied by St.
Thomas and more explicitly asserted by St. John of the Cross. Mari-

---

[6] *Ascent of Mount Carmel*, Bk. I, v. 4.
[7] St. John of the Cross, *Canticles* 2d redaction, str. 28.
[8] *Canticles*, str. 38.

tain himself speaks of the mystical experience as proving that the soul can "break through the entanglements of created things and establish itself in the nudity of spirit." [9]

The Biblical dialectic which is imperiled, if not destroyed, by this type of Christian thought is succinctly expressed in the words of St. Paul in which he admonishes the faithful to "walk worthy of the vocation wherewith ye are called, with all lowliness and meekness, with long suffering, forbearing one another in love, endeavouring to keep the unity of the Spirit in the bond of peace." He justifies this admonition by the observation that there "is one God and Father of all, who is above all, and through all and in you all," in other words by an affirmation of the basic Christian belief in the transcendence of God over, and His immanence in, the world. The dialectic is strengthened still further by attributing the grace of unity to the ascended Lord but with the observation "that He that ascended what is it but that he also descended first into the lower parts of the earth? He that descended is the same also that ascended up far above all heavens, that he might fill all things." [10] In this Pauline statement the Biblical conception of the relation of history to the perfection of Christ is stated symbolically in very clear terms. It is a conception which is constantly imperiled by theories which either place the norm of history too simply within history or which conceive of an eternal perfection as irrelevant to history and achieved only when thought transcends action, or when mystical consciousness transcends thought; and when the soul, freed of will and impulse, of distractions and responsibilities, contemplates the eternal.

These mystical heresies reveal by contrast to what degree the Christian conception of the love of Christ is ethically normative in Christian life because of the prior conception of the character of God, as revealed in Christ. The God of Christian revelation is not disengaged from, but engaged in, the world by His most majestic attributes; it is consequently not the highest perfection for man to achieve a unity of being from which all natural and historical

[9] *Degrees of Knowledge*, p. 394.   [10] Eph. 4:1–10.

vitalities have been subtracted. The highest unity is a harmony of love in which the self relates itself in its freedom to other selves in their freedom under the will of God.

v

SUMMARY

all of this very important

An analysis of the full implications of the Christian doctrine of the· "second Adam" and the perfection of Christ yields principles for interpreting historical reality which illumine, and are validated by, the facts of history. The paradoxical relation of perfection to inno- cency, to maturity and to eternity comprehended in terms of the relation of the Cross to history, illumines all the complex relations of history.

The state of innocency towards which the Christian doctrine of perfection casts a provisional glance is a state of nature or prehistory in which the harmony of life with life, as nature knows it, has not yet been broken. In this state neither the individual nor the com- munity has achieved sufficient freedom over historical process to be "anxious" or insecure, or to be tempted by this insecurity to the abortive strategies of sin. Yet, in so far as human history knows no absolute state of nature, it is not possible to find any such locus of innocency in the life of either the individual or the race.

As freedom develops, both good and evil develop with it. The innocent state of trust develops into the anxieties and fears of free- dom; and these prompt the individual and the community to seek an unjust security at the expense of others. On the other hand it is possible that the same freedom may prompt larger and larger structures of brotherhood in human society. This brotherly relation of life with life is most basically the "law of life." It alone does justice to the freedom of the human spirit and the mutual depend- ence of men upon each other, their necessity of fulfilling themselves in each other.

There is, however, no development towards larger realms of broth- erhood without a corresponding development of the imperial corruption of brotherhood. There is, therefore, no historical development which gradually eliminates those sinful corruptions of brotherhood which stand in contradiction to the law of love. The law of love is, therefore, not a norm of history, in the sense that historical experience justifies it. Historical experience justifies more complex social strategies in which the self, individual and collective, seeks both to preserve its life and to relate it harmoniously to other lives. But such strategies of mutual love and of systems of justice cannot maintain themselves without inspiration from a deeper dimension of history. A strategy of brotherhood which has no other resource but historical experience degenerates from mutuality to a prudent regard for the interests of the self; and from the impulse towards community to an acceptance of the survival impulse as ethically normative.

The *agape,* the sacrificial love, which is for Christian faith revealed upon the Cross, has its primary justification in an "essential reality" which transcends the realities of history, namely, the character of God. It does not expect an immediate or historical validation but looks towards some ultimate consummation of life and history. On the other hand the Christian doctrine of Creation does not set the eternal and divine into absolute contradiction to the temporal and the historical. There are, therefore, validations of *agape* in actual history, in so far as concern for the other actually elicits a reciprocal response.

This interpretation of the possibilities and limits of history is the fruit of natural experience and a natural (rational) analysis of experience. For any rigorous examination of the problems of man in nature-history clearly reveals that history points beyond itself and that it does so by reason of the freedom and transcendence of the human spirit. It is never completely contained in, or satisfied by, the historical-natural process, no matter to what level this process may rise.

But this interpretation is the fruit of faith and revelation in so far as there is no experience which points irrefutably to the particular divine ground and end of history which Christian faith discerns in Christ and the Cross. In the realm of ethics as in the realm of truth, the revelation of Christ is foolishness, in the sense that experience does not lead us to expect or anticipate the answer which it makes to the ethical problem. But it is "wisdom to them that are called" in the sense that, once accepted, it becomes an adequate principle for interpreting the ethical problem in history. It is the only principle of interpretation which does justice to the two factors in the human situation: Man's involvement in natural process, including the imperative character of his natural impulse of survival; and his transcendence over natural process, including his uneasy conscience over the fact that the survival impulse should play so dominant a role in all his ethical calculations.

CHAPTER IV

WISDOM, GRACE AND POWER

(THE FULFILLMENT OF HISTORY)

EVERY FACET of the Christian revelation, whether of the relation of God to history, or of the relation of man to the eternal, points to the impossibility of man fulfilling the true meaning of his life and reveals sin to be primarily derived from his abortive efforts to do so. The Christian gospel nevertheless enters the world with the proclamation that in Christ both "wisdom" and "power" are available to man; which is to say that not only has the true meaning of life been disclosed but also that resources have been made available to fulfill that meaning.[1] In Him the faithful find not only "truth" but "grace."[2]

The whole of Christian history is filled with various efforts to relate these two propositions of the Christian faith to each other, in such a way that the one will not contradict the other. These efforts are never purely academic; for the two sides of the gospel correspond to two aspects of historic reality. The two emphases are contained in the double connotation of the word "grace" in the New Testament. Grace represents on the one hand the mercy and forgiveness of God by which He completes what man cannot complete

[1] *Cf.* 1 Cor. 4:19: "The Kingdom of God is not in word but in power."

[2] John 1:17.

98

and overcomes the sinful elements in all of man's achievements. Grace is the power of God over man. Grace is on the other hand the power of God in man; it represents an accession of resources, which man does not have of himself, enabling him to become what he truly ought to be. It is synonymous with the gift of the "Holy Spirit." The Spirit is not merely, as in idealistic and mystical thought, the highest development of the human spirit. He is not identical with the most universal and transcendent levels of the human mind and consciousness. The Holy Spirit is the spirit of God indwelling in man. But this indwelling Spirit never means a destruction of human self-hood. There is therefore a degree of compatibility and continuity between human self-hood and the Holy Spirit. Yet the Holy Spirit is never a mere extension of man's spirit or identical with its purity and unity in the deepest or highest levels of consciousness. In that sense all Christian doctrines of "grace" and "Spirit" contradict mystical and idealistic theories of fulfillment.

The conception in Christian thought of a fulfillment and completion of life by resources which are not man's own, prevents Christian ideas of fulfillment by grace from standing in contradiction to the more fundamental conviction that human life and history cannot complete themselves; and that sin is synonymous with abortive efforts to complete them. It is furthermore in consistent relation with the proposition that man perceives the completeness beyond his incompleteness and the holiness beyond his sin only by faith. For if it is possible to become aware of the limits of human possibilities by a faith which apprehends the revelation of God from beyond those limits, it must also be possible to lay hold of the resources of God, beyond human limits, by faith. And this certainly is reinforced by the character of the Christian revelation, according to which God is not a supernal perfection to which man aspires, but has resources of love, wisdom and power, which come down to man. The very apprehension of the "wisdom of God," the completion of the structure of meaning by faith, must have connotations of "power" in it. For if we understand the possibilities and limits of life from beyond ourselves, this understanding has some potentialities of fulfilling the meaning of life. It breaks the egoistic and self-centred forms of fulfillment, by which the wholesome development of man is always arrested and corrupted. For this reason it is not possible to give a fully logical or exactly chronological account of the relation of faith to repentance, of the apprehension of truth which is beyond our comprehension to the shattering of the self by a power from beyond ourself. If a man does not know the truth about God, who is more than an extension of his self (a truth to be known only by faith), he cannot repent of the premature and self-centred completion of his life around a partial and inadequate centre. But it can be, and has been, argued with equal cogency, that without repentance, that is, without the shattering of the self-centred self, man is too much his own god to feel the need of, or to have the capacity for, knowing the true God. The invasion of the self from beyond the self is therefore an invasion of both "wisdom" and "power," of both "truth" and "grace." The relation of insight to will, of wisdom to power in this experience is too intricate to be subject to precise analysis.

Yet whatever "newness of life" flows from the experience of repentance and faith is, when governed by true Christian faith, conscious of a continued incompleteness and a certain persistence of the strategy of sin. For this reason the peace which follows conversion is never purely the contentment of achievement. It is always, in part, the peace which comes from the knowledge of forgiveness.

II

THE BIBLICAL DOCTRINE OF GRACE

When we turn to the New Testament doctrine of grace, more particularly to the Pauline interpretation of it, it becomes apparent that both facets of the experience of grace—the conquest of sin in the heart of man on the one hand, and the merciful power of God over the sin which is never entirely overcome in any human heart, on the other—are fully expressed in the Pauline doctrine. The relation

between them is not always made explicit. It is therefore possible for
the various Christian traditions, which emphasize the one or the
other facet of grace, to find support in this or that Scriptural text.
In this way St. Paul's thought has become the fountain source of
both perfectionist theories of grace and of the protest of Reformation
thought against them.[1]

Schlatter describes the twofold aspect of the Pauline experience
of grace with the right circumspection and impartiality: "He has a
sense of sin, as including and comprehending all his actions, and
yet at the same time and in the same consciousness he has a good
conscience which is at peace with itself and is conscious of the nor-
mality of its actions. Both of these aspects of his consciousness are
rooted and united in the awareness of the divine forgiveness and the
sense of a righteousness which divine grace has imparted."[2]

There are texts in the Pauline epistles which lean to the one or the
other side of the interpretation of grace. The contrast between the
old life and the new is described again and again in terms which
seem to make an absolute[3] distinction between the two.

But it must be observed at once that some of the very assertions

---

[1] Paul Wernle observes quite correctly: "All gnostic and methodistic
sects which have insisted upon or sought after the sinlessness of the
redeemed, have merely exaggerated a true element in the Pauline tradition." *Der Christ und die Suende bei Paulus*, p. 24.

[2] A. Schlatter, *Der Glaube im Neuen Testament*, p. 503.

[3] Cf. *inter alia*: Romans 6:8 ff. "Now if we be dead with Christ we
believe that we shall also live with him. Knowing that Christ, being
raised from the dead, dieth no more; death hath no more dominion over
him. For in that he died, he died unto sin once; but in that he liveth he
liveth unto God. Likewise reckon yourselves dead indeed unto sin but
alive unto God through Jesus Christ our Lord." The death and resurrection of Christ as symbolic of the death of sin and the resurrection of the
new life of righteousness is a perennial theme in Pauline thought.
 Romans 8:6. "To be carnally minded is death; but to be spiritually
minded is life and peace."
 Romans 6:22. "But now, being made free from sin and become servants to God, ye have your fruit unto holiness and the end everlasting
life."
 Eph. 4:24. "That ye put on the new man, which after God is created
in righteousness and true holiness."

which lend themselves to perfectionist interpretations are immediately followed by injunctions which cast doubt upon such an exposition. These injunctions declare in effect: you are now sinless. Therefore you must not sin any more. The exhortation implies that the original statements have a slightly different meaning than their obvious connotation. They really mean: self-love has been destroyed in principle in your life. See to it now that the new principle of devotion to God in Christ is actualized in your life.[4] The qualifying statements, following immediately upon affirmations which suggest, or might suggest, complete holiness, raise the question whether St. Paul's conception of holiness ever connotes complete freedom from sin. He does undoubtedly maintain that there is a radical difference between "carnal-mindedness" and "spiritual-mindedness" and this difference might be defined as the contrast between the life which is governed by the *principle* of self-centredness and one which is governed by the *principle* of devotion and obedience to God. But his injunction to the sinless, not to sin any more, implies that he understands the possibility of sinning for those who have broken with sin in principle.[5]

[4] Cf. *inter alia*: Romans 6:11–12. "Likewise reckon ye also yourselves to be dead indeed unto sin . . . *let not sin therefore reign* in your mortal body."

In Eph. 4: 17–32, the logic of the Christian life is said to demand that "ye henceforth walk not as the other Gentiles walk, in the vanity of their mind." The fact that they have renounced sin in principle demands that they break with it in fact, and the redeemed are admonished to conquer very obvious sins: "Let him that stole steal no more," etc.

Eph. 5:8: "For ye were sometimes darkness but now are ye light in the Lord: walk as children of the light."

Gal. 5:24–26: "And they that are Christ's have crucified the flesh with the affections and lusts. If we live in the spirit, *let us also walk* in the spirit. Let us not be desirous of vainglory, provoking one another, envying one another."

[5] The Johannine epistles state the idea of sinlessness more unqualifiedly and have, therefore, always been favorite sources of proof texts for sanctificationist doctrines, particularly in the Eastern church. *Cf.* 1 John 3:6: "Whosoever abideth in him sinneth not." 1 John 3:9: "Who-

This interpretation is reinforced by the well-known Pauline disavowal of perfection: "Not as though I had already attained, either were already perfect; but I follow after, if that I may apprehend that for which also I am apprehended of Christ Jesus,"[6] in which the newness of life in principle is regarded as a gift, which must subsequently be realized progressively in volition and aspiration.

These qualifications make it quite apparent that there are no essential contradictions in Pauline thought, however much the emphasis may shift from one to the other aspect of grace. The insistence upon the radical difference between the old and the new life is not in conflict with what must be regarded as the primary Pauline emphasis; his idea of grace as "justification," as the assurance of divine forgiveness. On this side of Pauline thought the disavowal of perfection is explicit and precise. The very burden of the Pauline message is that there is no peace in our own righteousness. The final peace of the soul is gained on the one hand by the assurance of divine forgiveness; and on the other hand by "faith." The Christ who is apprehended by faith, *i.e.* to whom the soul is obedient in principle, "imputes" his righteousness to it. It is not an actual possession except "by faith."[7]

---

soever is born of God doth not commit sin; for his seed remaineth with him; and he can not sin because he is born of God." The Johannine literature asserts sinlessness of actual acts because its conception of the new life, influenced by Hellenistic thought, connotes an almost metaphysical distinction between the new and the old life. Yet even here we find important reservations. Cf. *inter alia*: 1 John 1:8: "If we say we have no sin we deceive ourselves and the truth is not in us."

[6] Phil. 3:12.

[7] Cf. *inter alia*: Romans 5:1: "Therefore being justified by faith, we have peace with God, through our Lord Jesus Christ."
Romans 3:22 ff.: "There is no difference: for all have sinned and come short of the glory of God; being justified freely by his grace through the redemption that is in Christ Jesus, whom God has set forth as a propitiation through faith in his blood, to declare his righteousness for the remission of sins that are past, through the forbearance of God."
Eph. 2:8: "For by grace are ye saved through faith. . . . It is the

This doctrine of the "imputation of righteousness" has always been offensive to moralistic interpreters of Christian faith. They have made much of the non-moral character of such imputation. But forgiveness, as a form of love which is beyond good and evil, is bound to be offensive to pure moralists. The Pauline doctrine really contains the whole Christian conception of God's relation to human history. It recognizes the sinful corruption in human life on every level of goodness. It knows that the pride of sin is greatest when men claim to have conquered sin completely. ("Not of works lest any man should boast.") It proclaims no sentimentalized version of the divine mercy. It is possible to appropriate this mercy only through the Christ, whose sufferings disclose the wrath of God against sin, and whose perfection as man is accepted as normative for the believer, by the same faith which sees in Him, particularly His Cross, the revelation of the mystery of the divine mercy triumphing over, without annulling, the divine wrath. The doctrine is, of course, subject to corruption, and has been corrupted innumerable times in the Christian ages. It can become a vehicle of complacency, prompting men to "continue in sin that grace may abound." It may be interpreted in juridical and legalistic terms in such a way that it never conveys the religious truth which strikes man in the very centre of his spiritual being. But all this does not change the profundity of the conception of "justification by faith" and its complete conformity with the conception of life, God and history as we have it in the gospels.

There is a possibility that the balance which St. Paul maintains between the two facets of the experience of grace—the power of

---

gift of God, not of works, lest any man should boast. For we are his workmanship, created in Christ Jesus unto good works."

Gal. 5:4: "Christ is become of no effect unto you, whosoever of you are justified by the law; ye are fallen from grace."

Phil. 3:8–11: "I have suffered the loss of all things, and . . . do count them but dung . . . that I may win Christ, and be found in him not having my own righteousness, which is of the law, but that which is through the faith of Christ, the righteousness which is of God by faith."

God within the life of man, making for newness of life, and the power of God's love over man, annulling his sin by His mercy—is slightly imperiled in some Pauline ideas, which are strongly influenced by his polemic against Jewish legalism. In these he suggests that the forgiveness of sins applies particularly to the sins of the past [8] and seems to identify the "works" of the law which justify no man, particularly with the works of the historic Jewish law.[9]

The Pauline emphasis upon forgiveness of past sins lies at the basis of the whole Catholic-Medieval interpretation of the relation of justification and sanctification, in which justification is made the prelude of subsequent sanctification, and in which the complex and paradoxical relation between the two is imperiled or destroyed, thus leading to a new form of self-righteousness. Possibly, St. Paul did not carry his own thought through to its ultimate conclusion and ages of Christian experience were required to disclose that a righteousness "by grace" may lead to new forms of Pharisaism if it does not recognize that forgiveness is as necessary at the end as at the beginning of the Christian life.

The profound confession of St. Paul in Romans 7 has sometimes been used to refute the interpretation of Pauline thought, according to which justification applies only to past sins in the state before conversion. These refutations argue that a man who confesses to such inner tensions as are expressed in the words: "For the good that I would I do not: but the evil which I would not, that I do," could certainly not have believed that the forgiveness of sins applied only to sins before conversion. The difficulty with this refutation is that there is no certainty that St. Paul intended to describe his spiritual state after conversion in the words of Romans 7. Whether this con-

---

[8] *Cf.* Romans 3:24: "Being justified freely by His grace through the redemption that is in Christ Jesus: whom God hath set forth to be a propitiation . . . for the remission of sins *that are past."*

[9] Gal. 3:11: "But that no man is justified by the law in the sight of God it is evident: for the just shall live by faith."

Romans 3:20: "Therefore by the deeds of the law there shall no flesh be justified in his sight; for by the law is the knowledge of sin."

fession was intended to be purely retrospective, or was meant to express a tension which even the redeemed experience, is an exegetical problem which is answered according to previous doctrinal presuppositions. With our own doctrinal preconceptions of the problem involved we cannot believe St. Paul meant to confine his confession to the state before conversion. The record of Christian history proves that no living man is ever completely emancipated from the inner contradictions, which the chapter so eloquently portrays.

As for the suggestion that St. Paul meant to confine the "deeds of the law," which failed to justify, merely to the Jewish law and suggested thereby that the righteousness of grace fulfilled a more perfect law, namely the law of love, this theory is refuted by the fact that contrast in the relevant passages is between "law" and "faith." Undoubtedly St. Paul was thinking particularly of Jewish legalism, when he elaborated the thesis that law, of itself, was a curse, since no man fulfilled it; and that "deeds of the law" were a source of delusion, since they pretended to a perfection which no man could achieve. But there is no reason why the condemnation of legalistic righteousness should be interpreted in the thought of St. Paul as applying only to the explicit Jewish law. He, himself, extends the whole principle of the law beyond the Jewish legal and moral tradition and asserts that "when the Gentiles, which have not the law, do by nature the things contained in the law, these, having not the law, are a law unto themselves." [10]

It is true of course that a higher than the traditional law is implied in the "gospel." The New Testament is critical of the law not only because it does not furnish the resources to fulfill its own demands, but also because its demands are not high enough and do not exhaust the possibilities of good in any given situation. These possibilities are comprehended only in the law of love, which transcends and fulfills all law. But this is not the point which St. Paul is

[10] Romans 2:14. This argument significantly precedes the discussion of the relation of "law" and "faith" in Romans 3.

making when he criticizes the deeds of the law, though it may be implied in the criticism. It may be implied because the keeping of the law may give men a false sense of virtue and obscure the unrighteousness of those who are legally righteous.

A survey of Pauline thought must thus lead to the conclusion that there is no contradiction in his elaboration of the doctrine of grace. There is, at least, no final contradiction. There is, on the contrary, a profound understanding of the complexities of the spiritual life of man with its possibilities of genuine newness of life in "love, joy and peace" for those who have broken with self-love in principle; and yet of the possibility of sin even on this new level of righteousness.

III

GRACE AS POWER IN, AND AS MERCY TOWARDS, MAN

An analysis of the relation of grace as power and grace as pardon in Biblical thought, though it may prove Biblical doctrine to be essentially consistent, will hardly convince modern man of the relevance of the doctrine. All modern theories of human nature whether Christian, semi-Christian or non-Christian, have arrived at simpler solutions for the moral problem. These simpler solutions are, broadly speaking, comprehended in the one strategy of increasing the power and the range of mind and reason against the narrower impulses of the body. It is necessary therefore to apply the Biblical doctrine to the facts of experience in order to establish its relevance. This can be done most conveniently in terms of the application of a very comprehensive and profound Pauline text to the moral and spiritual experience of men: "I am crucified with Christ: nevertheless I live; yet not I, but Christ liveth in me: and the life which I now live in the flesh I live by the faith of the Son of God who loved me, and gave himself for me."[1]

[1] Gal. 2:20.

It will be well to consider the implications of this description of the process of regeneration in order:

1. *"I am Crucified with Christ"*

We have previously noted that St. Paul is fond of interpreting the destruction of the old life and the birth of the new in the symbolism of the death and resurrection of Christ. The first assertion of his interpretation is that the old, the sinful self, the self which is centred in itself, must be "crucified." It must be shattered and destroyed. It cannot be redeemed merely by extending the range of mind against the inertia of the body. The Christian doctrine of grace stands in juxtaposition to the Christian doctrine of original sin and has meaning only if the latter is an accurate description of the actual facts of human experience. It will not be necessary to reconsider this doctrine here.[2] But it may be helpful to restate the human situation very briefly in terms of the doctrine. The plight of the self is that it cannot do the good that it intends.[3] The self in action seems impotent to conform its actions to the requirements of its essential being, as seen by the self in contemplation. The self is so created in freedom that it cannot realize itself within itself. It can only realize itself in loving relation to its fellows. Love is the law of its being. But in practice it is always betrayed into self-love. It comprehends the world and human relations from itself as the centre. It cannot, by willing to do so, strengthen the will to do good. This weakness is partly due to finiteness. The propulsive powers of the self, with its natural survival impulse, do not suffice to fulfill the obligations which the self as free spirit discerned. But the weakness is not merely one of "nature." It is also spiritual. The self never follows its "natural" self-interest without pretending to be obedient to obligations beyond itself. It transcends its own interests too much

---

[2] We have sought to do this in Vol. I, Chs. VII–IX.

[3] "For to will is present with me: but how to perform that which is good I find not." Romans 7:18.

to be able to serve them without disguising them in loftier pretensions. This is the covert dishonesty and spiritual confusion which is always involved in the self's undue devotion to itself.[4]

The self in this state of preoccupation with itself must be "broken" and "shattered" or, in the Pauline phrase, "crucified." It cannot be saved merely by being enlightened. It is a unity and therefore cannot be drawn out of itself merely by extending its perspective upon interests beyond itself. If it remains self-centred, it merely uses its wider perspective to bring more lives and interests under the dominion of its will-to-power. The necessity of its being shattered at the very centre of its being gives perennial validity to the strategy of evangelistic sects, which seek to induce the crisis of conversion.[5] The self is shattered whenever it is confronted by the power and holiness of God and becomes genuinely conscious of the real source and centre of all life. In Christian faith Christ mediates the confrontation of the self by God; for it is in Christ that the vague sense of the divine, which human life never loses, is crystallized into a revelation of a divine mercy and judgment. In that revelation fear of judgment and hope of mercy are so mingled that despair induces repentance and repentance hope.[6]

[4] Described by St. Paul in the words: "Their foolish heart was darkened." Romans 1:21.

The Augustinian definition of the plight of the self as a "defect of the will" is correct in pointing to the necessity of an accession of power from beyond the self; but it is incorrect, or at least subject to misinterpretation, in so far as it suggests mere weakness, rather than spiritual confusion as the cause of the vicious circle of self-centredness.

[5] There is of course no absolute necessity for a single crisis. The shattering of the self is a perennial process and occurs in every spiritual experience in which the self is confronted with the claims of God, and becomes conscious of its sinful, self-centred state.

[6] While Christians rightly believe that all truth necessary for such a spiritual experience is mediated only through the revelation in Christ, they must guard against the assumption that only those who know Christ "after the flesh," that is, in the actual historical revelation, are capable of such a conversion. A "hidden Christ" operates in history.

notice that Paul says
"I am" rather that "I was"

2. *"Nevertheless I Live"*

The Christian experience of the new life is an experience of a new selfhood. The new self is more truly a real self because the vicious circle of self-centredness has been broken. The self lives in and for others, in the general orientation of loyalty to, and love of, God; who alone can do justice to the freedom of the self over all partial interests and values. This new self is the real self; for the self is infinitely self-transcendent; and any premature centring of itself around its own interests, individually or collectively, destroys and corrupts its freedom.

The possibility of a reconstruction of the self is felt to be the consequence of "power" and "grace" from beyond itself because the true analysis of the plight of the self revealed it to be due to impotence rather than to lack of knowledge. The current and contemporary ideas of salvation by knowledge (even as the gnostic ways of salvation in the ancient world) rest upon a dualistic interpretation of human personality, which separates mind from body, and spirit from nature. They obscure the unity of selfhood in all its vital and rational processes. Wherever this dualism prevails "spirit" is devitalized, and physical life is despiritualized.

The assertion, "nevertheless I live," may be taken to refute two alternative schemes of salvation. In the one the self is indeed invaded by "spirit" as "power" but it is not the "Holy Spirit" and therefore it destroys the self. In the other the spirit of the self seeks to extend itself into its most universal and abstract form until all power, and ultimately the self itself, is lost.

The possession of the self by something less than the "Holy Spirit" means that it is possible for the self to be partly fulfilled and partly destroyed by its submission to a power and spirit which is greater than the self in its empiric reality but not great enough to do justice

---

And there is always the possibility that those who do not know the historical revelation may achieve a more genuine repentance and humility than those who do. If this is not kept in mind the Christian faith easily becomes a new vehicle of pride.

to the self in its ultimate freedom. Such spirit can be most simply defined as demonic. The most striking, contemporary form of it is a religious nationalism in which race and nation assume the eminence of God and demand unconditioned devotion. This absolute claim for something which is not absolute identifies the possessing spirit as "demonic"; for it is the nature of demons to make pretensions of divinity; just as the devil "fell" because he sought the place of God.[7] The invasion and possession of the self by spirit, which is not the Holy Spirit, produces a spurious sense of transfiguration. The self is now no longer the little and narrow self, but the larger collective self of race or nation. But the real self is destroyed. The real self has a height of spiritual freedom which reaches beyond race and nation and which is closer to the eternal than the more earthbound collective entities of man's history. Such demonic possession therefore destroys and blunts the real self and reduces it to the dimensions of nature.[8]

However terrible the consequences of modern demonic possessions, particularly in political life, they furnish the useful lesson of proving that human life is actually subject to power and not merely to mind. Modern political religions captured men partly because our liberal culture had become devitalized and "rationalized" to the point where salvation or the fulfillment of life was universally regarded as no more than the extension of mind. Men felt certain that they possessed themselves; and sought in the complacency of their self-possession to extend the range of the self and to make it more inclusive. But a self which possesses itself in such a way never escapes from itself. Human personality is so constructed that it must be possessed if it is to escape the prison of self-possession. The infinite regression of its self-transcendence represents possibilities of freedom

[7] *Cf.* Vol. I, p. 180.

[8] *Cf.* Erich Fromm, *Escape from Freedom* for a psychological discussion of what is involved in modern demonic politics. It goes without saying that loyalty to nation and other historical communities is not destructive of freedom when these do not make final and absolute claims upon the human spirit.

which are never actualized in self-possession; for self-possession means self-centredness. The self must be possessed from beyond itself.

Yet such possession of the self is destructive if the possessing spirit is anything less than the "Holy Spirit." For in that case spirit represents some partial and particular vitality in life and history and therefore does not deserve the unconditioned devotion which is consequent upon being thus possessed. According to the Christian faith, Christ is the criterion of the holiness of spirit.[9] He is the criterion of holiness because the revelation of God in Christ is on the one hand an historical focus of the divine, through which the mystery of the divine becomes morally and socially relevant to human nature, involved in finiteness and unable to comprehend the eternal. On the other hand it is the unique character of the revelation of God in Christ that it makes the divine and eternal known in history without giving any particular or partial force, value or vitality of history a sanctity or triumph which its finite and imperfect character does not deserve. Christ is thus both the criterion of the holiness of spirit and the symbol of the relevance between the divine and the human.

The Pauline word, "nevertheless I live," is set not only against the fulfillment of self by demonic possession through which the self is really corrupted and destroyed; it also marks the contrast between Christian conceptions of fulfillment and mystic doctrines of salvation in which the final goal is the destruction of the self. We have previously considered the tendencies towards self-destruction in various types of naturalistic, idealistic and mystic philosophies and religions.[10] We need only to emphasize at this point that the contrast between mystic-idealistic and Christian conceptions of self-fulfillment is determined by the "existential" character of the

[9] *Cf.* 1 John 4:1–2: "Beloved, believe not every spirit, but try the spirits whether they are of God; because many false prophets are gone out into the world. Hereby know ye the Spirit of God. Every spirit that confesseth that Jesus Christ is come in the flesh *is* of God."

[10] *Cf.* Vol. I. Ch. III.

self in Christian doctrines. The self is a unity of finiteness and free-dom, of involvement in natural process and transcendence over process. There is, therefore, not one particular level of the self, either in its consciousness or its reason, which can be extricated from flux and thereby achieve redemption. But on the other hand the unity of the self is so conceived in the Christian faith that it is not destroyed in the process of its fulfillment. Mystic doctrines of salva-tion might be expressed in a paraphrase of the Pauline word: "The Christ in me has been resurrected; therefore I have ceased to live."[11] According to these doctrines the real self is never threatened, judged, crucified or destroyed in any first step of salvation. Yet it is destroyed and lost in the final step. According to these doctrines there are various selves, and more particularly two: one immersed in finiteness and the other transcending it;[12] yet neither is a real self.

According to the Christian doctrine the sinful self must be de-stroyed from beyond itself because it does not have the power to lift itself out of its narrow interests. It cannot do so because all of its transcendent powers are intimately and organically related to its finiteness. It is tempted by this situation to pretend emancipation; but this pretension is its sin. Yet when the sinful self is broken and the real self is fulfilled from beyond itself, the consequence is a new

[11] This contrast between Christian and mystic doctrines is analysed profoundly in James Denney's *The Christian Doctrine of Reconciliation* and summarized in his phrase: "I would rather be saved in Christ than lost in God."

[12] One could multiply examples of this destruction of selfhood in various idealistic and mystic schools of thought. It may be helpful to offer a single example from the thought of Francis H. Bradley: "The finite is more or less transmuted and as such disappears in being accomplished. This common destiny is assuredly the end of the good. The ends sought by self-assertion and *self-sacrifice* are each alike unat-tainable. The individual can never himself become a harmonious system. In the complete gift and dissipation of his personality *he as such* must vanish; and with that the good as such is transcended and submerged. . . . Most emphatically no self-assertion or self-sacrifice nor any goodness or morality has as such any reality in the absolute." *Appearance and Reality*, pp. 419–20.

life rather than destruction. In the Christian doctrine the self is therefore both more impotent and more valuable, both more dependent and more indestructible than in the alternate doctrines.[13]

3. *"Yet not I; but Christ Liveth in Me"*

The last of the Pauline assertions about the reconstruction of the self in the experience of conversion and "self-realization" could be defined as a "negation of a negation"; for the denial that the self has been destroyed is now made subject to another denial on another level. Just what does St. Paul mean by this final denial "Yet not I; but Christ liveth in me"?

There is an ambiguity in this final explication of the relation of the self to Christ which may well be an expression of the double aspect of the Christian experience of grace, to which we have previously alluded, and with which all the Christian ages are concerned. The "yet not I" could be intended to assert merely the "priority of grace," to be a confession by the converted self that its new life is the fruit, not of its own power and volition, but of an accretion of power and an infusion of grace. It could also be intended as an affirmation that the new self is never an accomplished reality; that in every historic concretion there is an element of sinful self-realization, or premature completion of the self with itself at the centre; that, therefore, the new self is the Christ of intention rather than an actual achievement. It is the self only by faith, in the sense that its dominant purpose and intention are set in the direction of Christ as the norm. It is the self only by grace, in the sense that the divine mercy "imputes" the perfection of Christ and accepts the self's intentions for achievements.

The double negation could mean either one or the other of these two affirmations. But why could it not mean both? Is it not fun-

---

[13] We shall have to consider in a later chapter how this Christian conception of selfhood is emphasized, guarded and expressed in the paradoxical Christian hope of the "resurrection of the body."

damental to Pauline thought that these two aspects of grace are always involved, in varying degrees of emphasis in the various interpretations of the life of the spirit? And is it not the testimony of human experience that in the final experience of "love, joy and peace," it is not possible to distinguish between the consciousness of possessing something which we could not have possessed of ourselves and the consciousness of not possessing it finally but having it only by faith?

We shall proceed upon the assumption that both affirmations are contained in the Pauline "negation of the negation" and scrutinize them in turn.

a. Grace as the power not our own.

Whenever the power of sinful self-love is taken seriously there is a concomitant sense of gratitude in the experience of release from self. It is felt that this is a miracle which the self could not have accomplished.[14] The self was too completely its own prisoner by the "vain imagination" of sin to be able to deliver itself. Just as the truth of God which breaks the vicious circle of false truth, apprehended from the self as the false centre, can never be other than "foolishness" to the self-centred self until it has been imparted by "grace" and received by faith; so also the power which breaks the self-centred will must be perceived as power from beyond the self; and even when it has become incorporated into the new will, its source is recognized in the confession: "I, yet not I."

Yet a difficult problem confronts us in this confession. If divine

---

[14] Augustine expresses this continued sense of gratitude and humility in the new life in a classic passage: "How is it then that miserable men dare to be proud, either of their free will before they are freed; or of their own strength, if they have been freed? . . . If therefore they are slaves of sin, why do they boast of free will? For by what a man is overcome to the same is he delivered as a slave. But if they have been freed why do they vaunt themselves as if it were by their own doing and boast as if it had not been received?" "On the Spirit and the Letter," Ch. 52, in *Nicene and Post-Nicene Fathers,* First Series, Vol. V.

grace alone were the source of the new life Christian faith would be forced to accept a doctrine of divine determinism which would seem to imperil every sense of human responsibility. This is exactly the danger which Reformation theology, and more particularly Calvinistic theology, runs in its doctrines of predestination; and this tendency has been reaffirmed in the modern radical Reformation thought of Barth. It cannot be denied that the doctrine has some Scriptural authority. St. Paul did not hesitate to affirm, on occasion, the almost capricious character of the divine mercy.[15]

The possible consequences of moral irresponsibility which may arise from such conceptions of the divine determinism are illustrated by an example admitted by Augustine himself. He reports that a group of monks, upon being taken to task for their moral sloth into which their piety had degenerated, declared: "Why do you preach to us about our duties and exhort us to fulfill them, since it is not we who act but God who worketh in us both to will and to do? ... Let our superiors be satisfied to point out our duties ... but let them not reprove us when we are at fault, since we are such as God has foreseen us to be and his grace has not been given us to do better." [16]

The moral and spiritual irresponsibility of these monks is an example of a constant peril to the spiritual life arising from too deterministic conceptions of redemption, though it is fair to observe that some Christian traditions have achieved a sense of responsibility in practice which their own doctrines of predestination denied.   ·

It may be relevant to note that the Pauline text, of which the monks availed themselves in part, contains in its full form a more paradoxical statement of the relation of grace and free will. St. Paul writes: "Work out *your own* salvation with fear and trembling; for *it is God* which worketh in you both to will and to do of his

[15] Cf. *inter alia*: Romans 9:18: "Therefore hath he mercy on whom he will have mercy, and whom he will he hardeneth."

[16] St. Augustine, *De corruptione et gratia*, 4-10.

good pleasure."[17] This statement of the relation of divine grace to human freedom and responsibility does more justice to the complex facts involved than either purely deterministic or purely moralistic interpretations of conversion.

If it be true, as we have maintained,[18] that no sinful self-centredness can ever destroy the structure of freedom and self-transcendence in man, it must follow that there is some inner testimony from the very character and structure of the human psyche against the strategy of sinful egotism. The finite mind has some understanding of its own finiteness; and therefore it cannot escape an uneasy conscience over its sinful effort to complete its own life about "itself and its own" (Luther). This is the "point of contact" between grace and the natural endowments of the soul, which even Luther, despite his doctrine of total depravity, admits and which Karl Barth seeks desperately to deny. As long as there is such a point of contact there is something in man to which appeal can be made; though it must be admitted that men may be driven to despair, rather than repentance, either by the events or the appeals which shake the self-confidence of the sinful self.

The careful effort of Catholic theology to do justice to both grace and free will would therefore seem to be more correct than the tendency in Augustinian and Reformation theology to deny all human activity in, and responsibility for, repentance or faith. Thomas Aquinas defines the relation between the two in the well-known metaphor of the light of the sun and the seeing of the eye. The analogy for grace is the light which comes from the sun and without which man could not see at all. But the necessity and possi-

---

[17] Phil. 2:12–13. A word of the Book of Revelation contains the same double emphasis: "Behold, I stand at the door and knock; if any man hear my voice and *open the door*, I will come in to him, and will sup with him, and he with me." Rev. 3:20.

[18] Particularly in the discussion of *Justitia Originalis* in Vol. I, Ch. X.

bility of human action is expressed in the analogy: "He who has his eyes turned away from the light of the sun prepares himself to receive the light of the sun by turning his eyes thither."[19]

The weakness of this Catholic "synergism" is that it defines the limits of human activity and responsibility and of divine grace too precisely and exactly, and places them too much on the same level; a weakness which pertains to all Thomistic analyses of the final mysteries. Thereby the profundity of the experience of conversion tends to be obscured. The real situation is that both affirmations—that only God in Christ can break and reconstruct the sinful self, and that the self must "open the door" and is capable of doing so—are equally true; and they are both unqualifiedly true, each on its own level. Yet either affirmation becomes false if it is made without reference to the other.

From the level of the sinful self, surveying its own situation, it is always true that it has the possibility of, and therefore responsibility for, becoming conscious of the undue character of its self-love. But when the self stands beyond itself "by faith," it is conscious of the fact that nothing it has done or can do is free of debt to the miracle of grace. It cannot explain why this tragic event, or that impulse towards the life of another, or this word of truth from the gospel should have shattered its old self-confidence and made conversion and reconstruction possible. From that perspective everything is a miracle of grace and every form of newness of life justifies the question: "What hast thou that thou hast not received?"

Whenever this apprehension of the situation by faith becomes dimmed, a careful balancing of the two factors of redemption on the same level easily, and almost invariably, leads to new forms of self-righteousness. Thus St. Gregory, the theologian, began a description of his father's Christian life with a nice balance of the two factors: "I do not know which to praise more: the grace which called him or his own choice." But he ended his appreciation of his father's Christian faith with an analysis in which grace and gratitude for

[19] Treatise on Grace, Question 109, Art. 6.

mercy have really disappeared: "He belonged to those who anticipate faith by their disposition; and possessing the thing itself, lacked only the name. . . . He received faith itself as a reward for his virtue." [20]

The conception of the relation of grace and human resources in Reformation theology does justice to the ultimate and religious level of the problem; but it is in danger of obscuring the complexity of the relation by denying the reality of human freedom. The Catholic conception on the other hand seeks to do justice to both elements in the relation but it tends to comprehend them upon the same level and to measure the exact limits of each.

b. Grace as the forgiveness of our sins.

We have proceeded upon the assumption that the "negation of the negation" in the Pauline text: "Yet not I, but Christ liveth in me" has a double connotation; the second suggests that the new life is not an achieved reality. It is directed to Christ as the norm of life "by faith," and it accepts the divine grace which imputes his perfection to the believer. This second meaning is supported by the words with which the passage continues: "And the life which I now live in the flesh I live by the faith of the Son of God, who loved me, and gave himself for me." [21]

It may be prudent to note that whether or not the particular text under review contains both connotations is of no great importance, though there is no reason to assume that it does not. The thought of St. Paul, taken as a whole, certainly illumines both aspects of the experience of grace. But at the moment our concern is not with Pauline thought but rather with the relevance of the Biblical doctrine of grace to the experiences of life. Does experience validate this double conception?

It would be wrong to look for validation of the Biblical doctrine

[20] Quoted by Nicholas N. G. Gloubosky, Ch. II in the symposium, *The Doctrine of Grace*, S. C. M. Press, London, p. 78.
[21] Gal. 2:20.

in some natural experience of grace. If our analysis of the relation of faith to reason, and of the "Holy Spirit" to the spirit of man be correct, the experience which validates the doctrine can only be prompted by the doctrine itself. For without the "wisdom of God" apprehended in faith, and standing partly in contradiction to human wisdom, men are never conscious of the seriousness of sin; for the judgment of God against their sinful pride and self-assertion is not perceived.

There is indeed a counterpart of the doctrine of justification by faith in idealistic philosophy which illustrates the precise limits of concurrence and difference between "natural theology" and a theology which rests upon a Biblical basis. According to this doctrine there must be some kind of consummatory experience in life, some sense of achieved perfection, even when it has not been achieved, some anticipation of the goal, even while still involved in process. But none of these doctrines takes sin seriously. The consummatory experience bridges the gap between the imperfection which is involved in process and the transcendent goodness. In them man justifies himself by anticipating the eternity, to which the eternal element in his spirit entitles him.[22]

Without the radical sense of judgment in Biblical religion it is always possible to find some scheme of self-justification. Man may judge himself; but this capacity for self-judgment supposedly proves the goodness of that self which pronounces the judgment upon the empirical self. This judging self can, therefore, declare, "I am thereby justified." It is the self for which the end of evolution is already attained. It lays hold on eternity. Man's ability to judge

[22] B. Bosanquet's version of the doctrine is: "Religion justifies the religious man. It does not abolish his finiteness, his weakness or his sin. It denies that they are real." In *What Is Religion*, p. 49.

Francis H. Bradley's conception is similar. He says: "For the faith of religion the end of evolution is already evolved." *Ethical Studies*, p. 279.

J. Caird expresses the same idea in the words: "Religion rises above morality in this, that whilst the ideal of morality is only progressively realized, the ideal of religion is realized here and now." *Introduction to Philosophy of Religion*, p. 284.

himself is proof of a goodness in him which has final justification. But according to Biblical faith the confession always runs: "I know nothing by myself; yet am I not hereby justified; but he that judgeth me is the Lord." [23]

Such an experience is itself the fruit of grace in the sense that it represents a "wisdom" about life which is "foolishness" in prospect and wisdom only in retrospect. Experience as such may not yield it, and yet justify it in the end. In this context we must inquire particularly whether experience justifies the assertion that the conscience remains uneasy even in the highest reaches of achievement in the new life. Is it true that sin, though broken "in principle," is never broken in fact in the new life? Is it true that peace is never solely a sense of having realized what life should be; but always contains an element of hope and an assurance of forgiveness? Is the final peace dependent upon the certainty that there are divine resources which are able to cope with the continued contradiction between human self-love and the divine purpose?

Modern Christianity has not been concerned with the relevance of this interpretation of human experience, for reasons which we shall have occasion to examine more thoroughly presently. The study of the relevance of this doctrine must therefore confront the indifference and even hostility of "modern" men, whether Christian or unChristian.

The real question is not whether we are able to achieve absolute perfection in history; for even the most consistent perfectionist sects do not deny that human life remains in process. The question is whether in the development of the new life some contradiction between human self-will and the divine purpose remains. The issue is whether the basic character of human history, as it is apprehended in the Christian faith, is overcome in the lives of those who have thus apprehended it.

That question would seem to find one answer in logic and another in experience. It is logical to assume that when man has be-

[23] 1 Cor. 4:4.

come aware of the character of his self-love and of its incompatibil-
ity with the divine will, this very awareness would break its
power. Furthermore, this logic is at least partially validated by
experience. Repentance does initiate a new life. But the experience
of the Christian ages refutes those who follow this logic and without qualification. The sorry annals of Christian fanaticism, of unholy religious hatreds, of sinful ambitions hiding behind the cloak
of religious sanctity, of political power impulses compounded with
pretensions of devotion to God, offer the most irrefutable proof of
the error in every Christian doctrine and every interpretation of the
Christian experience which claim that grace can remove the final
contradiction between man and God. The sad experiences of Christian history show how human pride and spiritual arrogance rise to
new heights precisely at the point where the claims of sanctity are
made without due qualification.

A tragic and revealing aspect of the experience of the Christian
ages is that, again and again, "publicans and sinners" have had to
rescue an important aspect of truth about life, and restore whole-
someness into human relations, against the fanaticism of Christian
saints, who had forgotten that sainthood is corrupted whenever
holiness is claimed as a simple possession. A full appreciation of the
profundities of the Christian faith must therefore prompt gratitude
to these "publicans and sinners" for their periodic testimony against
the Christian Church whenever it has forgotten the full truth of its
gospel and has allowed itself to be betrayed into new forms of self-
righteousness. The publicans and sinners do not, of course, have the
full truth either. For when they turn from the moral scepticism,
which enables them to challenge religious fanaticism, they develop
fanatic furies of their own. They have no principle of interpreting
life which can save them from alternate moods of scepticism and
fanaticism. But that does not change the fact that a moral sceptic,
who regards all truth and all goodness as merely a cloak of self-
interest, does at least understand the perennial egoistic corruption

of truth and goodness. He is finally betrayed into moral nihilism because he knows nothing of the truth and goodness, not so corrupted, which are the possession of faith alone. The protest of secularism against Catholicism in all national cultures, in which Catholicism has played the dominant rôle and has invariably compounded the relativities of politics and history with the ultimate sanctities, is particularly instructive in this connection.

If we examine any individual life, or any social achievement in history, it becomes apparent that there are infinite possibilities of organizing life from beyond the centre of the self; and equally infinite possibilities of drawing the self back into the centre of the organization. The former possibilities are always fruits of grace (though frequently it is the "hidden Christ" and a grace which is not fully known which initiates the miracle). They are always the fruits of grace because any life which cannot "forget" itself and which merely makes brotherhood the instrument of its "happiness" or its "perfection" cannot really escape the vicious circle of egocentricity.[24] Yet the possibilities of new evil cannot be avoided by grace; for so long as the self, individual or collective, remains within the tensions of history and is subject to the twofold condition of involvement in process and transcendence over it, it will be subject to the sin of overestimating its transcendence and of compounding its interests with those which are more inclusive.[25]

[24] This "dialectical" element in the anatomy of morals is not understood at all in Mortimer Adler's neo-Thomist treatise, *A Dialectic of Morals*. Adler fails to comprehend the difference between *agape* and *eros*. He therefore does not see that the quest for happiness does not emancipate from egocentricity, even if perfection is regarded as the way to happiness. The individual who seeks his happiness through his perfection is still centred within himself.

[25] It is frequently asserted in Christian, particularly in Reformation, thought, that we will continue to sin so long as we are "in the body." This would make it appear that sin is the consequence of finiteness. But, whether explicitly or implicitly, Christian thought gives this phrase the same connotation as the Pauline conception of *sarx*. Historical existence

There are thus indeterminate possibilities of redeeming parent-hood from the lust of power and making the welfare of the child the end of family life. But there are also many possibilities of using the loving relationship of the family as an instrument of the parental power impulse on a higher or more subtle level. The "saints" may not be conscious of this fault; but the children who have to extricate themselves from the too close and enduring embrace of loving parents know about it. There are indeterminate possibilities of re-lating the family to the community on higher and higher levels of harmony. But there is no possibility of a family escaping the fault of regarding its own weal and woe as more important to the whole than it really is. There are unlimited opportunities of relating "our" nation more harmoniously to the lives of other nations; but there is no possibility of doing so without some corruption of national egoism.[26]

It is not easy to express both these two aspects of the life of grace, to which all history attests without seeming to offend the canons of logic. That is one reason why moralists have always found it rather easy to discount the doctrine of "justification by faith." [27] But

---

is never mere finiteness but finiteness and freedom; and a part of his-torical existence is therefore the temptation, and a yielding to the tempta-tion, of claiming ultimate significance for partial values and ultimate validity for partial perspectives.

[26] Even now genuine hopes for a new world order are compounded with anticipatory pride over the eminence which "Anglo-Saxon" civiliza-tion will have in it; or of the possibilities of achieving an "American Century" through American power.

[27] Emil Brunner defines the twofold character of grace as: "It is a having and yet not having, a standing beyond the contradiction and yet standing in it. It is justification of the sinner, who, though justified, con-tinues to the last days of his earthly life to be a sinner and is as much in need of forgiveness as on the day of his conversion." *Theology of Crisis,* p. 63.

Martin Luther expresses the paradox in many ways, as for instance: "The beneficiary of justification knows that now he serves the law of God and asks for mercy because he serves the law of sin" or "Both things are true, no Christian has sin and all Christians have sin" or "The saints are

here, as in many cases, a seeming defiance of logic is merely the consequence of an effort to express complex facts of experience. It happens to be true to the facts of experience that in one sense the converted man is righteous and that in another sense he is not.

The complexity of the facts not only makes it difficult to comprehend them in a formula which does not seem to offend canons of consistency. It is also difficult to express both aspects of the experience of grace without unduly suppressing one or the other side of it. The theologies which have sought to do justice to the fact that saints nevertheless remain sinners have frequently, perhaps usually, obscured the indeterminate possibilities of realizations of good in both individual and collective life. The theologies which have sought to do justice to the positive aspects of regeneration have usually obscured the realities of sin which appear on every new level of virtue. This has been true particularly of modern versions of Christian perfectionism; because in them evolutionary and progressive interpretations of history have been compounded with illusions which have a more purely Christian source.

We must trace the course of this debate in detail presently; for it embraces the whole history of western Christendom and it involves all the issues which are crucial for an understanding, and a possible reorientation, of the spiritual life of our day.

At the moment it is important to emphasize that the two sides of the experience of grace are so related that they do not contradict, but support each other. To understand that the Christ in us is not a possession but a hope, that perfection is not a reality but an intention; that such peace as we know in this life is never purely the peace of achievement but the serenity of being "completely known and all forgiven"; all this does not destroy moral ardour or responsibility. On the contrary it is the only way of preventing premature completions of life, or arresting the new and more terrible pride

always intrinsically sinners; that is why they are declared righteous extrinsically," or "We are sinners in reality but are righteous in hope." Quoted from *Works*, Ficker, ed., Vol. II, pp. 104, 105 and 176.

which may find its roots in the soil of humility, and of saving the Christian life from the intolerable pretension of saints who have forgotten that they are sinners.

The simple moralists will always regard this final pinnacle of the religious experience with little or no comprehension. They will assert that it is merely a formula which allows us "to continue in sin that grace may abound." But if the "foolishness of God" has been truly incorporated into the wisdom of faith the simple answer to this charge can be: "God forbid. How shall we that are dead to sin, live any longer therein?" [28]

[28] Romans 6:2.

CHAPTER V

THE CONFLICT BETWEEN GRACE AND PRIDE

IF OUR analysis up to this point be, in any fundamental sense, a correct one, the Pauline interpretation of grace and the new life is not a unique dogma which could or could not have been added to the gospels. Its significance lies in its explicit formulation of the problem of life and history, as it was apprehended negatively in the prophetic interpretation of history and as it was positively affirmed in Jesus' reinterpretation of prophetic expectations. It is closely related to Jesus' insistence that the righteous are not righteous before the divine judgment; and to his conception of the suffering Messiah as a revelation of the justice and the mercy of God.

If we now address ourselves to the task of tracing the interpretation of the central dogma of Christian faith through the Christian ages it becomes increasingly apparent that human self-esteem resists the truth of the Christian gospel almost as vigorously within the bounds of a faith which has ostensibly accepted it, as it was resisted by the pre-Christian ages. They expected a Christ but not the Christ who would vindicate God in his justice and mercy without including any man in that vindication. The Christian ages seek a new way of vindicating men who have become righteous through Christ.

This resistance takes many forms and avails itself of many current philosophies in various ages. While it is important to note the particular causes which prompted Christian theologians to deny or to obscure the fundamental paradox of the gospel's interpretation of life and history, it is more important to recognize that the motive which underlies all these various formulations is essentially the same. It is the unwillingness of man to admit the curious predicament of his existence by reason of his simultaneous involvement in, and transcendence over, temporal flux and finiteness; or, more exactly his unwillingness to admit that there is no escape from this predicament even on the level of the new life. The favourite strategy for denying the perennial character of the contradiction between the human and the divine is to interpret the revelation of God in Christ as the disclosure of the eternal in history resulting in a consequent translation of the believer from the historical and temporal to the eternal. Such a redemption involves the apprehension of the eternal truth; and this knowledge of the truth also presumably guarantees the realization of it in life; in other words, the achievement of perfection.

It is well to recognize at the outset that the perennial revolt in the Christian ages against the whole truth of the Christian gospel is the cause of the fanaticisms and religiously sanctified imperial lusts which have disfigured the history of Western civilization. In this revolt the invariable strategy is to set one part of the Christian truth against the whole of it. This revolt explains why a civilization, informed by a religious faith, which, alone among the faiths of the world, both encouraged historic creativity and responsibility and yet set the limits upon man's historic possibilities, must appear from the perspective of the more earthbound (Confucianism) and the more world-denying (Buddhism) religions of the East as a civilization of unbridled ambitions and heaven-storming passions.

This does not mean that the corruption of Christian truth by human self-esteem could have been avoided if this or that theological tendency had not gained ascendency, in this or that epoch. To say that the self-confidence of classical culture is the primary source of this corruption is to explain a general tendency historically but not profoundly. For human pride is more powerful than any instruments of which it avails itself. It must be regarded as inevitable that a religion which apprehends the truth about man and God by faith alone should be used as the instrument of human arrogance. This is done whenever the truth which is held by faith, because it is beyond all human attainment, comes to be regarded as a secure possession. In this form it is no longer a threat to man. It does not mediate judgment upon the false and imperial completions of human life. It becomes, rather, the vehicle of the pretension that the finiteness and sin of life have been overcome. The New Testament understands how inevitable this misuse of the gospel is. Its conception of the false Christs and of the Antichrist, who appear at the end of history expresses this understanding. But this tragic aspect of Christian history is understood only occasionally outside of the New Testament. For everywhere else in the Christian ages, the saints seek to refute the justified jeers of sceptics and sinners by pointing to the blamelessness of the life of Christians or by seeking to prove that the virtues of the church outweigh its vices. Yet Christianity can validate its truth about life and history only when it is possible, from the standpoint of that truth, to comprehend the rise of the false truths which use Christianity itself as their vehicle.

II

PRE-AUGUSTINIAN CONCEPTIONS OF GRACE

In tracing the resistance which the truth of the gospel meets in the ages we might begin with a period of Christian thought, from the Apostolic age to Augustine, in which the Pauline formulation of the ultimate religious problem was only imperfectly, if at all, apprehended. The thought of the period was moulded by the necessity of establishing and defending the Christian faith in, and against, the Græco-Roman culture. That culture regarded the time-eternity problem as the crucial issue in man's life and sought salvation in mystery religions, Gnostic sects, Mantic arts, Platonic and Neo-Platonic philosophies, in all of which the temporal could be translated into the eternal or the eternal purged of the temporal.

Christian faith had enough power to challenge the Hellenic doctrine of the chasm between the divine and the historical and to elaborate Christologies which broke with Greek dualism. But it did not have enough power to come to a clear perception of the problem of sin which was involved in the Christian interpretation of historical reality; or of the doctrine of the Atonement, which was the Christian answer to this problem. "Attempts at deducing the church's doctrinal position," writes Harnack, "from the theology of Paul . . . will always miscarry; for they fail to note that to the most important premises of the Catholic doctrine of faith belongs an element which we cannot recognize as dominant in the New Testament, viz. the Hellenic spirit."[1] The idea that baptism cured the believer of sin, a fruitful source of perfectionist illusions, had a very early beginning.[2] Salvation was frequently equated with the true knowledge of God through Christ, as contrasted with the errors of heathendom. The deeper problems of the Christian faith were partially obscured in some of the Apostolic Fathers and totally so in others.[3] The ideas of "eternal life," knowledge (*gnosis*) and law, particularly the new law of Christ, exhausted the meaning of the gospel. Nor does the situation change in the thought of the Apologists who follow the Apostolic Fathers. Justin Martyr regards Christianity as a "new law" and a "new philosophy." In this conception he does not simply capitulate to Platonism; for he does not believe that man has inherent capacities to arrive at the truth and to achieve virtue. These are gifts of grace. But the paradox of our having and not having them is not understood. The Biblical idea of the forgiveness of sins is of course never denied. But forgiveness

[1] *History of Dogma,* Vol. I, p. 48. Harnack's understanding of the loss of Pauline profundities in pre-Augustinian Christianity is the more remarkable and impressive because he, himself, does not fully appreciate the implications of Pauline thought.

[2] The Epistle of Barnabas (70–79 A.D.) gives the idea special prominence.

[3] Partially so in Clement, Barnabas, Polycarp and Ignatius; totally so in Hermas and the second epistle of Clement. *Vide,* Harnack, Vol. I, p. 172.

becomes a single remission *of sins that are past*[4] at a very early date. The Catholic formula of subordinating justification to sanctification is thus of very early origin.

The position of Tertullian on these issues is particularly significant. He was the protagonist of Biblical, particularly of Hebraic thought, against the Hellenizing tendencies of the early Christian philosophers and he sought to preserve the prophetic-eschatological interpretation of history against the corrosion of Hellenic interpretations. Furthermore he understood the doctrine of original sin. Yet he was confused in his understanding of the Christian doctrine of the justice and mercy of God. He regarded the idea of divine forgiveness as irrational and unjust, and declared that, "if we really needed to ascribe to God a goodness so at variance with reason, it would be better that there should be no God at all."[5]

The tendency to regard Christianity as a way to achieve the eternal and to realize perfection was even more pronounced in the Eastern than in the Western church. Origen the greatest of Eastern theologians, as indeed the most original of all pre-Augustinians, was both perfectionist and moralistic in his conception of the method of attaining holiness.[6] His predecessor, Clement of Alexandria, expressed the idea of the deification of man through Christ, which characterized all Alexandrian thought, in the words: "When we are reborn we receive straightway that perfect thing for which we are

[4] This limit upon grace is explicit in Barnabas 5:9 and 11 Clem. 2: 4–7.

[5] *Adv. Marcionem,* i, 25. Despite his polemic against Hellenizing tendencies Tertullian paid inadvertent tribute to the power of these ideas in the church by occasionally defining the significance of Christ in essentially Hellenic terms, as for instance: "God lived among us, that man might be taught to do the things of God. God acted on the level with man, that man might be able to act on the level with God." *Adv. Marcionem,* ii, 27.

[6] Origen declared: "The perfection of God's likeness a man must acquire for himself by his own zealous endeavors in imitation of God; because the possibility of being perfect is given to man at the beginning through the dignity of God's image; but the perfect likeness he must accomplish for himself through the fulfillment of works. *De princ,* III, vi, 1.

striving. For we are enlightened and that is to know God; he can therefore not be imperfect who has known that which is perfect."[7] The gnostic formulation of the way of salvation echoes in these words. Gregory of Nyssa believed that, "Man, restored to the fashion of pure Adam, attains the measure of the stature of the last and becomes even higher because he becomes deified."[8]

While the Biblical-Pauline conceptions are more prominent in the thought of less consistent Hellenists, such as Irenæus and Athanasius, it cannot be affirmed that the full meaning of the Biblical conception of sin and grace was understood by them. A modern historian is probably not far from the truth in the assertion that "the (pre-Augustinian) church never heartily accepted St. Paul's doctrine of justification by faith. . . . Sometimes it was wholly ignored; at other times even when the formula was respected it was interpreted in a way which would have been expressed more naturally by saying that men are saved by repentance."[9]

The Greek idea of *gnosis* thus dominated the pre-Augustinian centuries; and, though the church rejected the more explicitly dualistic forms of it as heresy, it capitulated to more modified Hellenistic conceptions of the way of salvation.[10] Greek Christianity sometimes capitulated so completely to Hellenism that the gospel became merely a higher form of knowledge. When more Biblical it recognized the necessity of "grace" and "power"; which is to say, it understood the human problem in volitional rather than in purely rationalistic terms. But even then it never rose to a full comprehension of the problem of man's historical existence as viewed in prophetic-Biblical thought and as culminating in the New Testament conceptions of sin and grace. Thus an Egyptian father writes: "The

[7] *Pædagogus*, I, vi.

[8] *De instituto Christiano.*

[9] Hastings Rashdall, *The Idea of Atonement in Christian Theology,* p. 206.

[10] Harnack writes: "It is therefore no paradox to say that Gnosticism, which is just Hellenism, obtained half a victory in Catholicism." *History of Dogma,* I, p. 227.

grace of God can purify a man in an instant and make him perfect; for all is possible to God; as happened in the case of the robber, who was transformed by faith in a moment of time and brought into paradise." [11]

Perfectionist illusions reach their most consistent proportions in the thought of St. John of Chrysostom, who, confining divine grace to the sacrament of baptism, declares: "Grace touches the soul itself and tears up sin by the roots. . . . The soul of him who is baptized . . . is purer than the rays of the sun, and such as it was originally begotten; nay rather far better than this; for it enjoys the Spirit which sets it on fire on all sides and extends its holiness. . . . The Holy Spirit recasting it by baptism as in a furnace and consuming its sins causes it to shine more purely than any pure gold." [12]

While the thought of the Latin church is never as consistently perfectionist as that of the Eastern church, and while subsequent developments lead the Western church to further modification of its position, the thought of the Eastern church bears the stamp of complete consistency from the Greek fathers to the dogmas of the contemporary Orthodox church. In terms of the history of culture this represents the triumph of Hellenism over Hebraism. In terms of religion it is the failure of the church to understand that part of the gospel which is directed against itself and its saints. [13]

[11] The Blessed Marcarius of Egypt, *De custodia cordis*, xii.

[12] Homil: In Epist. I and Cor. 15:1–2.

[13] As we shall not have occasion to trace perfectionist thought in the Greek church through the centuries to the present it may be relevant to quote a modern Orthodox theologian upon this dominant tendency in the Eastern church. He writes that "the Greek Fathers do rightly believe that when once God is acting through the sacraments, His action cannot have only temporary character or partial effect. The power of Divine Grace is manifested through the Sacraments and its effect is eternal." Hamilcar S. Alivisatos in symposium, *The Doctrine of Grace*, S. C. M. Press, London, p. 267.

One of the most authoritative Orthodox theologians of recent times, Chrestos Androustos, states the Greek doctrine of sanctification in most unequivocal terms. He writes: "The two elements of forgiveness of sins and justification are not separate from each other, as if sanctification

III

THE CATHOLIC CONCEPTION OF GRACE

The realization within the post-apostolic church that the primary issue of life and history is the relation of grace to sin, rather than the subordinate problem of eternity to time, comes to its first clear and explicit expression in the thought of Augustine. Scriptural authority had prevented the prophetic-Biblical concepts from ever being completely lost; but they had certainly been obscured in the preceding centuries. With Augustine's elaboration of the Pauline doctrine of original sin, the Christian ages arrive at a full consciousness of the fact that it is not finiteness but the "false eternal" of sin, the pretension that finiteness has been or can be overcome, which brings confusion and evil into history.[1]

------

followed upon cleansing from sin, but they are two aspects of the same thing. . . . The remission of sin is not the mere imputation of freedom from sin,—but the actual effacement of it. . . . God, in judging a sinner, does not regard him as righteous while he remains a sinner, but makes him actually righteous. The state of sin is removed entirely by God's power in the act of justification. . . . The principle and basis of sin in the perversion of the will is entirely removed and the regenerate will is born godward." In his "Dogmatike" quoted in Frank S. B. Gavin's *Some Aspects of Contemporary Greek Thought,* p. 227.

It may be relevant to call Tolstoi to witness against the moral consequences and spiritual confusion which results from such perfectionist pretensions. He writes in *"My Confession"*: "The Orthodox church: with this word I no longer connect any conception than that of a few hirsute men, extremely self-confident, deluded and ignorant, in silk and velvet with diamond panagias, called bishops and metropolitans; and other thousands of hirsute men, who under the guise of performing certain sacraments are busy fleecing the people. Instead of humility there is grandeur; instead of poverty there is luxury, instead of forgiving offenses, hatred and wars. And all men deny one another but not themselves."

These strictures are not entirely fair because Tolstoi was a perfectionist of sectarian persuasion who was convinced that, if only a more rigorous strategy were adopted, men could be freed of sin. He understood the perennial factors of historic existence as little as the sacramental perfectionists.

[1] *Cf.* Vol. I, Ch. VI.

The neo-Platonic influence in Augustine's thought slightly obscures the Biblical paradoxes. His analysis of the human situation
is Biblical, though his conception of sin as a "defect" of the will—
as a lack of power to do good—is partly derived from Plotinus and
is not in complete conformity with his profound understanding of
the inevitable tendency towards self-love in the expression of human
freedom. Perhaps this slight admixture of Hellenistic thought in his
doctrine of sin contains the roots of his error in the doctrine of grace,
which is the Biblical answer to the problem of sin. For Augustine's doctrine of grace blunts and obscures the complex relation
between grace as power and grace as pardon. He does not question
the traditional conception of the relation between the two. We have
seen that the idea of God's forgiveness and justification, preceding
and laying the foundation for sanctification, began very early. According to this theory, the divine mercy, mediated through Christ,
destroys the sinful contradiction between man and God, and turns
the soul from self-love to obedience; whereupon it may grow in
grace and achieve constantly higher stages of sanctification. This
subordination of justification to sanctification becomes definitive for
the whole Catholic conception of life and history. It contains the
roots of a new self-righteousness and a new pretension that man is
able to complete life and history. The difference between it and
Hellenistic conceptions is that it expresses man's consciousness of his
inability to realize the good by his own power; but it assumes that
it can be accomplished by the aid of divine power. "It is certain,"
declares Augustine, "that we can keep the commandments if we
so will; but because the will is prepared by the Lord we must ask
him for such force of will as to make us act by willing. It is certain
that it is we who will when we will but it is he who makes us will
what is good; . . . it is he who makes us act by supplying efficacious
power to our will." [2] It must be quite apparent that this exposition
does full justice to the relation of a power not our own to our own
power. In his polemic against Pelagian moralism, this is the point

[2] *On Grace and Free Will*, xvii, 32.

which Augustine is intent upon guarding. But he does not fully recognize the persistent power of self-love in the new life. He knows that love is no simple possibility for human nature; but he is certain that it is God's possibility in the heart of man.

His classical treatise on the subject of Christian perfection is an exposition of the Pauline text: "Not as if I had already attained, either were already perfect." In expounding this text he recognizes, as do most Christian perfectionists, that there is no possibility for finite nature of arriving at a goal; for man is in history and history is a process of becoming. But he is convinced that the seeking of the goal may be perfect. "Let us," he says, "as many as are running perfectly, be thus resolved that, being not yet perfected, we pursue our course to perfection along the way which we have thus far run perfectly." [3]

He does not, of course, affirm the sinlessness of Christians. He sees no possibility of conquering sin absolutely. He is certain that concupiscence remains and that consequently divine forgiveness is necessary up to man's last hour. [4] But he is convinced that the sins which remain are "venial" rather than "mortal"; which is to say that he regards expressions of self-love, after redemption, as incidental, and not as the expression of a basic attitude. "He is not unreasonably said to walk blamelessly," according to Augustine, "not who already has reached the end of his journey, but who is pressing on to the end in a blameless manner, free from damnable sins and at the same time not neglecting to cleanse by almsgiving such sins as are venial." [5] The distinction between damnable and venial sins is, and remains, an important one in Catholic thought. The idea that almsgiving can cleanse the soul of venial sins is the camel's nose of "righteousness by works" entering into the tent of grace.

The important point at issue in the Augustinian conception is whether the destruction of sin "in principle" means that the power

[3] *On Man's Perfection in Righteousness*, Ch. 19.
[4] *Enchiridion*, lxiv.
[5] *On Man's Perfection in Righteousness*, Ch. 20.

of inordinate self-love is broken in fact. It is the thesis of both Augustine and all the Catholic ages that this is the case; and that residual sin represents the eruption of vagrant desires and impulses which have not yet been brought completely under the control of the central will. The thesis is plausible enough; for if destruction of self-love "in principle" does not also mean "in fact" in some basic sense, what does it mean? Certainly there must be some facts which reveal the new principle by which the soul lives. Surely there must be "fruits meet for repentance"!

But here the complexities of the moral life are obscured by too simple statement of them. The actual situation is that man may be redeemed from self-love in the sense that he acknowledges the evil of it and recognizes the love of God as the only adequate motive of conduct; and may yet be selfish in more than an incidental sense. The pride of a bishop, the pretensions of a theologian, the will-to-power of a pious business man, and the spiritual arrogance of the church itself are not mere incidental defects, not merely "venial" sins. They represent the basic drive of self-love, operating upon whatever new level grace has pitched the new life. Pure love is "by faith" in the sense that only when man, in prayer and contemplation, is lifted beyond himself does he have a vantage point from which self-love does not operate. In action the power of self-love is mixed with the new power of the love of God which grace has established.

This tragic quality of the spiritual life was never clearly apprehended until the Reformation. Its apprehension gives the Reformation its particular and unique place in the history of the Christian life. Augustine's failure to understand it had the consequence of making him the father of Catholicism in his doctrine of grace; while he became at the same time the ultimate source of the Reformation in his doctrine of sin. The Reformation discovered that there was in the Pauline-Biblical and in the Augustinian analysis of the human situation a problem too profound to be solved by the Augustinian answer to that problem.

The Augustinian portrayal of the collective, as well as the individual, historical situation remains within the limits of this qualified perfectionism. The conflict in history is between the *civitas Dei* and the *civitas terrena,* the one being animated by the "love of God" to the point of contempt for the self, the other by "the love of self" to the point of contempt of God. He acknowledges that in history the two cities are "commingled" and he has no simple perfectionist solutions for the problems of relative justice which arise even for the Christian in a sinful world. But on the whole he identifies the *civitas Dei* with the historical church, of which he asserts that only there is true justice to be found. He does surround this identification with all kinds of qualifications, which later Catholic ages did not have the prudence to maintain. He distinguishes between the *civitas Dei* as it is here on earth and the *civitas superna* as it is in heaven. He differentiates between the church as it is and as it will be.[6] He declares explicitly that "wherever in these books I have mentioned the church as not having a spot or wrinkle, it is not to be taken as now existing but of the church whose existence is being prepared."[7]

Nevertheless the church is, despite these qualifications, in some sense the Kingdom of God on earth. It had not achieved the ultimate perfection; and moreover there is, in his thought, no guarantee that all members of it are saved. But the conception of its perfection corresponds essentially to his idea of the perfection of the saints. He thought of it as "pursuing its course to perfection" along the way which it has "thus far run perfectly."[8] But he could not con-

---

[6] *"Ecclesia qualis nunc est"* and *"ecclesia qualis tunc erit."* De civitas Dei, Book XX, Ch. 9.

[7] *Retract,* II, xvii.

[8] Bishop Gore rightly affirms that Augustine did not originate the idea of the visible church; or the belief that salvation is by the church alone; or the conviction that "he cannot have God for his Father who has not the church for his Mother." In all these convictions he merely entered into the general Catholic heritage. Charles Gore, *The Church and the Ministry,* pp. 13 ff.

A. Robertson agrees with Gore that Augustine did not originate the idea of the visible church and adds that "it would be truer to say that

ceive of it as standing itself under divine judgment. In other words the church was the historic *locus* where the contradiction between the historical and the divine was overcome in fact; rather than that *locus* where the judgment and the mercy of God upon the historical are mediated, and where, therefore, the contradiction of the historical and the holy is overcome in principle. This conviction governs Augustine's whole philosophy of history. The historical conflict between self-love and the love of God is essentially a conflict between the church and the world; and the commingling of church and world never means that the church might, as an historic institution, become the vehicle of evil. The church does not, in other words, really stand under the judgment of God. Rather it reigns with Christ. "Even now," he declares, "the church is the Kingdom of Christ, and the Kingdom of heaven. That is to say even now *his saints reign with him,* not indeed in the same way as they will reign then. Nor yet do the tares reign with him, although in the church they are growing with the wheat." [9]

It may well be that subsequent Catholic ages weakened the Augustinian analysis of the human situation and transmuted it into semi-Pelagian doctrine. But they did not have to change his conception of the Christian solution of the human situation. For the Augustinian and the Catholic doctrine of grace are one; and the one doctrine runs consistently through the Catholic centuries. According to it sin is essentially the loss of an original perfection, rather than the corruption of the image of God in man; and grace is the completion of an imperfect nature. The fulfillment of what is good but incomplete in nature is emphasized, as against the element of cor-

---

he originated the idea of the invisible church." A. Robertson, *Regnum Dei*, p. 187.

Augustine's reservations about the church did contain the Reformation idea of the invisible church, which became the instrument of placing the historic church under divine judgment; just as his basic idea about the church, without reservations, was in conformity with accepted Catholic belief before and after his time.

[9] *De civ. Dei*, Book XX, Ch. 9.

Catholic concept —
Subordination to Sanctification — forgiveness
of justification only applies to "sins past"

140   *Conflict Between Grace and Pride*   [CH. V]

ruption which always places "nature" and "grace" in contradiction. In the analysis of the situation of man in history the Biblical-paradoxical element is slightly stronger in Augustine than in the official Catholic doctrine as ultimately defined by Thomas Aquinas; but in the definition of what grace accomplishes there is no difference between Augustine and Aquinas.

In this definition the self-esteem of classical man and the Biblical sense of the contradiction between man and God are nicely merged. The Biblical view of man-in-history overcomes the classical concept of the sufficiency of human (particularly rational) powers. In the Catholic view it is always through grace that man is able to do the good. But the classical view overcomes the Biblical in the sense that the redeemed man actually stands beyond the sin of history in fact as well as in principle. The precise formulation of this qualified uneasiness about the human situation is the subordination of justification to sanctification and the assertion that forgiveness is needed and meant primarily for "sins that are past."

The final and symbolically most revealing form of this new Catholic self-righteousness is the belief held in Catholic faith that in the final judgment man is saved by merit; only he must realize that the merit is achieved by the grace of God. On this point Aquinas is able to agree perfectly with Augustine. He writes: "Man by his own will performs works which are worthy of eternal life; but, as Augustine says, for this it is necessary that the will of man should be prepared by grace. As the gloss on the 'Grace of God is life eternal' (in Augustine) says: 'It is certain that eternal life is given as a reward for good works; but those works for which it is granted belong to the grace of God.' " [10]

The point at issue may seem academic to the casual student. It may even appear to the critical as a case of that futile theological hairsplitting, which seems to make theological debate so fatuous. But all important issues, whether in philosophy or theology, are finally defined in very precise distinctions, which may easily hide

[10] Thomas Aquinas, *Treatise on Grace*, Quest. 109, Art. v.

from the unwary, even as they reveal to the initiated, the importance of the issue which is at stake. The issue at stake here is whether man's historical existence is such that he can ever, by any discipline of reason or by any merit of grace, confront a divine judgment upon his life with an easy conscience. If he can it means that it is possible for a will centred in an individual ego to be brought into essential conformity with the will and power which governs all things. On this question the Catholic answer is a consistently affirmative one.[11]

There were Catholic mystics who tended to go beyond the bounds of the Catholic synthesis in their assertion of the perfectibility of man by grace. This strain of medieval thought must be considered presently as one of the roots of modern perfectionism. At the moment it is not important to consider it but rather to recognize the significance of the Catholic doctrine in which a balance is struck between the Biblical idea that man cannot complete his own life and history, and that he involves himself in evil in the pretense of doing so; and the classical (and generally non-Biblical) confi-

---

[11] It must be emphasized that the Catholic doctrine never asserts absolute but essential conformity between the redeemed will and the will of God.

Aquinas asserts that "the gift of habitual grace is not given us that we may be in no further need of divine help; for every creature needs that God should preserve it in that goodness which it received from him."

He declares, however, that in the redeemed state, "man can keep from mortal sin, which is grounded in reason, yet he cannot avoid venial sins because of the disorder of the *lower sensual desires,* the movements of which the reason can indeed severally repress . . . but he cannot repress all, for while he represses one, another perchance arises." According to this formulation the conformity of the human to the divine will is well nigh absolute, and the only sin which remains is occasioned by vagrant impulses below the level of the will. This conception might seem to be purely classical rather than Biblical. But Aquinas' syntheses of the two are always as perfectly proportioned as it is possible to make them. Thus he saves this interpretation of the residue of sin from purely classical connotations by declaring that the vagrancy of the lower desires is due to lack of perfect submission of the will to God: "Because man's will is not wholly subject to God it follows that there must be many disorders in the acts of reason." From *Treatise on Grace,* Quest. 109, Art. ii.

Catholic view —
a balance between
the classical & Biblical
views

dence that some capacity in man, which transcends finiteness and process, is able to realize the vision which he apprehends by such transcendence.

The Catholic synthesis is expressed in many ways. It is summarized perfectly in Bernard of Clairvaux's assertion that man has freedom from necessity in the state of nature, freedom from sin in the state of grace and freedom from misery in the state of glory.[12] This is to say that the difference between the consummation of life in history and the consummation of life beyond history is merely that the former is still subject to the conditions of finiteness.

The only explicit variation from this consistent Catholic doctrine is contained in the Formula of Ratisbon, in which the desire to come to terms with the Reformation prompted the, from the Catholic standpoint, remarkable thesis that, "We are not just or accepted of God on account of our own works of righteousness, but are reputed just on account of the merits of Jesus Christ only." But after possibilities of compromise with the Reformation had been dissipated the Catholic church defined its position in different terms at the Council of Trent. Then it declared: "If any man shall say that the good works of man that is justified are in such wise the gifts of God that they are not also *the good merits* of him that is justified, or that the said justified by the good works that are performed . . . does not *truly merit increase of grace and eternal life,* . . . let him be anathema."[13]

[12] St. Bernard of Clairvaux, *Concerning Grace and Free Will*, Ch. iii. Trans. by Watkins Williams, SPCK.

[13] Council of Trent, Canon xxvii. It would be wrong to create the impression that the Council of Trent was always wrong in defining its position in opposition to the Reformation. Very frequently it was rightly concerned to guard one side of the paradox of grace: that it is a power of righteousness, against the tendency towards moral defeatism and antinomianism in the Reformation. Canon xxii is thus rightly directed against Protestant antinomianism: "If any shall say that Christ Jesus was given to men as redeemer and in whom they should trust and not also as legislator whom they should obey, let him be anathema."

Canon xi contains an equally valid protest against the idea that grace

It took its position solidly on the ground that no real contradiction remained for the redeemed between what man is and what he ought to be, and insisted that: "If any man shall say that the commandments of God are, even for a man that is justified and constituted in grace, impossible to keep, let him be anathema." [14]

Whatever reservations Catholic thought may make in regard to "venial" sins, it never has any serious question about the actual coincidence of grace as pardon and grace as power or about the essential sinlessness of the redeemed man. In the words of Cardinal Newman, it believes that, "Justification is the fiat of Almighty God which breaks upon the gloom of our earthly state as the Creative Word upon chaos. It declares the soul righteous and in that declaration on the one hand conveys pardon *for its past sins* and on the other makes it actually righteous." [15]

The Catholic doctrine of grace is the foundation of a total theological structure, which exhibits the same consistent logic in all of its parts. In all of them the Biblical-prophetic view of life and history is provisionally accepted, though frequently weakened by the definition of sin as the privation of an original perfection, rather than as a positive corruption. But even when the definition of the human situation is more Biblical than classical (as in the case of Augustine) the proposed solution of the situation defies the limits

---

is pardon only: "If any man shall say that men are justified either by the sole imputation of the righteousness of Christ, or by the sole remission of sins to the exclusion of the grace and charity which is shed abroad in their hearts by the Holy Ghost, and is inherent in them, or even that the grace by which we are justified is *only the favour of God,* let him be anathema."

[14] Canon xviii.

[15] Lectures on Justification, p. 83. It might be added that the Anglo-Catholic position never varies significantly from the Roman one. In one of the ablest treatises on grace from an Anglo-Catholic theologian, Robert C. Moberly writes: "There is no ultimate distinction between 'to justify' and 'to make righteous'; between a man's being pronounced righteous by the Truth of God and being in the Truth of God righteous." *Atonement and Personality,* p. 335. Moberly's book is a masterly analysis of the relation of grace to the freedom of human personality.

of human possibilities, as the Bible conceives them. It seeks for a place in history where sin is transcended and only finiteness remains. In seeking for that place it runs the danger of falling prey to the sin of spiritual pride and of illustrating in its own life that the final human pretension is made most successfully under the aegis of a religion which has overcome human pretension in principle.

All Catholic errors in overestimating the sinlessness of the redeemed reach their culmination, or at least their most vivid and striking expression, in the doctrine of the church. Here the reservations of Augustine are forgotten; and the church is unreservedly identified with the Kingdom of God. It is the *societas perfecta*. It is the sole dispenser of grace. Its visible head assumes the title: "Vicar of Christ" which appears blasphemous from the perspective of a prophetic view of history.[16] The title and the claim of papal infallibility reach such heights of human pretension that the Reformation indictment of the Pope as "Anti-Christ" may be regarded as something of an historical inevitability. Indeed political opponents of the Pope anticipated the Reformation in making the indictment during the Catholic ages. Non-Roman Catholics may regard papal, and indeed hierarchical pretensions in general, as corruptions, rather than expressions of, essential Catholic doctrine. It is indeed true that the councils once held the authority which the Pope now claims; and that Augustine's conception of the "saints who reign with Christ" was less pretentious than the claims of actual political dominion which Hildebrand derived from these words. But this merely means that the rulers of a perfect society have usurped the sanctity which was once claimed for the society as such. In the final religious analysis either claim is equally monstrous, though the earlier is more plausible than the later one.

The deification of the church is spiritually dangerous, however conceived. The Catholic doctrine that the church is an "extension

[16] The title dates from Innocent III. In earlier centuries it was the Holy Spirit who was Vicar of Christ and the Pope was only St. Peter's Vicar.

of the Incarnation" represents a significant shift of emphasis from the Pauline-Biblical doctrine that the church is the "body of Christ." For when conceived as the body it is clear that it remains subject to the laws of historical reality. Its ideal and norm is, that all its members should be perfectly coordinated to one another by being subordinated to the "head" which is Christ.[17] But the actual realities always betray some of the contradictions which characterize historical existence. In history there is always "another law in my members, warring against the law of my mind." [18] This war is certainly as apparent in the collective, as in the individual, life of the redeemed.

When an institution which mediates the judgment of God upon all the ambiguities of historic existence claims that it has escaped those ambiguities by this mission, it commits the same sin which the prophets recognized so clearly as the sin of Israel. This sin becomes particularly apparent—and intolerable—when it expresses itself in political will-to-power; and it is mitigated only slightly by the achievements of universality which the historic church and papacy have to their credit. A "Vicar of Christ," who represents one among many competing social and political forces in history, cannot be a true representative of the Christ, who was powerless in history and in whom no particular cause or force in history triumphed or was vindicated. The fact that the papal-ecclesiastical power actually achieved a measure of impartiality and transcendence over warring nations and competing social forces and was thereby enabled to play a creative rôle in the history of the Western world may be recorded with gratitude. But it does not prove that the church was able to escape the mixture of creativity and corruption which characterizes all historic striving.

History clearly reveals how curiously and tragically the "spirit of Christ" and the "genius of Caesar" were compounded in the motives and methods of the great popes and in the whole history of ecclesiastical achievement and pretension. The ecclesiastical-religious con-

[17] 1 Cor. 12.   [18] Romans 7:23.

trol of economic life was at once a harmonization of conflicting economic interests from an impartial perspective; and an intolerable alliance between priestly and feudal forces. The rising middle classes found this religious sanctification of the justice and injustice of the feudal order vexatious; and they came to the inevitable conclusion that the order could not be changed without challenging the religious authority which supported it.

The papal political control of Europe was on the one hand an effort to bring the self-will of nations under the dominion of the "law of Christ"; and it was on the other hand a claim of dominion shared with, and precariously maintained against, the empire. In this contest with the empire the alleged superiority of the "spiritual" over the "temporal" power was constantly used as a weapon of the ecclesiastical authority for the purpose of establishing "temporal" dominion. But this claim was not sufficient to maintain the precarious eminence of the papacy. It also availed itself of very "temporal" diplomatic and political strategies. These were finally subordinated to the primary pattern of using the rising French power as a counter-weight against the German emperors. The religious collapse of the imposing structure was caused by the revolt against the religious pretensions inherent in the papal power. The political collapse was occasioned by the increasing subservience of papal power to these same French interests, which served originally as a counter-weight against the empire. The details and complexities of this struggle go beyond our present interest. It is important to recognize, however, that the ultimate outcome corresponds to the prophetic prediction of doom upon historical dominions which seek to usurp the majesty of God.[19]

The theological-religious control over the cultural life of Europe exhibited the same ambiguities as the economic and political dominion of the church. It was on the one hand an effort to bring all

[19] It may be relevant in this connection that in Ezekiel's impressive prophecies of doom upon all the nations of the world because "they have set their heart as the heart of God," ends with a prophecy of doom upon the spiritual leaders, "the shepherds of Israel," because they "fed themselves, and fed not my flock." Ezekiel 34:8.

truth of science, philosophy and culture under the authority of the truth of the gospel, in which partial truth finds its fulfillment and the sinful corruptions of truth are revealed and purged. It was on the other hand the expression of the pride of priests, seeking to transmute an ultimate religious position, which can be held only by faith, into a human possession and into an instrument of authority over other types of knowledge.   *its inevitableness*

One need not be a fatalist to regard this whole development of Catholic doctrine as practically inevitable in the history of Christian thought and life. It was inevitable because man's self-esteem resists that part of the truth of the gospel which is set against all human achievements and discovers the sinful element of self-aggrandisement in them. That resistance was obvious before Christ came in the inadequacy of the solutions offered by Messianic hopes for the problem of history as disclosed by prophetic interpretation. They could not find a solution because they looked for a vindication of God which would include the vindication of the hopeful. The resistance was obvious in the circle of Jesus' own disciples, who found the idea of a suffering, rather than triumphant, Messiah offensive.[20] It was apparent in the early church which found the part of the gospel, which promised the completion of incomplete human life, more sympathetic than the Atonement, as an answer to the problem of sin.

Furthermore the complexities of the religious life, particularly the twofold aspect of grace, were sufficiently perplexing, even without the confusion prompted by human pride. Reason was bound to find difficulty in understanding that the faith and the grace by which we stand beyond the contradictions and ambiguities of history is no simple possession; that it is a having and not having; and that, claimed as a secure possession, it becomes a vehicle of the sin from which it ostensibly emancipates. For all these reasons the effort to achieve a perfection which stands beyond the contradictions of history was inevitable in Christian life; and it was equally inevitable

[20] *Cf.* Mk. 8:31-38.

(granted the actual problem of man-in-history) that this effort should involve the church in new sins on the very pinnacle of its spiritual achievements. This is the pathos of the glory and the decline of medieval Christianity.

IV

THE DESTRUCTION OF THE CATHOLIC SYNTHESIS

The historic reaction to these achievements and pretensions was equally inevitable. In a sense the full truth of the gospel was never fully known, or at least never explicitly stated in the church until history had furnished incontrovertible proof of the error of simpler interpretations. Here lies the significance of the Reformation. It is the historical locus where that side of the gospel, which negates and contradicts historical achievements, became more fully known. This truth invaded the historical consciousness of Western man with a tempestuous fury and changed the whole history of Christendom. The polemical interests of the historic controversy, which was thereby initiated, were bound to prompt a frequently one-sided presentation of the rediscovered truth of the gospel. In this one-sided emphasis the other side of the gospel, embodied in the Catholic "synthesis" was frequently obscured or lost. But no polemic or other weaknesses of the Reformation can derogate from the fundamental character of the insights embodied in the Reformation doctrine of "justification by faith." This doctrine, which appears so irrelevant to modern men, who are strangers to both the Catholic and the Reformation interpretations of the Christian faith, represents the final renunciation in the heart of Christianity of the human effort to complete life and history, whether with or without divine grace. It represents the culmination of the prophetic interpretation of history; for it admits those aspects of historic reality without reservation, which the prophets first disclosed. It understands that human history is permanently suspended between the flux of nature and finiteness and its eternal source and end; that every effort to escape this situation involves man in the sinful pride of seeking to obscure the conditioned character of his existence; and that even the knowledge of this fact, which man may have "by grace" is no guarantee of immunity from sin.

The Reformation understands that therefore we are "justified by faith" and "saved in hope"; that we must look forward to a completion of life which is not in our power and even beyond our comprehension. It realizes that the unity of human existence, despite its involvement in, and freedom from, natural process, is such that it cannot be "saved" either by disavowing its freedom in order to return to nature, or by sloughing off its creaturely character so that it may rise to the "eternal." This is a final enigma of human existence for which there is no answer except by faith and hope; for all answers transcend the categories of human reason. Yet without these answers human life is threatened with scepticism and nihilism on the one hand; and with fanaticism and pride on the other. For either it is overwhelmed by the relativity and partiality of all human perspectives and comes to the conclusion that there is no truth, since no man can expound the truth without corrupting it; or it pretends to have absolute truth despite the finite nature of human perspectives.

But before considering the meaning of Reformation doctrine more fully it is important to recognize that that curious compound of human self-confidence and gospel humility which was effected in the "medieval synthesis" was challenged not merely by the Reformation but also by the Renaissance. The spiritual life of recent centuries is determined by interactions between these two forces. Modern historians of culture have had some difficulty in relating these two great spiritual movements to each other. Frequently they are presented as merely two concurrent movements of "emancipation" from ecclesiastical control and superstition. At other times they are interpreted as successive movements of emancipation; and in that case the Renaissance is usually regarded as the more thorough. In such interpretations the logical order does not agree with the chronological one; for the Renaissance began two centuries earlier than the Reformation. It is significant, moreover, that it developed in the heart of Catholicism. Fifteenth-century Vatican life was the very centre of Renaissance spirituality. The fact is that the Renaissance was at once more Catholic and more "modern" than the Reformation.

This fact will seem paradoxical if it is not recognized that the Renaissance and Reformation represent partly contradictory historical forces, released by the disintegration of the medieval synthesis. For the Renaissance the Catholic interpretation of the human situation is too pessimistic; and for the Reformation it is too optimistic. But since the Catholic synthesis is more optimistic than pessimistic there is more affinity between the Renaissance and Catholicism than between Reformation and Renaissance or between the Reformation and Catholicism. The line between Catholic and Renaissance perfectionism is comparatively unbroken, though the Renaissance dispenses with "grace" as a prerequisite power for the fulfillment of life. It finds the capacities for fulfillment in human life itself. The Reformation on the other hand represents a more complete break with the medieval tradition; for it interprets "grace" primarily, not as the "power of God" in man; but as the power (forgiveness) of God towards man. It denies that either an individual life or the whole historical enterprise can be brought to the degree of completion which Catholic theories of grace imply.

The Renaissance opposes the ecclesiastical control of all cultural life in the name of the autonomy of human reason and thereby lays the foundation for the whole modern cultural development. The Reformation opposes the dogmatic control of religious thought by the church in the name of the authority of Scripture, insisting that no human authority (not even that of the church) can claim the right of possessing and interpreting the truth of the gospel, which stands beyond all human wisdom and which is invariably corrupted (at least in detail) by these interpretations. Each one of these protests against the church's pretended sole right or ability to interpret

The character of religious dogma

and to apply the final truth has its own validity. But they are drawn from completely different levels of experience.

The Renaissance protest, in the name of the autonomy of reason, is much less conscious of the ultimate human problem. It knows that human perspectives are partial and finite; but it would overcome this finiteness progressively by the extension of the power of mind. It does not understand how invariably the paradox of finiteness and freedom leads to the more serious problem of sin. Its protest against ecclesiastical authority is nevertheless valid upon its own level. For religious dogma always tends to regard the ultimate sense of meaning, which it embodies, as a substitute for all the subordinate realms of meaning which the human mind discerns and discovers by tracing the causal sequences of nature and by bringing all phenomena into some realm of meaning by the power of coherence inherent in human reason.

It is significant that the greatest achievement of Renaissance culture lay in directing rational inquisitiveness towards the elaboration of modern natural science. For in the study of nature the human mind may really approximate that god-like objectivity which it fondly, but erroneously, imagines itself to possess when it studies the facts of human history. In the field of history it is no pure mind which observes the facts, but an anxious reason, organically related to an anxious ego, reacting with pity or scorn, with fear or pride, to the greatness or the weakness, to the promised support or the threatened peril, of this or that competitive expression of human vitality.

The Reformation protest against ecclesiastical authority is conscious only of the ultimate human problem which transcends all the particular and subordinate realms of meaning in human life. It knows that human life cannot complete itself; that "the world by its wisdom knew not God"; and that the world involves itself in evil by finding some inadequate centre of meaning for its whole realm of coherence. It detects in the church control of religious dogma a new form of idolatry on the Christian level. Here a human

this may be the case w/ C of C

institution centres life and history around itself; it does this by "possessing" the truth which transcends all truth and by pretending to dispense the "grace" which is a power beyond all human power and is operative only when human powers recognize their own limits.

The Reformation insistence upon the authority of Scripture, as against the authority of the church, bears within it the perils of a new idolatry. Its Biblicism became, in time, as dangerous to the freedom of the human mind in searching out causes and effects as the old religious authority. But rightly conceived Scriptural authority is meant merely to guard the truth of the gospel in which all truth is fulfilled and all corruptions of truth are negated. This authority is Scriptural in the sense that the Bible contains the history, and the culmination in Christ, of that *Heilsgeschichte* in which the whole human enterprise becomes fully conscious of its limits, of its transgressions of those limits, and of the divine answer to its problems. When the Bible becomes an authoritative compendium of social, economic, political and scientific knowledge it is used as a vehicle of the sinful sanctification of relative standards of knowledge and virtue which happen to be enshrined in a religious canon.

The Renaissance and Reformation conceptions of liberty which emerge from this struggle with authority also move on different levels, but they are not as diametrically opposed to each other as are the conceptions of life which underlie them. The Renaissance is interested primarily in freeing human life, and more particularly the human quest for knowledge, from inordinate social, political and religious restraints and controls. It is, therefore, the direct source of the struggle for freedom in human society, which has characterized the modern age. The Reformation means by freedom primarily the right and the ability of each soul to appropriate the grace of God by faith without the interposition of any restrictive institution of grace. It is interested in a freedom which transcends all social situations and may express itself even within and under tyranny.

Since, however, the same religious authority which claims to dispense "grace," and to control and mediate the divine mercy, also claims ultimate authority in the social-historical situation, the struggles for religious and social liberty tend to converge and to support each other. It is this fact which gives a certain plausibility to those interpretations of Renaissance and Reformation according to which both are diverse expressions of a common impulse towards liberty.

The struggle of the Renaissance and Reformation against religious authority, though more opposed to each other in basic principle than in actual expression, do not, however, reveal the full contrast between the two types of spirituality generated in each movement. That contrast may well be defined in terms of the "sanctification" and "justification" aspects of the Christian doctrine of grace.

The Renaissance is, when considered from the standpoint of Christian doctrine, "sanctificationist" in principle. In it all the reservations upon the hope of fulfilling life and realizing its highest possibilities, expressed in the prophetic-Christian consciousness, are brushed aside. If Catholic doctrine unduly subordinates the element of Christian truth symbolized in the concept of "justification," the Renaissance dismisses the idea completely, because it does not seem to correspond to any reality in its experience. One might add that on this issue the Renaissance has been definitive for the spirituality of modern man. For no typical modern man has any appreciation of the truth about life and history contained in the doctrine.

But the Renaissance goes further. It not only destroys the paradox of "justification" and "sanctification" but it dismisses the whole idea of "grace"; for it does not recognize any hiatus between the knowledge of the good and the power to do it. On that issue it represents a conscious return to classical conceptions of the human situation. It believes that man has capacities within himself (either rational or mystical) adequate for the fulfillment of life's most transcendent goals.[1] Here the Renaissance is equally definitive for modern spirit-

---

[1] The early Italian Renaissance expressed this confidence in human capacities in many forms: "I have made myself," said Potano. "Man can

uality. The only exception to this general tendency is to be found in "sectarian" Protestantism. Though the sects of the Reformation define salvation in essentially Renaissance and "perfectionist" terms, rather than in terms of the Reformation, they do retain the Christian concept of grace. The pietist sects believe that grace is required for the realization of individual perfection; and the apocalyptic sects depend upon the interposition of divine providence for the culmination of the whole historical process in an ideal society.[2]

It must be observed that while the perfectionism of the Renaissance was consciously based upon classical interpretations of the human situation it unconsciously added a Christian-Biblical element to its world view. Without this element it could not have taken its optimistic attitude towards the whole historical process. Its concept of history as a meaningful process, moving towards the realization of higher and higher possibilities is derived from Biblical-Christian eschatology. But the Renaissance, and with it the whole of modern culture, changed the Biblical conception of history at two important points. It did not conceive the fulfillment of history as transcending history and as therefore representing also its "end." Nor did it regard an ultimate "judgment" as a part of the "end" as in Biblical eschatology. It had, in other words, no consciousness of the ambiguous and tragic elements in history; or at least it knew of none which would not be progressively eliminated by the historical process itself. The whole of modern utopianism is thus implicit in Renaissance spirituality. The "idea of progress," the most characteristic and firmly held article in the *credo* of modern man, is the inevitable philosophy of history emerging from the Renaissance. This result was achieved

---

make whatever he will of himself," declared Alberti. "The nature of our spirit is universal," boasted Palmieri; and Ficino believed that "man seeks everywhere and always to be like God."

This assertion of human powers is less conscious or explicit in the later Renaissance because it is no longer under the necessity of stating it in opposition to Christian conceptions of grace.

[2] The relation of sectarian Christianity to Renaissance spirituality will be considered more fully in the next chapter.

by combining the classical confidence in man with the Biblical confidence in the meaningfulness of history. It must be observed, however, that history is given a simpler meaning than that envisaged in the prophetic-Biblical view.

One of the tasks which confront us in re-assessing the human situation today is to reject what is false and to accept what is true in the Renaissance world view. Human history is indeed filled with *endless possibilities*; and the Renaissance saw this more clearly than either classicism, Catholicism or the Reformation. But it did not recognize that history is filled with endless possibilities *of good and evil*. It believed that the cumulations of knowledge and the extensions of reason, the progressive conquest of nature and (in its later developments) the technical extension of social cohesion, all of which inhere in the "progress" of history, were guarantees of the gradual conquest of chaos and evil by the force of reason and order. It did not recognize that every new human potency may be an instrument of chaos as well as of order; and that history, therefore, has no solution of its own problem.

This tragic aspect of history, towards which the Renaissance was partly oblivious, was precisely that aspect of history which the Reformation most fully comprehended. This comprehension is contained in the Reformation polemic against all doctrines of sanctification, whether Catholic, secular or sectarian-Christian, in which it detects a too-simple confidence in historical possibilities. Its doctrine of "justification by faith" contains implications for an adequate interpretation of history which have never been fully appropriated or exploited, probably because most Protestant theologies which are interested in the historical problem, have drawn their inspiration from the Renaissance rather than from the Reformation.

It must be noted, however, that the understanding of the Reformation for the ultimate problem of historic existence was not (and probably could not) be elaborated without tendencies towards moral and cultural defeatism. Its consciousness of the ultimate frustration which faces every human enterprise inclined it towards indifference when dealing with all the proximate problems. When confronting these problems every moral situation, whether individual or collective, actually discloses, when fully analysed, unending possibilities of higher fulfillment. There is no limit to either sanctification in individual life, or social perfection in collective life, or to the discovery of truth in cultural life; except of course the one limit, that there will be some corruption, as well as deficiency, of virtue and truth on the new level of achievement.

This moral pessimism and cultural indifferentism of the Reformation was one cause of its defeat by the forces of the Renaissance. It must be recognized that the spiritual life of modernity has been primarily determined by this defeat. The indifference of the Reformation to the proximate problems and the immediate possibilities of human existence was, however, only one cause of this defeat. The other was that the phenomenal development of all the sciences and social techniques, of the conquest of nature and of the general extension of human capacities in the modern period were bound to emphasize what was true, and to hide what was false, in the Renaissance estimate of life.

In order to justify this interpretation of the modern situation it will be necessary to consider the Renaissance and the Reformation more fully. It is particularly important to understand why and how those aspects of the truth about human nature and destiny in which the Renaissance and the Reformation contradict each other, represent valuable insights into human nature and history, which are partially blunted and obscured in the medieval synthesis in which both were contained. The question is whether they can be so conceived and defined that they will not contradict or tend to defeat each other. If this were possible a philosophy of human nature and destiny could emerge which would reach farther into the heights and depths of life than the medieval synthesis; and would yet be immune to the alternate moods of pessimism and optimism, of cynicism and of sentimentality to which modern culture is now so prone.

CHAPTER VI

THE DEBATE ON HUMAN DESTINY IN MODERN CULTURE: THE RENAISSANCE

OUR ANALYSIS of the human situation in the light of Christian faith has brought us to the conviction that both the Renaissance and the Reformation embody insights which must enter into an adequate redefinition of the possibilities and limits of man's historical existence. In order to do this effectively it is necessary to reopen a debate which was brought to a premature conclusion in modern culture by the almost complete triumph of the Renaissance over the Reformation. This triumph was so great that the most characteristic insights of the Reformation were lost even to the consciousness of large sections of Protestant Christianity. Modern Protestantism frequently betrays greater indifference to, and ignorance of, the ultimate problems for which the doctrine of justification by faith was the answer than either Catholic Christianity or secular culture. The former may have solved the problem too easily; but it has never ceased to be aware of it. Secular spirituality, on the other hand, is frequently prompted by a wholesome common-sense to recognize the inevitable relativities and frustrations of history more generously than the perfectionist presuppositions of many modern Protestants permit them to do. Sometimes it develops a secularized version of the doctrine of justification to meet the problem of historical frustration; while liberal Protestantism remains enmeshed in sentimental and illusory historical hopes.[1]

Liberal Protestantism belongs, on the whole, to the Renaissance rather than the Reformation side of the debate on human destiny. *anglican thought* The spiritual situation in the Anglican church conforms to neither the Renaissance nor Reformation pattern of the other churches. Though its Thirty-nine Articles and the prayer book are informed by Reformation theology and piety, the characteristic insights of the Reformation are frequently obscured. The spiritual tension in the Anglican communion in recent centuries has been between Catholic emphases and a pre-Renaissance liberalism which is at least partly derived from the preoccupation of Anglican theology with patristic thought. The emphasis upon classical learning in the older English universities and the dependence of Anglican clergymen upon general university training rather than upon special theological studies, tends to increase the classical content of Anglican thought and to obscure the issues in which there is a contrast between Biblical and classical perspectives.

The debate within Anglicanism is thus between a pre-Augustinian theology and a post-Augustinian Catholicism. In this debate both parties betray strong perfectionist tendencies. The former group has affinities with modern liberalism; but prayer-book piety and the influence of Christian history prevent the secularization of this semi-Pelagianism. The Reformation content of the prayer book is meanwhile a constant resource, influencing the thought of the church in various ways. It would be difficult to assess how many sermons defy, and how many are inspired by, the spirit of the prayer of

[1] This judgment is more applicable to the spiritual situation in America than in Europe. European Protestantism has, generally speaking, remained in closer contact with its own Reformation roots. American Protestantism is predominantly sectarian in origin and has therefore inherited the perfectionism of the sects of the Reformation. This perfectionism belongs spiritually to the Renaissance rather than the Reformation. In America it is frequently compounded with the secular perfectionism, derived from the French enlightenment.

general confession in which the devout are prompted to confess that "there is no health in us."

At its worst Anglican thought is a compound of liberalistic moralism and traditional piety. At its best it manages to combine all facets of the Christian doctrine of grace more truly than other churches.

The conviction that the debate between Renaissance and Reformation must be reopened does not imply that the former was wholly wrong and the latter wholly right in defining the human situation. It implies only that the Renaissance was not as right, and the Reformation not as wrong, as the outcome of the struggle between them would seem to indicate. The debate has indeed been reopened already with the rise of "dialectical theology." This theology was a part of the general revolt against modern culture when the first World War prompted men to suspect that the facts of contemporary history were at variance with their interpretation in contemporary culture. But unfortunately this theological movement proceeded upon the assumption that the Renaissance was wholly wrong and that the Reformation was wholly right. In elaborating this conviction it stressed the most negative aspects of Reformation thought, even to the point of suppressing the emphasis upon sanctification and the fulfillment of life which the Reformation had retained.[2] In consequence the theological movement, initiated by Karl Barth has affected the thought of the church profoundly, but only negatively; and it has not challenged the thought outside of the church at all. It defied what was true in Renaissance culture too completely to be able to challenge what was false in it.

It seems necessary, therefore, to reopen the debate between Renaissance and Reformation by a different strategy, and to appreciate what was Christian and true in the Renaissance interpretation of life and history before we convict it of its errors.

[2] Adolf Koeberle's *The Quest of Holiness* is a significant Lutheran polemic against Barthian theology on the ground that it destroys the Reformation impulse towards sanctification.

II

THE MEANING OF THE RENAISSANCE

The Renaissance as a spiritual movement is best understood as a tremendous affirmation of the limitless possibilities of human existence, and as a rediscovery of the sense of a meaningful history. This affirmation takes many forms, not all of which are equally consistent with the fundamental impulse of the movement. But there is enough consistency in the movement as a whole to justify the historian in placing in one historical category such diverse philosophical, religious and social movements as the early Italian Renaissance, Cartesian rationalism and the French enlightenment; as the liberal idea of progress and Marxist catastrophism; as sectarian perfectionism and secular utopianism. In all of these multifarious expressions there is a unifying principle. It is the impulse towards the fulfillment of life in history. The idea that life can be fulfilled without those reservations and qualifications which Biblical and Reformation thought make is derived from two different sources; from the classical confidence in human capacities and from the Biblical-Christian impulse towards sanctification and the fulfillment of life, more particularly the Biblical-eschatological hope of the fulfillment of history itself.

These two sources determine the double connotation of the very word Renaissance. Just as the Renaissance is a conscious return to classical learning and to classical conceptions of the human situation, so also the more obvious connotation of the word "renaissance" is merely the "rebirth" of learning in general and of classical learning in particular. Though this is the only connotation recognized in most modern histories of culture, the word also meant something much more significant. It meant the rebirth of the earth and of human society. It was an expression of Christian eschatological hopes. This profounder meaning may have been less conscious than the former; but it must be observed that, in the early Renaissance at least, the more profound and far-reaching connotation of "renaissance" was more explicit than later theories of the meaning of the word and of the movement implied.[1]   *Resources*

Renaissance conceptions of both individual and historical fulfillment drew partly upon resources of the Catholic ages. The Renaissance idea of the infinite possibilities of individual life was ostensibly based upon classical conceptions; but these classical conceptions were never completely lost in Catholic rationalism, and they expressed themselves with particular force in the perfectionism of Catholic mysticism and monasticism. An unbroken line runs from the medieval mystics to Protestant pietists. The Renaissance idea of the fulfillment of history, which was finally elaborated in the idea of progress of the seventeenth and eighteenth century, was at least partly derived from Franciscan radicalism.

Franciscan piety, arising in the thirteenth century, has the distinction of being both the final flower of monastic perfectionism and the beginning of a new sense of historical fulfillment. The charm of its individual perfectionism was derived from the absolutism of the gospel ethic rather than from the world-denying dualism and mysticism which partly informed traditional medieval monasticism. Its sense of a dynamic and meaningful history, moving towards the establishment of the Kingdom of God on earth, was the result of a merger between the apocalypticism of Joachim of Flores and St. Francis' ideas of sanctification. Joachim of Flores may be regarded as the first thinker of the medieval period who challenged the static conception of history which had resulted from the identification of the church with the Kingdom of God in Catholic doctrine. According to Joachim, the history of the world was divided

merger between Joachim of Flores + St. Francis

---

[1] Konrad Burdach in his *Reformation, Renaissance, Humanismus* adduces convincing proof of the conscious intention of Renaissance thinkers to indicate something much more than a revival of learning by their hope of rebirth. When they spoke of *"nova vita,"* of *"renovatio,"* *"renovari," "renasci"* and *"regeneratio"* they thought of the regeneration, sometimes of the individual life, sometimes of the church, sometimes of Roman and Italian civilization and sometimes of the world.

into three periods, that of the Father, of the Son and of the Holy Spirit. The period of the Son was his own contemporary ecclesiastical epoch and was drawing to a close. But he looked forward to the epoch of the Holy Spirit in which the law of Christ, only contained as a promise in Catholic sacramentalism, would be inwardly fulfilled.

The radical wing of Franciscanism claimed that the apocalyptic hopes of Joachim had been realized in the perfection of Francis' life and would be fulfilled in the ideal order which Franciscan monasticism would establish. The thought of the "spirituals" of the type of Frater Peter John Olivi, who frequently claimed a spiritual eminence for Francis which challenged the very centrality of Christ in Christian dogma, may be regarded as the real emergence of historical consciousness from the a-historical and non-historical piety of mysticism. This is where Biblical eschatological thought, long submerged by the classical and ecclesiastical ingredients in the medieval synthesis, came into its own once again. It is significant, however, that a new modern element is subtly compounded with Christian eschatology. According to Olivi, history itself is *Heilsgeschichte*. The modern confidence in the redemptive power of the historical process itself is evident in embryonic form in the thought of the Franciscan spirituals.[2]

Franciscan theologians mediated both the individual perfectionist urge and the hope of historical fulfillment to the Renaissance. The greatest of Franciscan theologians, Bonaventura, was the special mediator of the one, and Roger Bacon of the other. Bonaventura's ambitious words: "He who loves God with perfect love is transformed into Him" were re-echoed, and frequently secularized in the "titanism" of the Renaissance. Bonaventura always remained

---

[2] The most authoritative historical analysis of this extraordinary merger of mystical and eschatological-historical consciousness in the confluence of the Joachimite and Franciscan thought is to be found in Ernst Benz, *Ecclesia spiritualis*.

[handwritten margin note: Renaissance — combination of Christian eschatology + classic conceptions of Franciscans]

conscious of man's dependence upon grace; while the Renaissance regarded the marvellous intellectual powers, inherent in human nature, as the source of all those limitless possibilities of human life which its literature celebrated. The relation between Franciscan perfectionism and Renaissance hopes is nevertheless real.

Roger Bacon's passion for learning frequently prompts modern historians to celebrate him as the "first modern," as the harbinger of the spring of a new age in the winter of the Middle Ages. But it is not always observed that he justifies learning primarily as the best method of providing men with weapons for meeting the peril of the Anti-Christ, who is to appear in the fullness of time. Thus Franciscan eschatology and the new passion for learning are united in the thought of Bacon. Naturally the sense of a dynamic history, moving towards its fulfillment in the present and the future, is not of purely Christian or Franciscan-Joachimite origin. The general awakening of the Renaissance, its sense of new powers and potencies, prompted a spontaneous generation of the sense of the fulfillment of history. Yet without the Christian eschatological presuppositions, the classical conceptions to which the Renaissance ostensibly returned, would not have provided adequate vehicles for this mood.

Actually the new and the old are strangely mingled in Dante's vision of both individual and political rebirth, in Petrarch's symbols of awakening from sleep, and in the sketches of utopia in the later Renaissance; Francis Bacon's *New Atlantis*, Sir Thomas More's *Utopia*, and Campanella's *Civitas solis*. There are echoes of Franciscan eschatology in the political Messianic pretensions of Carlo Rienzo, the unifier of Rome[3] and even in the ludicrous Messianic consciousness of Emperor Frederick II, pretensions which prompted ecclesiastical authorities to level the charge of Anti-Christ against him.[4]

The heightened sense of individuality and the urge towards the fulfillment of the highest possibilities of individual life in Renais-

[3] Burdach, *op. cit.*, Ch. II.   [4] Benz, *op. cit.*, p. 225.

ance spirituality have been considered in another connection.[5] It is therefore necessary to complete the picture of Renaissance thought here by sketching the development of theories of history through which Christian eschatological conceptions were transmuted into the modern idea of progress.

The chief agent of this development was undoubtedly the new confidence in developing reason, in cumulative knowledge and experience and in the rational conquest of nature. In this historical trend the classical confidence in rational man was disassociated from the historical pessimism of classical culture and made the instrument of historical optimism.[6] Even when, as in the case of Descartes, problems of the meaning of history were not consciously or explicitly considered, the passion for science is subtly related to historical optimism.[7]

Whatever form this confidence in reason as a force of historical progress may take, all the forms are expressions of a unified philosophical mood. The guiding principle of the philosophy which underlies the idea of progress is that of an immanent *logos* which is no longer believed to transcend history as an eternal form, but is thought of as operating in history, bringing its chaos gradually under the dominion of reason. Sometimes, as in the thought of Fichte and Hegel, this idea is profoundly conceived as a part of a whole metaphysical system; and history becomes, as in Fichte's thought, an indeterminate approximation of the receding goal of rational freedom, or, as in Hegel's thought, it is the gradual development of the self-consciousness of the eternal Spirit. Sometimes, as in the French enlightenment, the historical optimism merely rests upon the certainty that reason will generate individual virtue, or

[5] In Vol. I, Ch. III.

[6] This is particularly clear in the thought of Francis Bacon who protests against the cyclical interpretation of history, inherited from classicism, declaring that it is an obstacle to the advancement of learning.

[7] Descartes had originally intended to give his *Discourse on Method* the title: "The Project of a Universal Science, which can elevate our Nature to its highest degree of Perfection."

destroy the superstitions which hinder social progress,[8] or will prompt wise rather than foolish government.[9] Sometimes, particularly in the eighteenth-century Enlightenment, which was a less profound second chapter of the Renaissance, the historical hope rests altogether upon the idea that the rational conquest of nature will enhance physical welfare and increase physical comforts.[10]

Though the idea of progress as the most dominant and characteristic article in the creed of modernity is powerful enough to use the most diverse philosophies as its instruments, this basic confidence in an immanent *logos* principle never really varies. Even when Darwinism is used to express the mood of historical optimism in the nineteenth century, and the biological idea of the survival of the fittest becomes the bearer of historical optimism, a very naturalistic version of the *logos* principle is operative. For the law of survival in nature is thought of as a force of harmony and progress which will transmute even the most tragic conflicts of history into means of historical advance.

Neither the nineteenth nor twentieth century adds anything of importance to the general dogma of progress, as conceived from the

---

[8] Condorcet looks forward to the day "when tyrants and slaves, priests and their stupid hypocritical tools will have disappeared" and when men will be freemen with "no master save reason."

[9] Voltaire hopes for a period when "prejudices . . . will gradually disappear among all those that góvern nations" and when "philosophy universally diffused, will give some consolation to human nature for the calamities which it will experience in all ages." Voltaire, unlike many of his contemporaries, is never a consistent optimist.

[10] Sébastien Mercier asked: "Where will the perfectability of man stop, armed with geometry and the mechanical arts and chemistry?"

Priestley expressed this more vulgar idea of progress perfectly in the words: "Nature, including both its materials and its laws, will be more at our command; men will make their situation in this world abundantly more easy and comfortable; they will prolong their existence in it and will grow daily more happy. . . . Thus whatever the beginning of the world, the end will be glorious and paradisiacal beyond what our imagination can now conceive." Quoted by J. B. Bury, *The Idea of Progress*, pp. 197 and 221.

early Renaissance to the eighteenth century. Most modern socio-logical-historical philosophies take the idea for granted and elaborate it in terms which are derived from, or at least similar to, the thought of Comte or Spencer.

The relation between these modern ideas of progress and Christian eschatology is that in both cases history is conceived dynamically rather than statically or retrogressively.[11] The difference between them is twofold. The first difference is that the Renaissance thinks of the fulfillment of life, whether individually or in terms of total history, without "grace." It neither needs nor expects either an infusion of power for the fulfillment of individual life or the operation of "providence" in the fulfillment of history. The "laws" of nature and the "laws" of reason are its surrogates for providence. They give meaning to the whole of history, for they guarantee its growth. It does not deal with the problem of power, because it accepts the classical thesis that *logos,* reason, law or any forming principle of life inevitably bring the vitalities of history under its dominion.

The second difference is of even greater importance. The Renaissance regards history as dynamic; but it generally disregards the twofold dynamic in it. It assumes that all development means the advancement of the good. It does not recognize that every heightened potency of human existence may also represent a possibility of evil. The symbol for this difference is that in Christian eschatology the *end* of history is both judgment and fulfillment. The modern conception sees the end as only fulfillment.[12] Sometimes it is purely

[11] The identification of the church with the Kingdom of God led to a static conception of history in the middle ages. An even more dominant medieval idea, that the world was degenerating was probably compounded of classical pessimism and the negative side of the Christian expectation of the "end" of the world. The early Renaissance was continually engaged in the refutation of this retrogressive view of history.

[12] Marxist catastrophism comes considerably closer to Christian eschatology by its idea of a catastrophic judgment upon the evils of a capitalistic society which will usher in the period of fulfillment. But it cannot conceive of a judgment upon this new period of fulfillment.

utopian and anticipates the realization of the unconditioned good within the conditions of nature-history. But even when there are conceptions of an infinitely regressive goal, as for instance in the thought of Fichte,[18] the relation between the historical and the eternal is regarded as primarily the relation between "becoming" and "being." There is no sense of the historical being involved, on every level of achievement, in contradiction to the eternal. This tragic idea is expressed in Christian faith by its doctrine of a "final judgment," to which all history is subject.

The contradiction between the historical and the divine is created by the inevitable tendency of every individual and collective comprehension and realization of the meaning of history to complete the system of meaning falsely, with the self, individual or collective, as the premature centre, source, or end of the system. The inability of any age, culture or philosophy to comprehend the finiteness of its perspectives and the limit of its powers always produces a presumptuous claim of finality.

There is a curious pathos in the fact that modern interpretations of history almost invariably exhibit this tendency in their incidental errors and miscalculations. They identify their own age or culture, or even their own philosophy with the final fulfillment of life and truth and history. This is the very error which they have not taken into account or discounted in their basic principle of interpretation. It is not possible for any philosophy to escape this error completely. But it is possible to have a philosophy, or at least a theology, grounded in faith, which understands that the error will be committed and that it is analogous to all those presumptions of history which defy the majesty of God.[14]

[18] Cf. *Die Grundzuege des Gegenwaertigen Zeitalters* (1806).

[14] Benedetto Croce calls attention to the "fantastic idolization of France" in the thought of the French historian and philosopher of history, Michelet (Croce, *History as the Story of Liberty*, p. 24). Fichte believed that history would move from the fourth period of conscious reason and science to the fifth period of "regnant reason and art" chiefly through the mediation of German philosophy. Hegel was less nationalistic in his

"Our age," declared the French historian, Charles Perrault in 1687, "is, in some sort, arrived at the very summit of perfection. And since for some years the rate of progress has been much slower and appears almost insensible—as the days seem to cease lengthening when the summer solstice draws near—it is pleasant to think that there are probably not many things for which we need envy future generations." [15]

Historical fulfillment is not always claimed for the present. In its profounder moods modern philosophy of history makes the future rather than the present the surrogate for God and calls upon it to assume the divine functions of judging and redeeming the present. In this form it expresses the pride merely of man in general and not of a particular age and culture But even in this form the future is usually regarded as but a further extension of the present; and no further historical development is expected which might stand in contradiction to the achievements of the present.

In short the common and most grievous error in modern interpretations of history is their too simple conception of historical progress. They are right in conceiving history dynamically. Their understanding of the indeterminate possibilities of both individual and collective human existence is profounder than the alternate Catholic and Reformation conceptions; and this insight must be taken into account in any reformulation of the problem of human destiny. But they are wrong in conceiving the dynamic aspects of

----

conception but even more presumptuous. He believed that "the Germanic spirit is the spirit of the new world, whose object is the realization of absolute truth as endless self-determination of freedom which has its absolute form itself for content. The vocation of the Germanic peoples is to furnish bearers of the Christian principle" (*Philosophie der Geschichte in Werke,* Vol. ix, p. 415). The conception is not nationalistic for "Germanic peoples" means something more than "German." But it is more presumptuous than Fichte's thought, for it does not look forward to a final period of history. Rather it seems to contemplate present culture as having achieved the final good of history.

[15] Quoted by Bury, *op. cit.,* p. 87.

history too simply. They hope for an ever increasing dominance of "form" and "order" over all historical vitalities, and refuse to acknowledge that history cannot move forward towards increasing cosmos without developing possibilities of chaos by the very potencies which have enhanced cosmos.

III

SECTARIAN PROTESTANTISM AND THE RENAISSANCE

It is not possible to conclude the discussion of Renaissance spirituality without considering a form of Protestantism which has some remarkable affinities with the basic Renaissance attitude towards history, namely sectarian Protestantism. The Protestant sects, which arose contemporaneously with the Reformation, are critical of Catholicism for reasons which are in almost complete contrast to those of the Reformation. They do not protest against the claims of perfection which Catholicism makes. They are, themselves, usually extravagantly perfectionist. Their primary quarrel with Catholicism is that they suspect sacramentalism of achieving a pseudo-perfection and of "piping" and infusing grace too painlessly into the soul of the sinner and thus failing to induce a genuine change towards a new life.[1]

Sectarian Protestantism draws its inspiration from more Biblical sources than the Renaissance, though some forms of it have a common root in medieval mysticism. But it expresses a common impulse toward the completion of life and history.

In order to explore the genius of sectarianism more fully it is advisable to distinguish between two types of sects, or at least between two impulses in sectarianism: (*a*) The impulse towards the

---

[1] Robert Coachman, a sectarian leveller of the Cromwellian period, makes this typical criticism of sacramental grace: "When all manner of graceless men are fed with seales and pledges of God's favor and are invested with the full privileges and highest prerogatives of the most godly in the church, and are daily told that here is the body and blood of Christ given for them, how presumptuous they grow." *The Glory of the Stone* (1641), p. 15.

perfection of individual life expressed in the pietistic sects and (*b*) the impulse towards the fulfillment of history expressed particularly in the Anabaptist and socially radical sects.

a. The Pietistic Sects. The pietistic-mystical sects combine a mystical and a Biblical element in varying proportions. Where the mystical element is strongest, redemption is conceived as a restoration of some original unity of life, which must be achieved by contemplation. Where the Biblical element is strongest conversion is by "grace." The emphasis on grace is strongest in the evangelistic sects. Here the conversion experience is regarded not so much as the development of some inner power within the self as a shattering of the old and sinful self and its reconstruction by the Holy Spirit. The belated pietistic-evangelistic sect of Methodism insisted most consistently on the strategy of creating a conversion crisis by confronting the soul with the spirit of Christ. This crisis affects the total self and generates that creative despair, that "Godly sorrow" which makes it possible for the "power" of the Holy Spirit to reconstruct the self on a higher level.

The perfectionist impulse in sectarian Christianity is informed by the same logic which we have studied in pre-Augustinian Christianity. Sometimes it is expressed in extravagant terms, as in the words of George Fox: "For all the sects of Christendom that I discoursed with I found none that could bear to be told that any should come to Adam's perfection, into the image of God, that righteousness and holiness that Adam was in before he fell; to be pure and clean without sin as he was. Therefore how shall they be able to bear being told that any shall grow up into the full measure of the stature of Christ, when they cannot bear to hear that any shall come, while on earth, into the same power and spirit that the prophets and apostles were in." [2]

[2] George Fox, *Journal,* p. 101. Fox does not hesitate to make explicit sanctificationist claims for his own redeemed state: "I knew nothing," he writes of his conversion, "but pureness and innocency and righteousness, being renewed in the image of Christ Jesus so that I say I was come up to the state of Adam, which he was in before he fell. . . . But imme-

Sectarian perfectionism is constantly in peril of destroying the paradox of sanctification and justification in Biblical religion. Its experience of grace is conceived entirely as *"Christus in nobis"* and not as *"Christus pro nobis."* In common with George Fox, most sectarian perfectionists imagine that orthodox Christians, whether Catholic or Protestant, fail to achieve perfection only because they do not try hard enough or do not define perfection as the goal of the Christian life with sufficient rigour and consistency.[3]

If we study the conceptions of human nature which underlie sectarian doctrines and isolate the mystical, rationalistic and Biblical elements which are expressed there, it becomes quite apparent that the perfectionist idea of salvation is intimately related to and dependent upon previous conceptions of human nature. These conceptions, though influenced by Biblical thought in varying degrees, are essentially mystical or rationalistic. In common with both classicism and medieval mysticism, pietism believes in a universal and divine element in human nature which can be freed from the temporal. It has little understanding of the paradox that sin is the fruit of spirit and is possible only in that freedom; for it regards spirit the divine quality in man.[4] In terms of the symbols of Christian doctrine this mistake could be defined as mistaking the image of God in man for God Himself. "The Kingdom of God is within

---

diately I was taken up in spirit to see another and more steadfast state than Adam's innocency, even into the state of Christ Jesus that should never fall." *Ibid.,* p. 286.

[3] In Rufus M. Jones' *Spiritual Reformers,* the most eminent contemporary Quaker philosopher assumes that the perfectionist sects represent the real Reformation and that the actual Reformation movement was arrested by its refusal to follow the logic of Christian sanctification to its real conclusion.

[4] A contemporary critic of Fox saw this error very clearly; he wrote: "The light within, say they, is the only judge we must follow, the only Pilot we must steer by, the voice whereunto we must give ear, the only sanctuary to which we must fly for resolution, never remembering how this sanctuary is profaned by continual acts of idolatry and fornication therein committed." Richard Sherlock, *The Quakers Wilde Questions* (1654), p. 66.

you," declared Hans Denck, the father of both pietistic and apocalyptic sectarianism, "and he who searches outside himself will never find it, for apart from God no one can either seek or find him, for he who seeks God already in truth has him." [5]

The idea of the "inner light" and of the "hidden seed" always suggests that the divine element in human life may be found at the deepest level of consciousness or the highest level of mind. The idea is sometimes more mystical and sometimes more rationalistic. Sebastian Franck gives it a purely mystical connotation: "This inner light," he declared, "is nothing else than the word of God, God himself, by whom all things are made and by whom all men are enlightened. . . . No one can know God outside himself, outside of that region where *he knows himself in the ground of himself.*" [6]

The typical mystical strategy of introversion, the "journey towards the centre" is again and again commended as the way of salvation. Peter Balling, leader of the Dutch sectarian "Collegiant" movement, defined the technique of introversion in terms known in every type of mysticism: "We direct thee to within thyself," he wrote. "Thou oughtest to turn into, to mind and have regard to, that which is within thee, to wit, the light of truth, the true light which enlighteneth every man that cometh into the world." [7] Peter Sterry, one of Cromwell's court preachers, has a similar conception of the divine element in man lying at the depth of human consciousness, which is to be found by introversion. He wrote: "There is a spiritual man which lies hid under the natural man as seed under the ground. . . . If thou *go into thyself* beyond the natural man, thou shalt meet the Spirit of God." Any one who "would know the soul to its depths would know God." [8]

In the thought of the Dutch pietist and humanist, Cornhert, the

[5] Rufus M. Jones, *Spiritual Reformers of the Sixteenth and Seventeenth Centuries,* p. 24.
[6] *Ibid.,* p. 54.
[7] Peter Balling, *The Light of the Candlestick* (1662). Balling was in intimate relation with Spinoza.
[8] Rufus M. Jones, *op. cit.,* p. 283.

divine principle in man is interpreted in more purely rationalist terms. He believed that "through reason man partakes of the word of God which is reason itself, revealed and uttered. Therefore man may know of his own salvation with a certainty which far transcends the lower knowledge which we possess of external things." [9]

The Quaker, John Norris, defined the inner light with a confused combination of Biblical and rationalistic terms: "I think," wrote Norris, "that (a) that there is a light in man otherwise how can he know or perceive anything; (b) that he is not his own light or a light unto himself; and (c) that God is his light. That divine light is to be consulted and its answers carefully attended to." [10]

The confusion appears again and again in Quaker thought. The treatises do not always make clear whether "Christ" and "Spirit" are meant in the Biblical or the mystical sense. Sometimes they are used to designate merely native endowments of the soul; and sometimes they are used ambiguously, as for instance in Barclay's "Apology," one of the ablest of Quaker systematic treatises. "By this seed," he writes, ". . . we understand a spiritual and heavenly and invisible principle in which God as Father, Son and Spirit dwells, a measure of which divine and glorious life *is in all men as a seed* which of its own nature draws and *invites us to God;* and this we call *vehiculum Dei* or the spiritual body of Christ because it is never separated from God nor Christ . . . therefore as it is resisted God is said to be resisted; and on the contrary as it is received in the heart and suffered to bring forth its proper and natural effect, Christ comes to be formed and raised." [11]

In the thought of the various sectarian perfectionists, Wesley's conception, despite his indebtedness to such mystics as Thomas à Kempis, William Law, Theologia Germanica and Tauler, contains the largest Biblical element. Wesley is quite clear that deliverance must be from sin and not from finiteness; and he thinks of the

[9] *Ibid.,* p. 108.
[10] William C. Braithwaite, *Second Period of Quakerism,* p. 392.
[11] Robert Barclay, *An Apology for the True Christian Divinity,* p. 136.

process in existential rather than in purely contemplative terms. Furthermore his thought is rooted in the New Testament doctrine of forgiveness and justification. However, he regards justification in essentially Augustinian terms: as forgiveness for sins that are past; and he thinks of sanctification as the higher stage of redemption.

Wesley was in continual debate with the German pietists, particularly the Moravians, in regard to the doctrines of justification and sanctification, the latter, particularly Zinzendorf, being strongly under the influence of Reformation thought. Wesley records a debate with Zinzendorf in his journal as follows: Z: "I acknowledge no inherent perfection in this life. This is the error of errors. I pursue it through the world with fire and sword. Christ is our sole perfection. Whoever follows inherent perfection denies Christ." W: "But I believe that the spirit of Christ works this perfection in true Christians." Z: "By no means; all our perfection is in Christ. Our whole Christian perfection is faith in the blood of Christ. All Christian perfection is imputed and not inherent. We are perfect in Christ. In ourselves we are never perfect." W: "We strive about words." [12]

In this debate between Wesley and the Moravians all the significant issues between Reformation and perfectionist spirituality emerge. Wesley is primarily intent to guard against antinomianism in Reformation thought. He protests against the doctrine that "there is only one commandment in the New Testament, *viz.* to believe." He calls this assertion a "gross, palpable contradiction to the whole tenor of the New Testament, every part of which is full of commandments from St. Matthew to Revelation." [13] In a letter to the church at Herrnhut he writes: "I have heard that some of you affirm that it [salvation] implies liberty from the commandments of God so that one who is saved through faith is not obliged to obey them." In this same letter in which the moral tension of sectarian Christianity is rightly set against the antinomianism, to which Reforma-

[12] Wesley's *Journal*, Vol. II, p. 487.   [13] *Journal* II, p. 356.

tion thought is prone, he also wrongly attacks what is true in Reformation thought and declares: "I have heard some of you affirm that it [salvation] does not imply the proper taking away of our sins, the cleansing of our souls from all sin but only the tearing of the system of sin to pieces." [14]

This debate, in which each side is right on one point and wrong on the other, may be taken as a miniature of the whole controversy between the Renaissance and Reformation.[15] The one rightly maintains the moral imperatives of the gospel and wrongly imagines that they can be completely realized; the other rightly understands the limits of historic existence but is wrongly tempted to an antinomianism, which allows men "to continue in sin that grace may abound."

[14] *Ibid.*, II, 491. The same issue arises in a conversation with two Moravians, Boehler and Spangenberg. The latter asserts that "the old creature or old man remains with us till the day of our death." But "the new man is stronger than the old; so that while corruption continually strives, yet while we look to Christ it cannot prevail." Wesley asked him: "Is there then corruption in your heart?" and Spangenberg answered with the proper paradox: "In the heart of my old man there is but not in the heart of my new man. . . . Inward corruption cannot be taken away till our bodies are in the dust." Wesley records this conversation and adds the observation: "Was there inward corruption in our Lord; And cannot the servant be as his master?" *Ibid.*, p. 452.

[15] It is not possible to consider all the complexities of Wesley's perfectionism. It ought to be mentioned, however, that some of his perfectionist claims arise from a Pelagian doctrine of sin. He defined it as a "voluntary defiance of a known law." Perfection as conscious compliance with known laws is of course possible. Meanwhile Wesley was too much of a realist to be able to deny the reality of those sinful elements in the life of the redeemed which are neither fully conscious nor yet completely unconscious. (Cf. *Nature and Destiny of Man*, Vol. I, Chs. VII and VIII.) There is thus a conflict in Wesley's thought between his realism and his defective doctrine of sin, which results in such equivocal statements as "I do not contend for the term sinless though I do not object against it." He resolved the conflict by a rather neat theological device. He declared that there was no moment in life for which real perfection could be claimed except the moment just before death. His disciples have not always had the prudence to set the same limits.

Sectarian pietism, representing an amalgam of Biblical and mystical presuppositions, never externalizes the fulfillment of life in the manner of secular spiritual movements which had their rise in the Renaissance. It is significant nevertheless that it makes perfectionist claims which obscure the realities of historic existence as effectively as secular utopianism; and sometimes it indulges in even more deleterious sentimentalities. The root of the error of sectarian perfectionism is to be found in a conception logically and historically related to those held by secular perfectionists. The "hidden seed" and the "inner light" is an immanent Christ, which corresponds to the immanent *logos* of the main stream of Renaissance thought. The immanent Christ may be conceived more dynamically than the immanent *logos;* and conversion and redemption may therefore involve the total personality to a larger degree than the various secular *logos* doctrines do. But the idea of an immanent Christ in man, just as a completely immanent *logos* in history, obscures the real dialectic between the historical and the eternal. It fails to recognize that the freedom of man in history, whether conceived in rational or mystical terms contains possibilities of both good and evil.

b. The Eschatological Sects. The perfectionist impulse of the Reformation sects was not confined to the hope of individual sanctification in the pietistic-individualistic sects. It expressed itself also in the eschatological hopes for the fulfillment of history and the realization of a perfect society of the social radical sects, particularly the Anabaptists of the continent and the Cromwellian sects of seventeenth century England. Some of these were "suffering" sects and some were "fighting," to adopt Troeltsch's distinction. This is to say that some were more purely apocalyptic, waiting upon God to usher in the "Kingdom of Christ," while others were ready to engage the enemy in order to bring in the Kingdom of God upon earth. Whatever the differences between them they are all expressions of the impulse towards the fulfillment of life and history, which belongs to Renaissance spirituality.

If the pietist sects revealed the Biblical element in their thought and life by their idea of individual conversion through "grace" and "power," the eschatological sects betrayed their relation to the Biblical thought-world by conceiving of the historical process as moving towards a critical conflict between Christ and Antichrist rather than as a gradual process of the triumph of good over evil.[16]

The conceptions of continental Anabaptists of the sixteenth century and the "Fifth Monarchy" men of seventeenth century England were explicitly apocalyptic.[17] This led on the continent to absurd attempts at the realization of the Kingdom of God upon earth, the best known of which was the experiment at Münster, where Jan Bockelson, finally proclaimed himself "King of the whole earth."[18] The apocalyptics of England, unfortunately, or perhaps fortunately, were never able to claim the realization of the Kingdom. They had, in consequence, a much more creative relationship to all the democratic and equalitarian movements initiated in Cromwellian England. This distinction between continental and English apocalyptics

[16] The Quakers, in so far as they hoped for the social realization of the Kingdom of Christ on earth, came nearest to an evolutionary or progressive view of history, for they regarded the realization of love in individual life as at the same time the force which would gradually redeem society. The continental pacifist sects, on the other hand, particularly the Mennonites, were more purely apocalyptic. Menno Simons initiated the protest against the "fighting" sects of the Anabaptist movement on the continent. But he was never under the illusion that "suffering love" would gradually become historically successful and would overcome the world. He thought of it rather as a sign and symbol of the Kingdom of God, which God would have to usher in in his good time. The problem of historical evil was, according to his faith, beyond the comprehension and the power of man.

[17] The "Fifth Monarchy" men discerned five great periods of history, four of which had been dominated by the great empires of history and the fifth of which would be the period in which all kingdoms of the world would be subordinated to the Kingdom of Christ. This apocalyptic idea was not confined to a closely knit sect but spread through the other Cromwellian sects. *Cf.* George P. Gooch, *Democratic Ideas in Seventeenth-Century England.*

[18] *Cf.* E. B. Bax: *The Rise and Fall of the Anabaptists,* and Eduard Bernstein, *Cromwell and Communism.*

prompts the observation that what is legitimate in the perfectionist urge is always most perfectly expressed *in spe*. It is a good thing to seek for the Kingdom of God on earth; but it is very dubious to claim to have found it. In that claim some new relativity of history and some new egoistic force make pretensions of sanctity which, at best, are merely absurd and, at worst, unleash new furies and fanaticisms. That is why Marxism is so much better as leaven in history than the realized Marxism of Stalinism.

Even when the apocalyptic mood was less explicit in sectarian life, most of the English sects, who constituted the left-wing of Cromwell's army were implicitly eschatological. They were inclined to regard the political and economic system from which they suffered as the final form of historical evil and to hope, therefore, that victory over it would usher in the final period of social perfection.

Thus while Biblical eschatology was responsible for their view of history, as moving towards a final crisis, the general mood of historical optimism prompted them to seek for the Kingdom of God, without reservation, in history. They disregarded the Biblical idea of a "final" judgment and a "final" fulfillment beyond all possible historical realizations.

Their affinity with Renaissance thought is furthermore revealed in their inclination to identify God and "Spirit" with reason, and reason with the "natural law" of justice, which they used as a principle of criticism against historic forms of injustice. Gerrard Winstanley, the leader of the Diggers, wrote: ". . . the spirit which will purge mankind is pure reason. . . . Though men esteeme this word reason to be too meane to set forth the Father by, yet it is the highest name that can be given him. . . . For it is reason that made all things and it is Reason that governs the whole creation." [19]

Winstanley, who is probably the profoundest as well as the most radical of the Cromwellian sectaries, exhibited another extremely

[19] *The Saint's Paradise*, p. 78.

significant conflict between Biblical and modern conceptions in his thought. He had on the one hand a Biblical conception of the fall, according to which the fall is synonymous with the rise of "particular love," against the principle of "universal love." His other theory makes him the real progenitor of the Marxist interpretation of history. The idea is that sin comes into the world through the rise of property; for "this particular propriety of mine and thine has brought in all misery upon the people. For first it has occasioned people to steal from one another. Secondly it hath made laws to hang those that did steal." [20] According to this theory it will be possible to abolish sin by returning to those conditions of "common treasury" which existed in the beginning of history.[21] Here, in the second interpretation is one of the first of the modern interpretations of historical evil, which seeks its origin in some specific *locus* of history and in a special historical "fall." Winstanley anticipates the Marxist interpretation of history.

All of the radical sects of the Cromwellian period looked forward towards an ideal society, though they did not define it in identical terms. The Levellers were more libertarian and the Diggers more equalitarian. Between them they anticipated the modern bourgeois ideals of liberty and the proletarian ideals of equality.

The insistence of sectarian Christianity that the Kingdom of God is relevant to all historical social problems, and that brotherhood is a possibility of history is certainly a part of the Christian gospel. The debate between the Reformation sects and the Reformation itself joins the issue between the Renaissance and the Reformation within the heart of Biblical Christianity. The sects prove how thoroughly

---

[20] *The New Law of Righteousness*, p. 61.
[21] For recent studies of Cromwellian left-wing thought see: A. S. P. Woodhouse, *Puritanism and Liberty*; David W. Petegorsky, *Left-Wing Democracy in the English Civil War*; and Professor G. H. Sabine's *The Works of Gerrard Winstanley*. Petegorsky is inclined to emphasize the secular-social theory of the origin of sin in Winstanley's thought and Professor Sabine the more religious-Biblical one.

Christian the impulse is to fulfill the will of God and to realize the possibilities of man in history. These impulses express, at least, one part of the gospel. But there is a part of the Christian interpretation of life which the sects do not understand; and it is precisely that side of the truth which the Reformation had rediscovered and which it guarded with such devotion that it became oblivious to the truth which the sects embodied and expressed.

The impulse to fulfill God's law in history and to bring the realities of history into greater conformity with the Kingdom of God related sectarian Christianity fruitfully to the whole history of political and economic democracy. Calvinism, which as Troeltsch rightly observes, is semi-sectarian in many of its characteristics, also made its contributions to the democratic cause, as did the combination of Catholic and Renaissance thought which became embodied in the Anglican church. The Lutheran reformation was betrayed meanwhile into the hands of social reaction.

But sectarian radicalism also expressed all the utopian illusions of modern culture, proving thereby that the whole truth of the gospel is not to be found here. The eschatological sects were superior to the main stream of Renaissance thought in possessing both a more social and more radical interpretation of historical tasks and possibilities. Both its social and its radical notes were undoubtedly derived from Bible prophetism. But the sects failed to comprehend the meaning of the profoundest element in this prophetism. They did not see that all history and all historic achievements must remain under the judgment of God; that the "Kingdom of God" which we achieve in history is never the same as the Kingdom for which we pray. The sectarians sought for an ideal society in which every contradiction to the law of love would be eliminated. But such a society is no more possible in history than are sanctified individuals who have no law in their members warring against the law that is in their mind.

The triumph due at least to historical optimism which advances produced.

IV

THE TRIUMPH OF THE RENAISSANCE

It is possible even before we consider Reformation thought more carefully to establish one of the causes of the remarkable triumph of the Renaissance over the Reformation in the past three centuries. Even if the Reformation had not failed to do full justice to those aspects of history which the Renaissance illumined, the latter would probably have triumphed because of the special circumstances of modern history. Since the dawn of modern history, the advance of science, the phenomenal increase of wealth and comfort which the applied sciences have made possible, the revolutionary changes in government and industry, the discovery and settlement of new continents, the expansion of commerce to the point where it encircles the globe, all these developments were conducive to the support of the spirit of historical optimism. It is not easy to understand that the perennial problems of man's existence in history will reappear on every level of historical achievement in a period when the changes in the conditions of his life are so great as to create the illusion that new conditions and achievements have eliminated the perennial problems.

While the bourgeois classes were in the process of establishing our democratic capitalistic society, it was natural that they should assume that all injustice had disappeared or would disappear when feudalism had been completely vanquished. It was equally natural, when the democratic dreams of the seventeenth and eighteenth century turned into the sorry realities of the nineteenth and twentieth century, that new revolutionists and utopians should arise who imagined that if only bourgeois injustice could be eliminated, it would be possible to establish perfect justice. This particular proletarian dream has, incidentally, not been completely subjected to historical disillusionment, though the contradiction between Marxist hopes and Russian realities has certainly initiated that process. The whole optimism of our culture is as natural as the sanguine spirit of the youth who imagines that the awakening of his mind and imagination, the growth of physical powers and the enlargement of responsibilities, all guarantee the successful realization of his life. The youth can hardly be expected fully to realize that each new power and potency of life creates its own new problem.

It was natural that when modern technology increased the intensity and extent of social cohesion and established something like brotherhood on wider and wider areas, men would be so enamoured of this achievement that the other side of the picture would not be discerned. It was not recognized that the same technology which would create a potential world community, might also produce international chaos, if the world community lacked adequate political instruments for the organization of its life. No one anticipated that, before such a world community could be created, mankind might be driven to the very edge of the abyss of destruction; that efforts would be made to harness modern technology to purely destructive and imperial ends; that nations would use these destructive possibilities of a technical society in an effort to unify the world upon a tyrannical basis; that they would come perilously near to success; and that part of their success would be due to a false sense of security and a parasitic dependence upon comforts created by a technical society in the remnants of the civilized world.

We are still so completely immersed in these tragic historic realities that it is not possible even to chart the course by which we may emerge from them. We can only know that the twentieth century has refuted the dreams of the earlier centuries of the modern era in the most tragic terms, and that modern culture is immersed in pathetic confusions by reason of this refutation. The confusion is so great partly because modern culture has no alternate perspectives upon life and history to which it might turn, when it finds the certainties of yesterday dissipated by the realities of today.

No alternate perspectives are available because the triumph of the Renaissance was so complete that it destroyed not only particular interpretations of the Christian religion, but submerged the Christian religion itself, as, in any sense, a potent force in modern culture. The Catholic form of the religion became discredited by the fact that all the liberties of modern life and all the achievements of social and political justice were established in defiance of Catholicism's premature identification of its feudal society with the sanctities of the Kingdom of God. The Reformation form of the religion was not so much discredited as simply lost. It lives on of course after a fashion; for nothing in history ever seems to die completely. It certainly does not live with any such vestigial vitality as Catholicism boasts.

If we inquire why the characteristic insights of the Reformation were lost to modern man so completely we must determine to what degree what was true in the Reformation was overwhelmed by what was false in the Renaissance by reason of the peculiar illusions of modern history. For the contemporary refutation of these illusions might also provide a contemporary validation of the truth of the Reformation.

But we have suggested that the Reformation did not present its truth without error; that it was inclined to destroy the paradoxical Biblical conception of grace, and the twofold aspect of historical fulfillment as much from one side as did the Renaissance from the other. For this reason our inquiry must be particularly careful to approach the affirmations of the Reformation critically. Otherwise we merely shall harness contemporary disillusionment to historical defeatism; even as past decades placed their characteristic optimistic illusions in the service of an historical utopianism. In that case we should not learn anything from our total experience; we should merely permit the alternate vicissitudes of history to prompt alternate moods of illegitimate hope and unjustified despair.

CHAPTER VII

THE DEBATE ON HUMAN DESTINY IN MODERN CULTURE: THE REFORMATION

THE ANALYSIS of the contemporary religious situation has prompted several anticipatory appreciations and criticisms of the Reformation which must now be more fully examined. We have assumed that the Reformation has a more significant place than is generally realized in the history of Christian thought and life. It was the historical *locus* where the Christian conscience became most fully aware of the persistence of sin in the life of the redeemed. This realization, and the consequent refutation of alternate and more optimistic conceptions, resulted in a new appreciation of that part of the gospel which found the final completion of life in divine mercy.

We have suggested that the Reformation was frequently tempted to destroy the Biblical paradox of "*Christus in nobis*" and "*Christus pro nobis*," of grace as power within us, and grace as power over us from one side, while sectarian Christianity destroyed the paradox from the other side. This criticism must be considered more fully.

It would be presumptuous to make such a criticism without a full appreciation of the effort of the Reformation to be true to the twofold Biblical conception of grace. Nor will the criticism stand without a careful discrimination between the Lutheran and the Calvinistic approaches to this central problem; for the two sides of the Reformation did not arrive at identical conclusions on this issue. It will be advisable therefore to consider each in turn.

II

THE LUTHERAN REFORMATION

Luther's approach to the ultimate problem of the Christian life was dominated by two considerations. The primary one was his conviction, established after bitter experience, that no final peace could be found by the effort to achieve righteousness. He had tried the method of monastic perfectionism and had failed; and the assurance of the Pauline word that "the just shall live by faith," therefore came to him as a happy release from the bondage of "the law," from the intolerable tension of an uneasy conscience which came the nearer to despair, the more imperious the demand for perfection appeared to it. The secondary consideration was the result of historical observation, rather than inner experience. He was convinced that the pretention of finality and perfection in the church was the root of spiritual pride and self-righteousness. His belief that the mystic-ascetic attempt at perfection was futile prompted his polemic against monasticism. His conviction that the pretension of finality was dangerous motivated his polemic against ecclesiasticism.

In elaborating his own theory of grace and the Christian life he was far from excluding that side of the paradox of grace according to which it is the source of a new life, of "love, joy and peace." Luther has his own relation to the mystical tradition,[1] and he followed the tendency of those who converted the classical mystical effort at union with God into a "Christ-mysticism." The soul of the believer, he claimed, became so united with Christ that all his virtues flow into it: "Since the promises of God are words of holiness, truth, righteousness, liberty and peace, and are full of universal goodness, the soul, which cleaves to them with a firm faith, is so united to

---

[1] *Cf.* Rudolf Otto, *Mysticism, East and West.*

them, nay thoroughly absorbed by them, that it not only partakes of, but is thoroughly saturated by all their virtues." [2]

Luther interprets the power of righteousness, psychologically, primarily as the motive of love and gratitude to God. This motive dispenses with the necessity of considering the gratitude or ingratitude, the praise or blame of fellowmen: "Thus from faith flow forth love and joy in the Lord, and from love a cheerful willing free spirit, disposed to serve our neighbour voluntarily, without taking into account any gratitude or ingratitude, praise or blame, gain or loss. Its object is not to lay men under obligation, nor does it distinguish between friends or enemies . . . but most freely spends its goods, whether it loses them through ingratitude or gains goodwill." [3] Here Luther comprehends the whole beauty and power of Christian *agape*, particularly its transcendent freedom over all the prudential considerations of natural ethical attitudes.

He does not deny, in other words, that the new life is capable of a new righteousness. He only insists that it is not justified by them: "A Christian, being consecrated by his faith, does good works; but he is not by these works made a more sacred person or more a Christian. This is the effect of faith alone." [4]

[2] *On Christian Liberty*, p. 261. Luther very frequently used the mystical, as also Pauline metaphor of marriage to describe the union of the soul with Christ: "The third incomparable grace of faith is this: that it unites the soul to Christ, as the wife to the husband, by which mystery as the Apostle teaches, Christ and the soul are made one flesh. Now if they are one flesh, and if a true marriage . . . is accomplished between them . . . then it follows that all they have becomes theirs in common, as well good things as evil things; so that whatsoever Christ possesses that the believing soul may take of itself and boast of as its own, and whatever belongs to the soul, that Christ claims as his." . . . "Christ is full of grace, life and salvation. The soul is full of sin, death and hell. These will belong to Christ and grace, life and salvation to the soul." It will be noticed that in the final phrases the imputed righteousness is integrally related to an achieved righteousness. *Ibid.*, p. 264.

[3] *Ibid.*, p. 270.

[4] This correct formulation in regard to the reality of good works also contains one of Luther's errors. For it is by "faith alone" rather than by

Many of the emphases in Luther's thought combine the classical Christian doctrine shared by Catholicism and the Reformation, on the priority of grace, with a new emphasis on the place of forgiveness in grace. The soul is the "poor little harlot" who brings nothing to the spiritual marriage but a "sackfull of sins" and her "rich bridegroom Christ" brings all the goodness. Or the soul is the "parched earth" which can bring forth no fruit unless grace as the "rain from heaven" water it. But with this rain the Christian will "as a good tree bring forth good fruits. For the believer has the Holy Spirit; and where He is He will not allow me to be idle but incites him to all exercises of piety, to the love of God, to patience in affliction, to prayer, thanksgiving and the showing of love towards all." [5]

In picturing the possibilities of this love towards all Luther displays the most profound understanding of the meaning of Christian *agape,* particularly of its completely disinterested motives. He regards the ethic of the Sermon on the Mount as definitive for Christians, always so long as he is dealing with personal attitudes and relationships.[6]

Despite these great merits of the Lutheran position there are quietistic tendencies in it, even when Luther is analysing the intricacies of personal religion, where he is on the whole most faithful to the Biblical paradox. Sometimes he lapses into mystic doctrines of passivity or combines quietism with a legalistic conception of the imputation of righteousness. "Without works" degenerates into "without action" in some of his strictures against the "righteousness

---

"grace alone" that peace is found. This means that man's acceptance of grace by faith, rather than grace itself, becomes determinative. This error betrayed Luther into a rejection of whatever goodness may be realized outside the Christian life. For he continues: "Nay, unless he has previously been a Christian, none of his works would have any value at all; they would really be impious and damnable sins." *Ibid.,* p. 275.

[5] *Works* (Weimar, ed.), Vol. 40, p. 265.

[6] *Cf.* Werner Betcke, *Luther's Socialethik.* Luther's understanding of the primacy of the love commandment in Christian ethics is certainly much profounder than Calvin's.

Luther's weaknesses:
passive righteousness
elimination of moral obligation

188   *Human Destiny: The Reformation*   [CH. VII]

of works." He writes: "This most excellent righteousness of faith
. . . which God through Christ imputeth to us without works, is
neither political nor ceremonial, nor the righteousness of God's law,
nor consisteth in works, but is clean contrary: that is to say, a *mere
passive* righteousness. . . . For in this we work nothing unto God,
but only receive and suffer another to work in us, that is to say,
God. Therefore it seemeth good to me to call this righteousness of
faith, or Christian righteousness, the passive righteousness." [7]

The mystic fear of action, because all action is tainted with sin,
has its counterpart in the Lutheran fear of action, because it may
tempt to a new pride. So Emil Brunner warns that "all energetic
ethical activity carries with it a great danger. It may lead to the
opinion that by such activity deliverance from evil is being accomplished." [8] The danger cannot be denied. But if moral action is dis-
couraged on that ground, the Reformation theologian is in no better position than the monastic perfectionist who disavows particular
moral and social responsibilities because of the taint of sin which
attaches to them. Ideally the doctrine of justification by faith is a
release of the soul into action; but it may be wrongly interpreted
to encourage indolence. The barren orthodoxy of seventeenth-century
Lutheranism, in which the experience of "justification by faith"
degenerated into a "righteousness of belief," was not an inevitable,
but nevertheless a natural, destruction of the moral content of the
Christian life, for which there was a certain warrant in Luther's own
thought.

Possibly a greater weakness in the Lutheran analysis of grace is
found in Luther's idea of the relation of grace to the law. His difficulty here is derived not so much from his theory of justification
as from his idea of sanctification. Luther's vision of the "love, joy
and peace" which the redeemed soul has in Christ, is of an ecstatic
transcendence over all the contradictions of history, including the
inner contradictions of the "ought," the sense of moral obligation.

[7] In Commentary on Galatians, xciii.
[8] Emil Brunner, *The Divine Imperative*, p. 72.

Agape, as the fulfillment of the law, results in a complete disappearance of the sense of obligation to the law, and in a consequent elimination of all the careful discriminations of justice which belong to "law" in the broadest sense.[9]

Emil Brunner's exposition of Reformation ethics leads to exactly the same result. He writes: "The chief emphasis of Scriptural ethics lies not in victory over lawlessness but in the fight against legalism. . . . If I feel that I ought to do right it is a sign that I cannot do it. . . . Willing obedience is never a fruit of the sense of 'ought' but only of love. . . . Freedom means release from the sense of 'ought' from the bondage of the law."[10]

In this exposition of a highly personal and interior sanctification, the Reformation obscures the wisdom inhering in its doctrine of justification. For according to the doctrine of justification the inner contradiction of the soul is never completely healed. There are undoubtedly ecstatic moments when the conflict between self-love and the love of God, between conscience and the anxious survival impulse of the ego are transcended. But these moments are merely "earnests" of the final fulfillment of life; and they do not describe the general condition of the life of the redeemed. In that condition the relation between law and grace is much more complex; for by the inspiration of grace the law is extended as well as overcome. Repentance and faith prompt a sense of obligation towards wider

[9] Luther's conception of the relation of grace to law is most clearly expressed in his Commentary upon Galatians in which he writes: "For when Paul saith that we are delivered from the curse of the law by Christ, he speaketh of the whole law and principally of the moral law, which only accuseth, curseth and condemneth the conscience, which the other two [judicial and ceremonial] do not. Wherefore we say that the Moral Law or the Law of the Ten Commandments has no power to accuse or terrify the conscience in which Jesus Christ reigneth by his grace, for he hath abolished the power thereof." Gal. 2:21.

Luther thinks of the law primarily in negative terms. Its purpose is "to reveal unto man his blindness, his misery, his impiety, ignorance, hatred and contempt of God, death, hell, the judgment and deserved wrath of God." *Ibid.*

[10] Emil Brunner, *The Divine Imperative,* pp. 72–78.

and wider circles of life. The need of this neighbour, the demands of that social situation, the claims of this life upon me, unrecognized today may be recognized and stir the conscience to uneasiness tomorrow. There is a constantly increasing sense of social obligation which is an integral part of the life of grace. To deny this is to be oblivious to one aspect of historic existence which the Renaissance understood so well: that life represents an indeterminate series of possibilities, and therefore of obligation to fulfill them. It is precisely because this is so that there can be no complete fulfillment; for "a man's reach should exceed his grasp" (Browning). The conception of the relation of grace to law in Luther need not lead to antinomianism, as is sometimes charged; but it is indifferent to relative moral discriminations. It does not relax moral tension at the ultimate point of moral experience; for there it demands the love which is the fulfillment, and not the negation of law. But it relaxes the tension at all intermediate points and does not deal seriously with all the possible extensions of justice to which men ought to be driven by an uneasy conscience.[11]

[11] In analysing this problem Brunner continually confuses the sense of moral obligation with "legalism," that is, with the limitation of moral obligation to a specific code of conduct. Thus he knows no middle ground between perfect love and legalism. He writes: "The legalistic type of person finds it impossible to come into real human personal contact with his fellow-man. Between him and his neighbor there stands something impersonal, the 'idea,' the 'Law' . . . something abstract which hinders him from seeing the other person as he really is." This might be a just condemnation of legalism in the narrow sense but Brunner subsumes all experiences of moral obligation under the term and continues: "The good that one does simply from a sense of duty is never the good. Duty and genuine goodness are mutually exclusive." *Ibid.,* pp. 73–74.

There would be little goodness in history by that standard. Suppose we grant that there is not much goodness in which all sense of obligation has been swallowed up in perfect love. It would still be important to achieve higher and higher forms of goodness by the extension of the sense of obligation. When we confront the claims of our fellow men we may not be "legalistic" at all in the sense that we do not try to measure those claims by some fixed standard of justice. Yet we might with uneasy con-

The weakness of the Lutheran Reformation in dealing with the problem of law and grace in it becomes even more apparent when the issue is transferred from the inner life to the complexities of culture and civilization, and all expressions of the collective life of man. Here the "defeatism" of the Reformation becomes much more apparent. Its understanding of the ultimate problem of historical existence seems to preclude any understanding of all the proximate problems. The Reformation understands that every possible extension of knowledge and wisdom falls short of the wisdom which knows God. It realizes that the "world by its wisdom knew not God" and it rejoices in the grace, apprehended by faith, which overcomes the sinful ego-centricity of all human knowledge. But it has no interest in the infinite shades and varieties of the amalgam of truth and falsehood which constitutes the stuff of science and philosophy, and of all human striving after the truth. The Renaissance was undoubtedly wrong in imagining that the final truth could be found by the cumulative process of the history of culture. It did not recognize the peril of new errors on each new level of wisdom; most particularly the error of assuming that an age which had a point of vantage over all preceding ages would thereby arrive at the final truth.

But was it not right, in comparison with the Reformation, to take the obligation towards the truth seriously? And was not the Reformation delivered into the sin of cultural obscurantism by its indifference towards the relative distinctions of truth and falsehood which are so important in the history of culture: Did it not put itself essentially in the position of the unprofitable servant who declared: "Lord I knew thee that thou art an hard man, reaping where thou hast not sown, and gathering where thou has not

---

science weigh those claims against our own interests and decide to do some justice to them. This whole moral process might proceed without any reference to any known "law." It could be extremely personal and individual too. But it would still fall short of that perfect love, which Brunner seems to regard as the only release from "legalism."

strawed; and I was afraid and went and hid thy talent in the earth; lo, there thou hast that is thine." [12]

In confronting the problems of realizing justice in the collective life of man, the Lutheran Reformation was even more explicitly defeatist. Human society represents an infinite variety of structures and systems in which men seek to organize their common life in terms of some kind of justice. The possibilities of realizing a higher justice are indeterminate. There is no point in historical social achievement where one may rest with an easy conscience. All structures of justice do indeed presuppose the sinfulness of man, and are all partly systems of restraint which prevent the conflict of wills and interests from resulting in a consistent anarchy. But they are also all mechanisms by which men fulfill their obligations to their fellow men, beyond the possibilities offered in direct and personal relationships. The Kingdom of God and the demands of perfect love are therefore relevant to every political system and impinge upon every social situation in which the self seeks to come to terms with the claims of other life.

Luther denies this relevance explicitly. He declares: "The way to discern the difference [between law and gospel] is to place the gospel in heaven and the law on the earth: to call the righteousness of the gospel heavenly, and the righteousness of the law earthly and to put as great a difference between [them] as God hath made between heaven and earth. . . . Wherefore if the question be concerning the matter of faith and conscience let us utterly exclude the law and leave it on earth. . . . Contrariwise in civil policy obedience to law must be severely required. There nothing *must be known* concerning the conscience, the Gospel, grace, remission of sins, heavenly righteousness or Christ himself; but Moses only with the law and the works thereof." [13]

[12] Mt. 25:24-25.

[13] Commentary upon Galatians. It is interesting to compare this complete severance between the religious and the civil idea of liberty with the observation of John Milton: "It will not misbecome the meanest Christian to put in mind Christian magistrates, and so much more freely

seperated between the spiritual kingdom + the worldly kingdom

Here we have the complete severance between the final experience of grace and all the proximate possibilities of liberty and justice, which must be achieved in history. This principle of separation leads to a denial that liberty can have any other meaning for the Christian than liberty from "God's everlasting wrath. For Christ hath made us free not civilly nor carnally but divinely; that is to say our conscience is now made free and quiet, not fearing the wrath of God to come." Social antinomianism is guarded against by the injunction, "Let every man therefore endeavour to do his duty diligently in his calling and help his neighbour to the utmost of his power." [14] But evidently no obligation rests upon the Christian to change social structures so that they might conform more perfectly to the requirements of brotherhood. In his attitude towards the peasant revolt Luther rigorously applied this separation between the "spiritual kingdom" and the "worldly" one; and met the demands of the peasants for a greater degree of social justice with the charge that they were confusing the two.[15] He took a complacent

---

by how much they desire to be known as Christians, that they meddle not rashly with Christian liberty the birthright and outward testimony of our adoption, lest they . . . be found persecuting them that are free born of the spirit . . . bereaving them of that sacred liberty which our Saviour by his own blood purchased for them." From *Of Civil Power in Ecclesiastical Causes.*

Milton declares it "impertinent to endeavor to argue us into slavery on the example of our Saviour" who did indeed take "in our stead the form of a servant but he always retained his purpose of being a deliverer." . . . "He asked for the tribute money. 'Whose image and superscription is it?' says he. They tell him it was Caesar's. 'Give then to Caesar,' says he, 'the things that are Caesar's.' . . . Our liberty is not Caesar's. It is a blessing we have received from God himself." From *Pro populo Anglicano defensio.*

This is another instance in which the sectarian conception of the relation of the gospel to social problems is right and the Reformation is wrong.

[14] *Ibid.*, 5, 2.

[15] Luther declared that the peasant demand for the abolition of serfdom "would make all men equal and so change the spiritual Kingdom of Christ into an external worldly one. Impossible! An earthly kingdom

attitude towards the social inequalities of feudalism and observed that on earth there will always be masters and slaves. Luther added an element of perversity to this social ethic by enlarging upon the distinction between an "inner" and an "outer" kingdom so that it became, in effect, a distinction between public and private morality. The rulers, as custodians of public morality, were advised to "hit, stab, kill" when dealing with rebels. For Luther had a morbid fear of anarchy and was willing to permit the *Obrigkeit* any instrument to suppress it. The peasants on the other hand, as private citizens, were admonished to live in accordance with the ethic of the Sermon on the Mount. They were told that their demand for justice violated the New Testament ethic of nonresistance.[16]

By thus transposing an "inner" ethic into a private one, and making the "outer" or "earthly" ethic authoritative for government, Luther achieves a curiously perverse social morality. He places a perfectionist private ethic in juxtaposition to a realistic, not to say

---

cannot exist without inequality of persons. Some must be free, others serfs, some rulers, others subjects." *Works* (Weimar, ed.), Vol. 18, p. 326. "It is a malicious and evil idea that serfdom should be abolished because Christ has made us free. This refers only to spiritual freedom given to us by Christ in order to enable us to withstand the devil." *Ibid.*, p. 333.

[16] "You will not bear," Luther wrote to the peasants, "that anyone inflict evil of injustice upon you, but you want to be free and suffer only justice and goodness. . . . If you do not want to bear such a right [the right of suffering] you had better put away your Christian name and boast of another name in accordance with your deeds or Christ himself will snatch away his name from you." *Works* (Weimar, ed.), Vol. 18, p. 309.

To the princes he wrote: "It will not help the peasants to claim (Genesis I and II) that all things were created free and common and that they are all equally baptized. . . . For in the New Testament Moses counts for nothing; but there stands our master Christ and casts us with body and possessions under the Kaisers and worldly law when he says, 'Give unto Caesar the things that are Caesars.' " *Ibid.*, p. 361.

In the one case Biblical perfectionism is avowed without reservation and in the other case it is as completely disavowed.

cynical, official ethic. He demands that the state maintain order without too scrupulous a regard for justice; yet he asks suffering and nonresistant love of the individual without allowing him to participate in the claims and counter-claims which constitute the stuff of social justice. The inevitable consequence of such an ethic is to encourage tyranny; for resistance to government is as important a principle of justice as maintenance of government.

Luther's inordinate fear of anarchy, prompted by his pessimism and his corresponding indifference to the injustice of tyranny has had a fateful consequence in the history of German civilization. The tragic events of contemporary history are not unrelated to it. His one-sided interpretation of the socio-political problem was also influenced by the exaggerated emphasis which he placed upon the Pauline injunction: "Let every soul be subject unto the higher powers. For there is no power but of God; the powers that be are ordained of God. . . . For rulers are not a terror to good works but to the evil." [17]

Even without this particular error, the Lutheran political ethic would have led to defeatism in the field of social politics. Its absolute distinction between the "heavenly" or "spiritual" kingdom and the "earthly" one, destroys the tension between the final demands of God upon the conscience, and all the relative possibilities of realizing the good in history. The spiritual and moral significance of various progressive realizations of justice is denied from two angles. On the side of its realism the Lutheran ethic finds all historical achievements equally tainted with sin and the distinctions between them therefore unimportant. On the side of its gospel perfectionism it finds them falling equally short of that perfect love of the Kingdom of God, which is alone the earnest of salvation. [18]

[17] Romans 13:1–3.
[18] The defeatism in the realm of social morality, prompted by radical Reformation thought, is strikingly illustrated by a modern dialectical theologian, Hans Asmussen, who writes: "As long as it is the message of the churches that this home [the world] shall be made as beautiful as possible through ethical action so long are we tools of secularism. . . . It

The Lutheran Reformation is thus always in danger of heightening religious tension to the point where it breaks the moral tension, from which all decent action flows. The conscience is made uneasy about the taint of sin in all human enterprise; but the conviction that any alternative to a given course of action would be equally tainted, and that in any case the divine forgiveness will hallow and

---

would be a better confession of faith if the churches said to the world and to the heathen: We wait. Put an end to all social injustice. Eliminate war. After you have done all that, we still wait. All this is not enough for us. Purify mankind to the highest degree of perfection, morally and spiritually. That also is not enough for us. . . . I will remain as one who waits. For I have a gospel, good news. I await the resurrection of the dead and life in the world to come." In *Zwischen den Zeiten,* July, 1930.

Here quite obviously the eschatological tension, which belongs to the Christian view of history, is allowed to destroy the meaningfulness of history and to rob all historic tasks and obligations of their significance.

Emil Brunner who is more interested in ethical action than the other dialectical theologians arrives nevertheless at similar defeatist conclusions. On the one hand he allows the ultimate religious perspective upon the sinful taint in all human actions to destroy all proximate distinctions: "We see," he says, "how the real purpose of life is being thwarted at every turn in all the 'orders' which constitute the framework of human life; the ends sought are so futile and empty and the means used to achieve these ends are so utterly contemptible."

On the other hand he interprets the doctrine of "justification by faith" in such a way as to lead to a complacent acceptance of all this injustice. "The judge," he declares, "must deliver his sentence in accordance to the law in its present state, even though he may be personally convinced that the law is unjust. He does not make a 'compromise' when he acts in this way, if he is acting in the spirit of faith. For he knows that he cannot create a better law and that in this world law is necessary; but he also knows that so long as the people who frame the laws are unjust . . . that is to the end of life on earth . . . there will be no truly just system of law." *Divine Imperative,* pp. 253–255.

The whole history of jurisprudence reveals the importance of maintaining life in a legal tradition by an imaginative juridical application of the law to new situations. Fortunately there have always been judges who have never heard of this doctrine of justification by faith and who have therefore been prompted by a sensitive conscience to apply the law as justly as possible.

sanctify what is really unholy,[19] eases the uneasy conscience prematurely. Thus the saints are tempted to continue in sin that grace may abound, while the sinners toil and sweat to make human relations a little more tolerable and slightly more just.

The weakness of the Lutheran position in the field of social ethics is accentuated to a further degree by its inability to define consistent criteria for the achievement of relative justice. Despite its conception of sanctification as an ecstatic love which transcends all law, and of its doctrine of justification which eases the conscience in its inability to realize the good perfectly, it is forced, nevertheless, to find some standards of relative good and evil. Since it rightly has less confidence than Catholicism in the untainted character of reason, it relegates the "natural law" that is, the rational analysis of social obligations, to the background, as an inadequate guide. But it has only odds and ends of systems of order to put in the place of "natural law." These consist primarily of two conceptions. The one is the order and justice which any state may happen to establish. This order is accepted uncritically precisely because a principle of justice, by which the justice of a given state could be criticized, is lacking. The other is the idea of a *Schoepfungsordnung* an "order of creation," which is presumably, the directive given by God in the very structure of the created world. The difficulty with this concept is that human freedom alters and transmutes the "given" facts of creation so much that no human institutions can be judged purely by the criterion of fixed principles of "creation.'

In the field of sex-relations for instance, bi-sexuality and those vocations of mother and father which are unalterably related to biological differentiation are the only factors which may rightfully be placed in the category of "order of creation." Monogamy can certainly not be placed there, or for that matter any other form of marital union or standard of sex-relation. In political relations Luther sometimes regarded government as belonging to the "order

[19] *Cf.* Brunner, *ibid.,* p. 246.

of creation," and at other times seemed to think that its authority was derived from a special "divine ordinance," Scripturally validated, particularly in Romans 13. Government, however, can be regarded as belonging to "creation" only in the sense that both human freedom and the abuse of human freedom require that human society have a cement of cohesion transcending the natural sociality of animal existence. But no particular government can be derived from the "order of creation"; nor is the uncritical obedience to government, which Luther demanded, a part of the requirement of such an "order."

III

THE CALVINISTIC REFORMATION

It is an indication of the complexity of the problem which the Reformation confronted, that while the Lutheran side of the Reformation always walks on the edge of the precipice of supramoralism, not to say antinomianism, the Calvinistic Reformation is imperilled by the opposite danger of a new moralism and legalism. Puritanism may be regarded as the historic capitulation to this danger. The inability of Reformation thought to sail perfectly between the Scylla of the one and the Charybdis of the other danger, must prompt us to diffidence and modesty in dealing with the ultimate problem with which the Reformation is concerned. It is no easy task to do justice to the distinctions of good and evil in history and to the possibilities and obligations of realizing the good in history; and also to subordinate all these relative judgments and achievements to the final truth about life and history which is proclaimed in the gospel. Every effort to do it involves the whole paradoxical conception in Biblical faith, of the character of history, of its meaningfulness on the one hand, and of the completion of its meaning only in the judgment and mercy of God, on the other.

When Calvin confronts Roman doctrines he elaborates Reformation thought in terms which are hardly distinguishable from the

Lutheran position. He insists that, "there never was an action performed by a pious man, which if examined by the scrutinizing eye of divine justice would not deserve condemnation." He thinks that, "this is the principal hinge on which our controversy with the papists turns" for "there is no controversy between us and the sounder schoolmen, concerning the beginning of justification"; but the Catholics believe, "that a man, once having been reconciled to God through faith in Christ, is accounted righteous with God on account of his good works, the merit of which is the cause of his acceptance" while "the Lord on the contrary declares that faith was reckoned unto Abraham for righteousness."[1]

He believes that, "there still remains in a regenerate man a fountain of evil, continually producing irregular desires. . . . that sin always exists in the saints till they are divested of their mortal bodies."[2] Perhaps his finest insight into the complexities of perfection and sin is expressed in the words: "When we denominate the virtue of the saints perfect, to this perfection belongs the acknowledgment of imperfection both in truth and in humility."[3]

But when he develops his own doctrine of sanctification, he arrives at conclusions hardly to be distinguished from the Catholic ones. "Do you wish," he asks, "to obtain the righteousness of Christ? You must first possess Christ; but you cannot possess him without becoming partaker of his sanctification, for he cannot be divided. . . . Union with Christ by which we are justified contains sanctification as well as righteousness."[4] He thinks that the rejection of the idea of justification by works means, "not that no good works can be done or that those which are performed may be denied to be good but that we may neither confide in them nor ascribe our salvation to them."[5]

Sometimes he comes rather close to the Catholic distinction between venial and mortal sins, as for instance when he declares that

[1] *Inst.,* III, xiv, 11.
[2] *Inst.,* III, iii, 10.
[3] *Inst.,* III, xvii, 15.
[4] *Inst.,* III, xvi, 1.
[5] *Inst.,* III, xvii, 1.

the state of sanctification means that, "our carnal desires are daily more and more mortified, and we are sanctified, that is consecrated unto the Lord unto real purity of life, having our hearts moulded to obey his law so that our *prevailing inclination* is to submit to his will." [6]

Here perhaps lies the crux of the matter. Whenever the Christian, in whom sin is broken "in principle," claims that the sins which remain are merely incidental "carnal desires" without recognizing that the sin of self-love is present in a more basic form, there is a corresponding dissipation of the "broken spirit and the contrite heart." The fulfillment of life is no longer subject to the paradox of having and not having it. Sometimes Calvin defines the paradox in Augustinian terms and believes saints to be essentially righteous though lacking the final attainment of perfection. The believers, he declares, "are denominated righteous from the sanctity of their lives; but as they rather devote themselves to the pursuit of righteousness than actually attain righteousness itself, it is proper that this righteousness, such as it is, should be subordinate to justification by faith, from which it derives its origin." [7]

The definition of the Christian paradox of justification and sanctification is probably made more carefully in Calvin's *Institutes* than in any other system of thought. If he errs on the side of claiming too much in the end it is an error which is difficult to correct without committing the opposite error. But that Calvin committed an error, in feeling too secure in the sanctification of the Christian, is attested not only by his other writings, where he does not always make such careful qualifications and reservations, but also by his own actions.

His frequent tendency to define sin as carnal desire rather than as primarily self-love, contributes to a new self-righteousness; for sainthood in terms of a completely disciplined life which has subordinated all desires to a dominant purpose is a simpler possibility than a perfection which has excluded all egoistic elements from the

[6] *Inst.,* III, xiv, 9.   [7] *Inst.,* III, xvii, 11.

dominant purpose. The history of Puritan self-righteousness reveals the weakness of Calvinism on this point. Calvin does not fully understand the law of love as the final law. That is at least one reason why he thinks of himself a little too confidently as standing on the other side of the sinful contradictions of existence, despite his protestations that he will not ascribe salvation to the goodness of the saints. He interprets the Pauline assertion, that love is the greatest of the three virtues of faith, hope and love, as meaning only that "charity is serviceable to more people since only a few can be justified by faith."[8] He places love not only under faith, but under "purity of faith" in his hierarchy of virtues. The purpose of this ordering is to justify his rigour against heretics. Yet it is precisely in his loveless attitude towards heretics, who are, in his opinion, guilty "of dishonouring the majesty of God," a sin more heinous than "to kill an innocent man or to poison a guest or to lay violent hands on one's own father"[9] that he reveals that lack of pity, which is the particular sin of the self-righteous, who do not know themselves as, in some sense, in the same condemnation with those whom they indict.[10] The final proof of the genuine spirit of humility in the "elect," of their "brokenness of spirit," is their capacity for mercy and forgiveness. Without consciousness of their own need of forgiveness, "good" people never show mercy towards "bad" people.

[8] *Opera*, I, 798. Calvin thinks that, "as our liberty should be subject to charity so our charity should be subservient to purity of faith. It becomes us indeed to have regard to charity, but we must not offend God for the love of the neighbor." *Inst.*, III, xix, 13.

[9] Commentary on Zech. 13:3.

[10] This matter will be dealt with more fully in the following chapter. Calvin's emphasis upon the suppression of carnal desires, his identification of righteousness with self-discipline is not in perfect conformity with his more Scriptural definition of sin as pride. (*Cf.* Vol. I, p. 187.) He is not completely lacking in an appreciation of love as the final good. "His is the best and most holy life," he writes, "who lives as little as possible for himself." *Inst.*, II, viii, 54.

But in his total thought both his passion for right doctrine and for the discipline of sensual impulses, outweigh his appreciation of the love commandment.

The difference between Calvin's conception of the relation of grace to law and the Lutheran doctrine of grace and law conforms to the general divergence between the two theologies; Calvin inclines towards legalism rather than supra-moralism. He does not, as Luther, believe that grace abrogates the law, for he does not think of sanctification as an ecstatic experience of love which transcends all law. He thinks of it rather as a rigorous obedience to law. But since it is impossible for the soul in its sinful state to know the perfect law, it is necessary for it to be guided by the "divine law," particularly as it is revealed in the Bible.

"Though the law of God," he says, "contains in it that newness of life by which His image is restored in us, yet since our tardiness needs much stimulation and assistance, it will be useful to collect from various places in Scripture a rule for the reformation of life, that they who cordially repent may not be bewildered in their pursuit."[11]

Calvin's "divine law," in which he finds an answer to every moral and social problem, is nicely defined here. For it is a compendium collected from "various places in Scripture," without reference to the historical relativities which are enshrined in a sacred canon. This is the ethical corollary in Calvin's system of his general Biblicism, not to say Bibliolatry. Just as Luther regards the Bible primarily as the "cradle of Christ" and therefore has a principle of criticism of Scripture itself in the Christ of Scripture, so he also understands that the love commandment transcends all other commandments in the Bible. He is thereby saved from the error of Biblicism in both theology and ethics. Calvin, on the other hand, commits both errors.

Calvin's conception of "divine law" has the advantage of consistency over Luther's sketchy directives in the field of social and political life. But it nevertheless combines the errors of both obscurantism and pretension. It is obscurantist in that it does not sufficiently engage man's rational capacities in determining what is just and unjust in his relation to his fellows. It appeals prematurely to Biblical

[11] *Inst.*, III, vi, 𝑡.

Calvin's weakness — views the Bible as authority for every conceivable moral & social problem & fails to take into account historical relativities

§ III]   *The Calvinistic Reformation*   203

authority for answers to every conceivable moral and social problem. Catholic social ethics, though informed by an unjustified confidence in the ability of a universal reason to define the norms of justice, are sometimes more discriminating than the Calvinistic appeal to "divine law." Calvin's ethical system is pretentious as well as obscurantist; for it gives the Christian an unjustified confidence in the transcendent perfection of the moral standards which he has derived from Scripture and obscures not only the endless relativities of judgment, involved in applying a Scriptural standard to a particular situation, but also the historical relativities which are imbedded in these Scriptural standards themselves.

Though Calvinism made some genuine contributions to the advance of democratic justice, as we shall see shortly, it is not surprising that possibly greater contributions towards higher justice in recent centuries were derived from the sectarianism and various versions of the Renaissance movement. These movements may have been even blinder than Catholicism to the egoistic corruption in every historic system of justice; but they did understand both the possibility and the obligation of rational men to use their reason in estimating the needs of their fellowmen and in defining tolerably just standards of division between "mine" and "thine." Both sides of the Reformation on the other hand either regarded the problem of justice as insoluble by reason of human sinfulness; or they solved it too simply by appeals to presumably transcendent standards of justice, which were supposedly untainted by human sinfulness. But appeals to these standards merely resulted in one more human effort to find an absolutely secure and safe position, beyond historical ambiguities and contradictions.

A survey of these various aspects of Reformation thought and life leads to the conclusion that, despite its polemic against the premature transcendence over history in Catholicism, it is as frequently tempted to commit the same error as Catholicism (though with the use of different instruments of pretension) as it is to commit the opposite error.

This fact suggests that Reformation insights must be related to the whole range of human experience more "dialectically" than the Reformation succeeded in doing. The "yes" and "no" of its dialectical affirmations: that the Christian is *"justus et peccator,"* "both sinner and righteous"; that history fulfills and negates the Kingdom of God; that grace is continuous with, and in contradiction to, nature; that Christ is what we ought to be and also what we cannot be; that the power of God is in us and that the power of God is against us in judgment and mercy; that all these affirmations which are but varied forms of the one central paradox of the relation of the Gospel to history must be applied to the experiences of life from top to bottom. There is no area of life where "grace" does not impinge. There are no complex relations of social justice to which the love of the Kingdom of God is not relevant. There are on the other hand no areas or experiences where historical insecurity and anxiety are completely transcended, except in principle. There are indeed moments of prayer and, perhaps, ecstatic achievements of *agape* in which men are caught up in the "seventh heaven"; but these moments are merely an "earnest" of the fulfillment of life and must not be claimed as a possession. There is, finally, the transcendence of man over history and sin by faith. But that is also an "earnest"; and is corrupted like the manna in the wilderness when stored up as a secure possession.

IV

A SYNTHESIS OF REFORMATION AND RENAISSANCE

The defeatism of the Lutheran, and the tendency towards obscurantism in the Calvinist, Reformation must be regarded as a contributory cause of defeat of the Reformation by the Renaissance. It failed to relate the ultimate answer of grace to the problem of guilt to all the immediate and intermediate problems and answers of life. Therefore it did not illumine the possibilities and limits of realizing increasing truth and goodness in every conceivable historic and social situation.

This defeatism is only a contributory cause of its defeat because the general atmosphere of historical optimism in the past centuries seemed to refute even what was true in the Reformation; just as it seemed to validate what was both true and false in the Renaissance. There was, therefore, little inclination to discriminate between the true and the false emphases in the Reformation; between the truth of its ultimate view of life and history and its failure to relate this truth helpfully to intermediate issues of culture and social organization.

But when we are confronted with the task of reorienting the culture of our day, it becomes important to discriminate carefully between what was true and false in each movement. There is of course a strong element of presumption in the effort to make such judgments which will seem intolerable to those who disagree with them; and which can be tolerable even to those who find them validated, at least partially, by contemporary history, only if it is recognized that they are made in "fear and trembling."

The course of modern history has, if our reading of it be at all correct, justified the dynamic, and refuted the optimistic, interpretation contained in the various modern religious and cultural movements, all of which are internally related to each other in what we have defined broadly as "Renaissance." It has by the same token validated the basic truth of the Reformation but challenged its obscurantism and defeatism on all immediate and intermediate issues of life.

The "logic" of modern history, for which this rather large claim is made, can be simply defined. On the one hand the extension of all forms of knowledge, the elaboration of mechanical and social techniques, the corresponding development of human powers and historical potencies and the consequent increase of the extent and complexity of the human community have indubitably proved that life is subject to growth in its collective and total, as well as in its individual, forms. On the other hand the course of history, particularly in the past two centuries, has proved the earlier identification of growth and progress to be false. We have, or ought to have, learned, particularly from the tragedies of contemporary history, that each new development of life, whether in individual or social terms, presents us with new possibilities of realizing the good in history; that we have obligations corresponding to these new possibilities; but that we also face new hazards on each new level and that the new level of historic achievement offers us no emancipation from contradictions and ambiguities to which all life in history is subject. We have learned, in other words, that history is not its own redeemer. The "long run" of it is no more redemptive in the ultimate sense than the "short run." It is this later development of modern history which has given the Reformation version of the Christian faith a new relevance. No apology is necessary for assigning so great a pedagogical significance to the lessons of history. The truth contained in the gospel is not found in human wisdom. Yet it may be found at the point where human wisdom and human goodness acknowledge their limits; and creative despair induces faith. Once faith is induced it becomes truly the wisdom which makes "sense" out of a life and history which would otherwise remain senseless. This is possible for individuals in any age, no matter what its historical circumstances.

But it cannot be denied that historical circumstances may be more or less favourable to the inducement of the "Godly sorrow" which worketh repentance. There are periods of hope in history in which the Christian faith would seem to be irrelevant, because history itself seems to offer both the judgment and the redemption which the Christian faith finds in the God who has been revealed in Christ. There are other periods of disillusionment when the vanity of such hopes is fully revealed. We have lived through such centuries of hope and we are now in such a period of disillusionment. The centuries of historical hope have well nigh destroyed the Christian faith as a potent force in modern culture and civilization. We do not

The lessons learned from history
are implied in the Biblical-prophetic
view of history — moving towards
an end

§ IV]   *A Synthesis of Reformation and Renaissance*   207

maintain that the period of disillusionment in which we now find ourselves will necessarily restore the Christian faith. It has merely reestablished its relevance. There is always the alternative of despair, the "sorrow of the world" to the creative despair which induces a new faith.

If, however, the modern generation is to be helped to find life meaningful without placing an abortive confidence in the mere historical growth, it is incumbent upon those who mediate the truth of the gospel to this generation, to accept and not to reject whatever truth about life and history has been learned in these past centuries of partial apostasy. This is the more important because the lessons which have been learned are implied in the whole Biblical-prophetic view of history, which, in its pure form, has always regarded history in dynamic terms, that is, as moving towards an *end*.

A new synthesis is therefore called for. It must be a synthesis which incorporates the twofold aspects of grace of Biblical religion, and adds the light which modern history, and the Renaissance and Reformation interpretations of history, have thrown upon the paradox of grace. Briefly this means that on the one hand life in history must be recognized as filled with indeterminate possibilities. There is no individual or interior spiritual situation, no cultural or scientific task, and no social or political problem in which men do not face new possibilities of the good and the obligation to realize them. It means on the other hand that every effort and pretension to complete life, whether in collective or individual terms, that every desire to stand beyond the contradictions of history, or to eliminate the final corruptions of history must be disavowed.

Because both Renaissance and Reformation have sharpened the insights into the meaning of the two sides of the Christian paradox, it is not possible to return to the old, that is, to the medieval synthesis, though we may be sure that efforts to do so will undoubtedly be abundant.

The medieval-Catholic synthesis is inadequate because it rested upon a compromise between the twofold aspects of grace. It arrested

the fullest development of each aspect. Its conception of the fulfillment of life was marred by its confinement of the power of grace
to a human-historical institution. In the realm of the spiritual and
moral life this meant that grace was bound to sacraments, institu-
tionally controlled and mediated. Since "grace" stands for powers
and possibilities beyond all human possibilities, this represents an
intolerable confinement of the freedom of God within human limits.
"The wind bloweth where it listeth," [1] said Jesus to Nicodemus;
and that is a picturesque description of the freedom of divine grace
in history, working miracles without any "by your leave" of priest
or church. Since some of the most significant developments in the
field of social morality have taken place in modern life in defiance
of a sacramental church, which had limited social justice unwit-
tingly to the essential conditions of feudal life, it is understandable
that modern culture should still be informed by a strong resentment
against the pretensions of such a church.

In the field of culture the Catholic synthesis is equally unavailing.
It is one thing to believe that no elaboration of philosophy or science can carry us beyond the truth which is contained in the gospel;
and another to allow a human institution to control the whole cultural process in order to prevent science and philosophy from defying the authority of the gospel. When the final authority of the
gospel over all human culture is thus transmuted into the authority
of a historical and human institution, the pride of priests is inevitably mixed with an authority which can be ultimate only when
it stands beyond all human situations and achievements. If a human
authority sets the limits and defines the conditions under which the
pursuit of truth shall take place, it is quite inevitable that significant
truth should be suppressed and valuable cultural ambitions should
be prematurely arrested under the guise of keeping them within the
confines of the final truth about life and history as apprehended by
faith.

The real situation is that the human mind can, in the various

[1] John 3:8.

disciplines of culture, discover and elaborate an indeterminate variety of systems of meaning and coherence by analysing the relation of things to each other on every level of existence, whether geological or biological, social or psychological, historical or philosophical. If these subordinate realms of meaning claim to be no more than they are they will add to the wealth of our apprehensions about the character of existence and the richness of our insights into reality. They are furthermore valuable guides to conduct and action, whether it be in the exploitation of nature, or the manipulation of social forces, or the discipline of individual life. If the effort is made to establish any one of these subordinate realms of meaning as the clue to the meaning of the whole, the cultural pursuit becomes involved in idolatry. A premature source and end for the meaning of life is found; which is to say that a god is found who is not truly God, a principle of final judgment is discovered which is not really final; or a process of salvation and the fulfillment of life is claimed which is not finally redemptive.

It is perhaps inevitable that the free pursuit of knowledge should lead to such various forms of idolatry. There will be philosophies, claiming to have comprehended the world in a system of meaning, superior to the tragic and paradoxical meaning which the Christian faith finds in it. There will be social philosophies certain that they have found a way to achieve perfect brotherhood in history. There will be psychiatric techniques which pretend to overcome all the anxieties of human existence and therefore all its corruptions. There will even be engineering schemes for fulfilling life by the mere multiplication of comforts.

The truth of the gospel cannot be maintained against these pretensions by the interposition of any human authority. The attempt thus to restrain culture from idolatry is unwise because truth is bound to be suppressed with the suppression of error. Here the injunction in the parable of the wheat and tares is relevant: "Let both grow together until the harvest; and in the time of harvest I will say to the reapers, Gather ye together first the tares, and bind them in bundles to burn them; but gather the wheat into my barn." [2]

The attempt must also prove abortive, for there is no way of validating the truth of the gospel until men have discovered the error which appears in their final truth; and are threatened with the abyss of meaninglessness on the edge of their most pretentious schemes of meaning. Christian faith must, in other words, be in a much freer play with all the powers and ambitions of the cultural life of man than was permitted in that synthesis of culture and faith which the medieval church established.

But on the other hand the inclination of the Reformation to disavow all intermediate cultural tasks on the ground that the final wisdom is not to be found there; and to be indifferent to the obligations for achieving a more tolerable brotherhood in history, on the ground that such achievements fall short of salvation, is equally inadmissible. The Renaissance spirits of our day have vaguely equated what they regard as the cultural and social obscurantism of the Catholic and the Protestant church. They have seldom understood how different the strategies of the two forms of Christianity are. If the one is obscurantist it is because it places premature limits and unjustified restraints upon the pursuit of knowledge and the development of social institutions. If the other is obscurantist, it is because it is either indifferent towards the problems of thought and life which all men must consider though they are short of the ultimate problem of salvation; or because it interposes a new authority, that of Scripture, in such a way as to make the ultimate meaning of life, as contained in the gospel a substitute for all subordinate realms of meaning or as obviating the necessity of establishing these subordinate realms.

Any workable synthesis between culture and the Christian faith, which is also a synthesis between the two aspects of grace, must not abstract the ultimate human situation from immediate and intermediate ones. There is no social or moral obligation which does

[2] Mt. 13:30.

of the Paradox of grace to the human situation

not invite us on the one hand to realize higher possibilities of good and does not on the other reveal the limits of the good in history. There is no mystery of life, or complexity of causal relations, which do not incite the inquisitive mind to try to comprehend them; and which do not upon careful scrutiny point to a mystery beyond themselves. There is, therefore, no way of understanding the ultimate problem of human existence if we are not diligent in the pursuit of proximate answers and solutions. Nor is there any way of validating the ultimate solution without constantly relating it to all proximate possibilities. On this issue Renaissance perspectives are truer than either Catholic or Reformation ones.

The one point at which the Reformation must make its primary contribution to the synthesis is in refuting both Catholic and Renaissance pretensions of fulfilling life and history either by grace or by natural capacities inhering in human nature or in the historical process. Here the Reformation has rediscovered the final truth about life and history, implied in Old Testament prophetism and made explicit in the New Testament. In this sense the Reformation has an insight which goes beyond the truth embodied in the Catholic synthesis, and which cannot be stated in the compromises between Hellenism and prophetism which that synthesis achieved. *Summary*

The double aspect of grace, the twofold emphasis upon the obligation to fulfill the possibilities of life and upon the limitations and corruptions in all historic realizations, implies that history is a meaningful process but is incapable of fulfilling itself and therefore points beyond itself to the judgment and mercy of God for its fulfillment. The Christian doctrine of the Atonement, with its paradoxical conception of the relation of the divine mercy to the divine wrath is therefore the final key to this historical interpretation. The wrath and the judgment of God are symbolic of the seriousness of history. The distinctions between good and evil are important and have ultimate significance. The realization of the good must be taken seriously; it is the wheat, separated from the tares, which is gathered "into my barn," which is to say that the good within the finite flux has significance beyond that flux.

On the other hand the mercy of God, which strangely fulfills and yet contradicts the divine judgment, points to the incompleteness of all historic good, the corruption of evil in all historic achievements and the incompleteness of every historic system of meaning without the eternal mercy which knows how to destroy and transmute evil by taking it into itself.

The Christian doctrine of the Atonement is therefore not some incomprehensible remnant of superstition, nor yet a completely incomprehensible article of faith. It is, indeed, on the other side of human wisdom, in the sense that it is not comprehensible to a wisdom which looks at the world with confident eyes, certain that all its mysteries can be fathomed by the human mind. Yet it is the beginning of wisdom in the sense that it contains symbolically all that the Christian faith maintains about what man ought to do and what he cannot do, about his obligations and final incapacity to fulfill them, about the importance of decisions and achievements in history and about their final insignificance.

Contribution of the Reformation
   grace — what man ought to do
     & his inability to completely
   do it.

Atonement — the symbolism
   of grace — judgment (wrath)
  and mercy

CHAPTER VIII

HAVING, AND NOT HAVING, THE TRUTH

IF THE CHRISTIAN conception of grace be true then all history remains an "interim" between the disclosure and the fulfillment of its meaning. This interim is characterized by positive corruptions, as well as by partial realizations and approximations of the meaning of life. Redemption does not guarantee elimination of the sinful corruptions, which are in fact increased whenever the redeemed claim to be completely emancipated from them. But the taint of sin upon all historical achievements does not destroy the possibility of such achievements nor the obligation to realize truth and goodness in history. The fulfillments of meaning in history will be the more untainted in fact, if purity is not prematurely claimed for them. All historical activities stand under this paradox of grace.

These activities may be roughly placed into two general categories: the quest for the truth and the achievement of just and brotherly relations with our fellowmen. These two categories comprise the cultural and the socio-moral problems of history. It will be well to study each of these forms of historical activity in turn to see how the paradox of our having, and yet not having either truth or justice in history conforms to the facts; and how our understanding of the paradox influences, or may influence, our actions.

II

THE PROBLEM OF THE TRUTH

The ideal possibilities and the sinful realities in the realm of culture have been previously discussed.[1] We know that the freedom of the human spirit over the flux of nature and history makes it impossible to accept *our* truth as *the* truth. The capacity for rational self-transcendence opens up constantly new and higher points of vantage for judging our finite perspectives in the light of a more inclusive truth. On the other hand our involvement in natural and historical flux sets final limits upon our quest for the truth and insures the partial and particular character of even the highest cultural vantage point. Thus human culture is under the tension of finiteness and freedom, of the limited and the unlimited.

Two complicating factors must be added to this tension: since human personality is an organic unity of its vital and rational capacities, rational apprehensions are subject not merely to the limits of a finite mind but to the play of passion and interest which human vitalities introduce into the process. Knowledge of the truth is thus invariably tainted with an "ideological" taint of interest, which makes our apprehension of truth something less than knowledge of *the* truth and reduces it to *our* truth. The cultural quest is furthermore confused by the premature claims of finality which men invariably make for their finite perspectives. This pretension is the sinful element in culture. It includes not merely the effort to deny the finiteness of our perspectives but to hide and obscure the taint of interest and passion in our knowledge. This pride is the real force of "ideology." Without it the partial character of all human knowledge would be harmless and would encourage men to invite the supplementation and completion of their incomplete knowledge from other partial perspectives. In so far as sin has not, and cannot, destroy the rational capacities of men or reduce them to

[1] *Cf.* Vol. I, Ch. VII.

"the ignorance of our ignorance" — a failure in our capacity for self-transcendence

a state of total depravity, such supplementation is a continuing factor in the cultural process.

The denial of the finiteness of our knowledge and the false claim of finality is always partly the ignorance of our ignorance. It is a failure in our capacity for self-transcendence. But since this capacity belongs to man's native endowment, the sinful claim of finality is always partly a conscious or semi-conscious effort to obscure the partial and interested character of our knowledge of the truth. We are not merely ignorant of our ignorance but we "hold the truth in unrighteousness."

the answer

The Christian answer to this problem is the apprehension of the truth "in Christ." This is a truth about life and history which fulfills what is valid and negates what is sinful in our knowledge of the truth. It fulfills what is valid, because man's self-transcendence enables him to hope for and desire the disclosure of a meaning which has a center and source beyond himself. It negates what is sinful because it disappoints that element in all human hopes and expectations, which seeks to complete the meaning of life around the self, individual or collective, as the inadequate center of the realm of meaning. Thus the true Christ is both expected and rejected. When the *logos* is made flesh it is the light that "shineth in darkness and the darkness apprehended it not." [2] Yet it is possible to accept this truth despite, and because of, its contradiction of all sinful truth. By such acceptance the believer is lifted in principle above the egoistic corruptions of the truth in history: "as many as received him, to them gave he the right to become children of God." [3]

We have already considered the difference between this Christian conception of the *logos* who is revealed in history and overcomes the darkness of the lie in history ("the light shineth in darkness") and the *logos* doctrines, particularly of classical culture, according to which the truth is achieved by the emancipation of the *logos* in man from the conditions of finiteness in history.

[2] John 1:1, 5–11. (Rev. ed.)   [3] John 1:12. (Rev. ed.)

At this point it is necessary to set the Biblical doctrine in contrast to two alternative doctrines which have emerged on the soil and ground of the Christian interpretation of life. The classical *logos* doctrine is an alternative to the Biblical doctrine only in those forms of Christian mysticism in which the eternal and divine element in man is abstracted from the conditions of finiteness in history. The more potent modern alternatives are subtly compounded with the Christian interpretation of the problem of truth. According to the one, truth is established not only *in principle* but in fact in the heart of those who have accepted Christ. They are no longer sinners in their apprehension of the truth. According to the other, more and more perfect truth is apprehended by the cumulative processes of culture in history. The first alternative is quite obviously the Catholic version of "sanctification" in the realm of culture, though one must hasten to add that it is fairly defined as "Catholic" only if it is understood that this pretension of achieving the truth without sinful corruption in history is not limited to the institution in which it has been most precisely defined. It is a perennial error in all forms of Christianity.

The second alternative is also obviously the "Renaissance" version of the answer to the cultural problem. Classical and Christian concepts are combined in it. It is a *logos* doctrine which has been changed by historical consciousness. The *logos* is no longer purified by emancipation from history. It is purified by the process of history itself. History is, in fact, the record of the gradual emergence and purification of the *logos*. Hegelianism is, in a sense, the most perfect statement of this "Renaissance" solution of the problem of the truth in history, though there are naturalistic versions of the cumulation of wisdom and truth in history which are also expressions of it, despite their rejection of "idealism."

If we set these alternatives in contrast to the "Biblical" doctrine it must be understood that the term "Biblical" is meant to embrace the explication of the Biblical paradox of grace in Christian history particularly in the Reformation. Christian history is filled not only

paradox of grace *(speaks to some in*
applied to truth *Cs of C who emphasize that*
we can know the
§ 11] *The Problem of the Truth* *truth* · 217

with all kinds of pretensions that Christians stand completely
beyond the egoistic corruption of the truth; it also contains, partly
as reaction to these pretensions, forms of awareness, in varying
degrees of explicitness, that "redemption" in the realm of culture
and truth is a having and a not-having of the truth; and that the
pretension of having it leads to a new lie. This is the paradox of
grace applied to the truth. The truth, as it is contained in the
Christian revelation, includes the recognition that it is neither possible for man to know the truth fully nor to avoid the error of
pretending that he does. It is recognized that "grace" always
remains in partial contradiction to "nature," and is not merely its
fulfillment.

The very apprehension of this paradox is itself an expression of
the twofold aspect of grace. It is a thought beyond all human
thought and can affect thinking only indirectly. For it is not possible to remain fully conscious of the egoistic corruption in the truth,
while we seek to establish and advance it in our thought and action.
But it is possible in moments of prayerful transcendence over the
sphere of interested thought and action to be conscious of the
corruption; and it is also possible to carry this insight into our
interested thoughts and actions so that it creates some sense of pity
and forgiveness for those who contend against our truth and oppose
our action. But "grace" enters and purifies our thought and action
fully only if the contradiction between it and "nature" (in this
case corrupted truth) is understood. Here lies the secret of forgiveness. Mercy to the foe is possible only to those who know themselves to be sinners.[4]   *the secret of forgiveness*

[4] Professor Tillich's analysis of this problem, to which I am greatly
indebted, arrives at a formal transcendence over the ambiguity of all historical truth by the following logic: "The doctrine of the character of
knowledge as a decision, like everything that makes truth relative, elicits
the objection that this doctrine makes itself relative and thus refutes
itself. . . . What is true, however, of all knowledge cannot be true of
the knowledge of knowledge, otherwise it would cease to have universal
significance. On the other hand, if an exception is admitted, then for one

But the same uneasiness, which prompts pity and forgiveness towards the protagonist of an opposing "truth," must also incite the soul to the most diligent possible purification of the truth which it holds and by which it acts. Thus the twofold aspects of grace,

---

bit of reality the equivocal character of being is broken. . . . Is that possible? It would be impossible if the removal of the ambiguity of existence were to occur at any place in existence. Whatever stands in the context of knowledge is subject to the ambiguity of knowledge. Therefore such a proposition must be removed from the context of knowledge. . . . It must be the expression of the relation of knowledge to the Unconditioned. . . . The judgment that is removed from ambiguity . . . can be only the fundamental judgment of the relationship of the Unconditioned and Conditioned. . . . The content of this judgment is just this—that our subjective thinking never can reach the unconditioned Truth. . . . This judgment is plainly the absolute judgment which is independent of all its forms of expression, even of the one by which it is expressed here. It is the judgment which constitutes truth as truth." Paul Tillich, *The Interpretation of History*, pp. 169, 170.

Professor Tillich's analysis of the thought which transcends all conditioned and finite thought, and proves its transcendence by its realization of the finiteness of thought, is a precise formulation of the ultimate self-transcendence of the human spirit, revealed in its capacity to understand its own finiteness. It is a philosophical formulation of this reality, and therefore deals with the problem of finiteness and not of sin. Sin is the refusal to admit finiteness. This refusal is sinful precisely because spirit has the capacity to recognize its finiteness. But when it refuses to do so its sinful self-glorification must be broken by the power of "grace."

What Professor Tillich describes could therefore be equated with what I have defined at another point (Vol. I, Ch. X) as "perfection before the fall," the perfection which hovers as possibility but not as actuality over all action. If this possibility is realized at all, it belongs to the realm of "grace" and cannot be merely ascribed to the native endowment of spirit: that is its capacity for self-transcendence. Without such a capacity there would indeed be no "point of contact" for "grace," that is, without a shattering of the false sense of self-sufficiency and universality of spirit, the effort would be made (as it is made in idealistic philosophy) to extend the pinnacle of self-transcendence in the human spirit until it becomes universal spirit, that is God.

This is why the real "dialectic" of the conditioned and the Unconditioned in human culture is taken seriously in principle only in the Christian faith.

VERY IMPORTANT

the test of how well the paradox is comprehended — a tolerant attitude + at same time ability to hold convictions

defined traditionally as "sanctification" and "justification" are no more in contradiction to each other in the field of culture, and in the search for truth, than in any other field.

If this approach to the problem of truth be defined as Biblical, and the Biblical paradox of grace be comprehended in the light of Christian history which culminated in the Reformation, it is necessary to add immediately that no claim is made for the success of the Reformation, as a particular historical movement, in dealing with the problem of truth and culture. The test of how well this paradox of the gospel is comprehended, and how genuinely it has entered into human experience is the attitude of Christians towards those who differ from themselves in convictions which seem vital to each. The test, in other words, is to be found in the issue of toleration. To meet the test it is necessary not merely to maintain a tolerant attitude towards those who hold beliefs other than our own. The test is twofold and includes both the ability to hold vital convictions which lead to action; and also the capacity to preserve the spirit of forgiveness towards those who offend us by holding to convictions which seem untrue to us. Judged by that standard, the Reformation has little advantage over other versions of the Christian faith. Furthermore we must admit that Christian history in general has frequently generated fanaticisms as grievous as the idolatries of other cultures.

The history of Christianity proves that such grace as is manifested in Christian life does not lift men above the finiteness of the mind; nor yet save them from the sin of claiming to have transcended it. The divisions in the church, caused by geographic and climatic conditions, by class distinctions and economic circumstances, by national and racial particularities and by historical qualifications of every kind, are proof of the continued finiteness of those who live by grace.[5] The fanatic fury of religious controversies, the hatred engendered in theological disputes, the bitterness of ecclesiastical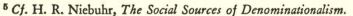

---

[5] *Cf.* H. R. Niebuhr, *The Social Sources of Denominationalism.*

rivalries and the pretentious claims of ecclesiastical dominion all reveal the continued power of sin in the life of the "redeemed"; and the use which sin makes of the pretension of holiness.

It is in fact not surprising that the enemies of Christianity should frequently regard it as the tool of inordinate historical claims and pretensions; rather than as a religion in which all such pretensions are broken in principle, and should sigh and hope for the destruction of religion as the only way of emancipating mankind from fanaticism. The enemies of religion do not, of course, understand that they are dealing with a more fundamental problem than anything created by this or that religion; that it is the problem of the relative and the absolute in history; that the problem is solved by Christian faith "in principle"; that Christian faith may aggravate the problem if it claims more than that; but that alternative solutions, as they are evolved in secular culture, present us either with the abyss of scepticism or with new fanaticisms.

III

THE TEST OF TOLERANCE

If we apply the test of toleration to the various versions of the Christian faith, in order to determine how closely they approximate to the wisdom of the gospel, we meet with some obvious results and with others which will seem surprising until they are more fully explored. The foregone conclusion is that the Catholic version of the Christian faith is intolerant in principle. This is not surprising because the Catholic idea of sanctification in regard to the problem of truth is consistent with its general theories of grace. The more surprising result of such an historical investigation is that Reformation theology has not, in fact, brought forth fruits of the contrite spirit and the broken heart in the field of intellectual controversy which would be consonant with its theory of grace and its doctrine of justification. The reason for this failure has been partially anticipated in our general survey but must be considered in the light of

the test of toleration. The chief source of toleration in modern ✗
history has been in the various forces of the Renaissance movement,
both sectarian and secular. But it is necessary to inquire whether
the tolerant attitude of the "liberal" spirit meets both, or only one,
of the two aspects of the test of toleration. Does it also maintain
a vital and organic relation between thought and action while it
achieves forbearance of contrary and contradictory views and
opinions?

1. *Catholicism and Toleration*

Catholicism is impelled by its whole history and by its peculiar
doctrine of grace to claim unconditioned possession of the truth.
In this claim in the realm of culture it obviously destroys the Biblical
paradox of grace. It pretends to have as a simple possession, what
cannot be so possessed. It may vary its attitude slightly towards
other versions of the Christian faith from time to time, but it is
completely consistent and unyielding in its conviction that it alone
possesses the truth and the whole truth.

One of the ablest exponents of Augustinian thought in contemporary Catholicism, Erich Przywara, writes about the Inquisition: "The Dominican order had become, willy-nilly, the servants of
the Inquisition, not on account of a sort of fanaticism (the great
Dominicans were all men of child-like humility and even tender
sensitiveness) but on account of an utter abandonment of all
individualism to the service of the everlasting truth. . . . God is just
the Truth (a genuine Augustinian phrase) and so service to the
Truth is service to God. . . . The Dominican type regards itself as
entrusted by an inscrutable providence with the sacred guardianship
of the one Truth in the midst of the world. It is of the type which
stands in the world . . . but yet while in the world it stands there
with the single task of subjecting the world . . . to the dominion of
this one everlasting truth. Truth remote from all fluctuations due to
individuality and existence."[1] The difficulty with this essentially

[1] Erich Przywara, *Polarity,* p. 106.

high-minded justification of the Inquisition is that it does not understand that the one everlasting truth of the gospel contains the insight that mere men cannot have this truth "remote from all fluctuations due to individuality and existence." This error is the root of all Inquisitions.

Catholics may indeed be individually humble and contrite, as Przywara avers; and may therefore compare favorably with Protestant individualists who have a fanatic zeal for their own individual interpretation of truth. But Catholicism is collectively and officially intolerant. Its intolerance expresses itself not only in blindness towards possible facets of truth contained in other than its own interpretations of the truth; but also in efforts to suppress the profession of other religions, including the profession of other versions of the Christian religion.

The Jesuit protagonist of intolerance in Elizabethan England, Robert Parsons, defined the logic of the Catholic position with rigorous consistency: "If every man which hath any religion and is resolved therein must needs suppose this only truth to be in his own religion, then it followeth necessarily that he must likewise persuade himself that all religions beside his own are false and erroneous; and consequently all assemblies, conventicles, and public acts of the same are wicked and dishonorable to God." Parsons carried this logic to the point of asserting that even if the other religions were really true, "yet would I be condemned for going among them, for that in my sight and judgment and conscience, by which only I must be judged, they must need seem enemies to God."[2]

The Catholic doctrine, which forces the church to seek for the monopoly of the public profession of religion in a state, is officially defined in the encyclical *Immortale Dei* of Pope Leo XIII: "Since no one is allowed to be remiss in the service due to God, and since the chief duty of all men is to cling to religion in both its teaching

[2] Quoted by W. K. Jordan, *The Development of Religious Toleration in England*, Vol. I, p. 390. Jordan's great work is invaluable for students of this problem.

and practice . . . not such religion as they may have preference for but the religion which God enjoins, and which certain and most clear marks show to be the only true religion . . . it is a public crime to act as if there were no God. So too it is a sin in the state not to have care of religion . . . or out of the many forms of religion to adopt that one which chimes in with the fancy, for we are bound absolutely to worship God in that way which He has shown to be His will." A modern Catholic theologian, commenting on these official words, underscores them as follows: "If the state is under moral compulsion to profess and promote religion it is obviously obliged to promote and profess only the religion that is true; for no individual, no group of individuals, no society, no State is justified in supporting error or in according to error the same recognition as to truth." [3]

The simple distinction between "truth" and "error," consonant with similar simple distinctions in Catholic teachings between "justice" and "injustice" is a convenient tool of the terrible and pathetic illusion that "our" truth must use every instrument of coercion, as well as persuasion, to destroy and suppress the "false-

[3] John A. Ryan and Francis J. Boland, *Catholic Principles of Politics,* p. 314. The authors admit that this position is "intolerant but not therefore unreasonable." For "error has not the same rights as the truth." They call attention to the fact that the official position requires the suppression of other religions only if the nation is Catholic by an overwhelming majority and that therefore, "Its practical realization is so remote in time and in probability that no practical man will let it disturb his equanimity." They warn Catholics in non-Catholic nations against denying this doctrine for the sake of averting animus against the church; for they believe that, "the majority of our fellow citizens will be sufficiently honourable to respect our devotion to the truth and sufficiently realistic to see that the danger of religious intolerance towards non-Catholics in the United States is so improbable and so far in the future that it should not occupy their time and attention." *Ibid.,* p. 321.

This curious and pathetic logic implies an admission that the intolerance to which the church is forced by its presuppositions is really dangerous to both civil peace and civil liberty. Non-Catholics are consoled with the assurance that religious diversity, once established historically, will prevent the church from putting its theory into practice.

hood" of an opposing belief. For the distinction ignores the ambiguous character of all knowledge in history and obscures the residual error in even the purest truth, and the saving truth in even the most obvious error. It supports Catholicism in its fury against the "enemies of God" and the "enemies of Christ." The church does not understand that rebellions and revolutions against its authority may be prompted not by hatred of God or Christ, but by resentment against the unjustified use of Christ as a "cover" for the historical relativities of culture and civilization in which it happens to be involved.[4] It is not the Christ but "my" Christ who arouses this fury.

The Greek Orthodox version of this Catholic error differs slightly from the Roman one. The difference is in the more mystical conception of "grace" which, in Eastern thought, is regarded as the triumph of eternity over time and finiteness. Thus an Orthodox theologian defines the unconditioned truth possessed by the church as the achievement of the eternal in time: "The Catholic nature of the church is seen most vividly in the fact," he writes, "that the experience of the church belongs to all times. In the life and

---

[4] The Pastoral of the Spanish Bishops during the Spanish Civil War (published September 1937) contains a vivid expression of this Catholic illusion. The Bishops described the hatred of the church among the communists as follows: "The hatred against Jesus Christ and the Blessed Virgin reached paroxysms . . . in the vile literature of the red trenches, ridiculing the divine mysteries, in repeated profanations of the Sacred Host we can glimpse the hatred of hell incarnated in our poor communists. . . . 'I have sworn to be revenged on you,' said one [soldier] to our Lord, enclosed in the tabernacle, and aiming at Him with a pistol, he fired at Him saying: 'Surrender to the reds. Surrender to Marxism.' "

The identification of Christ with the "Sacred Host" on the altar is the perfect fruit of the Catholic error. The host on the altar is an historically conditioned symbol of the ultimate sanctity. All historical symbols contain the taint of profanation; for they insinuate the partial and particular values of "my" civilization, culture, and values into the sphere of absolute sanctity. The profanation of the sacred by the enemy against which we complain is therefore always, at least partly, a protest against our own profanation of the sacred.

existence of the church time is mysteriously overcome and mastered. Time so to speak stands still. It stands still because of the power of grace which gathers together in catholic unity of life that which has become separated by walls built by the course of time." [5]

Anglo-Catholicism has been saved, by the lack of such actual historical universality as the Roman church can boast, from making as consistent pretensions as the Roman church. But it has the same difficulty in recognizing the contingent and sinful elements in the truth which the Church possesses. Due to this error it has introduced confusion into the ecumenical movement of the non-Roman churches by insisting that the basis of ecumenical unity must include both a common faith and a common "order." But the "order" of a church, its rites and its polity, belong clearly to the realm of the historically contingent. Failure to recognize this fact naturally leads the Catholic wing of the non-Roman churches to insist that its order is the only possible one for an ecumenical church. The logic of this sinful spiritual imperialism conforms to the logic of sin generally. It is the unconscious ignorance, and the conscious denial, of the finiteness of its own perspective. Anglo-Catholicism is not alone in displaying this sin, but it has been particularly blind to the finite perspectives in the realm of "grace" and therefore especially prone to refute its sanctificationist interpretations of the Church by its own actions.[6]

[5] Rev. G. V. Florovsky, quoted by J. H. Oldham in the symposium: *The Church of God: An Anglo-Russian Symposium*, p. 62.

[6] The pathos of this whole problem is most vividly portrayed in efforts to make the sacrament of the Lord's Supper into a genuine symbol of the unity of the church, above and beyond all distinctions and relativities which divide it. Any insistence that this sacrament must be administered according to a particular "order" inevitably leads either to new display of the division of the church, by preventing the common observance of the sacrament; or to a new display of imperialism, by forcing Christians of different persuasion to accept one order of administration as the price of unity. The Scriptural observation: "There are differences of administrations, but the same Lord; and there are diversities of operations,

2. *The Reformation and Toleration*

We have maintained that the Reformation doctrine of "justification by faith" in its relation to the doctrine of sanctification represents the final recognition within the Christian faith of the twofold aspect of grace in Biblical religion. Logically the paradox of grace, that it is a having and not having, applies to the realm of culture and truth with the same validity as to any other realm of life. But the Reformation failed to apply it to this realm. Its fanaticisms disturbed the peace of both the church and civil society no less than did Catholic intolerance. In its treatment of those who differed from its interpretation of the Gospel it was singularly barren of the "fruits meet for repentance," of the humility which betrays the "broken spirit and the contrite heart." It gave little indication of any consciousness that error might be mixed with the truth which it possessed; though the truth which it possessed contained the recognition of this very paradox.[7]

Martin Luther had some misgivings about the use of the death penalty for heretics as late as 1526 and declared: "I can in no wise

---

but it is the same God which worketh all in all" (1 Cor. 12:5–6) is clearly not heeded.

It may be observed that this sacrament can never become the effective symbol of the unity of the church if its original eschatological motif does not receive new emphasis. ("For as often as we eat this bread and drink this cup, ye do show forth the Lord's death, *till he come.*" (1 Cor. 11:26.) This eschatological emphasis in the sacrament is a true expression of the eschatological character of the church. It does not have the unity in fact which it desires in principle. The divisions of history and the chasms of nature and sin leave their mark upon it. It cannot overcome them completely in fact; but it would overcome them more completely than it does if it would recognize its inability to overcome them more contritely. It would thus live in memory ("This do in remembrance of me") and in hope ("till he come"). Such memory and such hope would not leave the present unaffected. The church could have the more of grace, if it admitted that the truth was subject to the paradox of having and not having.

[7] Professor Tillich has expressed this failure in the significant phrase that it never submitted the doctrine of justification by faith to the experience of justification by faith.

admit that false teachers ought to be put to death. It is sufficient to banish them." But only a year later the lust of battle against the Anabaptists had dissipated these scruples and he was urging the use of the sword to suppress them. In dealing with both the mystic and the radical-apocalyptic forms of sectarianism, Luther and Calvin were equally pitiless; and the Swiss reformer Zwingli had a similar attitude towards them. Calvin, writing to the Duke of Somerset (Protector during Edward VI's minority), demanded the suppression of heresy by the civil arm: "There are two kinds of rebels who have arisen against the king," he declared. "The one is a fanatical sort of people who under the color of the gospel would put everything to confusion. The other are those who persist in the superstitions of the papal Antichrist. Both alike deserve to be repressed by the sword, which is committed to you, since they not only attack the King but strive with God, who has placed him on his throne."

In the long history of religious controversy in England from the reign of Elizabeth to that of Cromwell, Presbyterianism pursued a policy very similar to that of Catholicism. It pled for liberty of conscience when it was itself in danger of persecution; and threat-ened all other denominations with suppression when it had the authority to do so. A contemporary Anglican critic of Presbyterianism charged that, "these men cried out for liberty of conscience and boasted that the oppression which was levied against them was the hallmark of their own sainthood. But directly they gained even partial authority, they instantly renounced their former tenderness of conscience and accomplished the destruction of the church with every instrument that a persecuting zeal could recommend."[8]

An impartial historian summarizes the position of both Catholics and Puritans in this long religious controversy: "It has been said that Puritans and Catholics were contending for liberty of conscience. To put it so seems misleading, if not altogether untrue. They were contending for the liberty of their own consciences, not for those of other people. . . . What they both claimed was freedom

[8] Quoted by Jordan, *op. cit.*, Vol. II, p. 365.

to dominate. So far as they were concerned it was merely an accident in the vast process of things, that their efforts to free themselves helped to enlarge human freedom." [9]

The intolerance of theologians of the orthodox Reformation was the more reprehensible because the sectaries, against which their fanaticism was particularly directed, emphasized the very truths which supplemented the insights of the Reformation. While it would be wrong to give a purely economic interpretation of the differences between the Reformation and sectarianism, it cannot be denied that the theological differences were partly occasioned by, and the expressions of, social and economic conflicts. Sectarianism was on the whole the religion of the poor; and their insistence that religious ideals were socially relevant was occasioned by the pressure of their economic and social disabilities. Meanwhile the orthodox Reformation frequently became the religious screen for higher middle class economic interests, as generally as Catholicism was involved politically and economically with the older feudal classes. The mixture of theological and economic perspectives, which theologians are prone to deny and which economic determinists emphasize to the point of making religion a mere tool of economic interest, is one aspect of historical reality which refutes the pretensions of pure idealists, whether religious or secular. Even the most abstract theological controversy, as also the seemingly most objective scientific debate, is never free of accents which interest and passion have insinuated into the struggle. These interests are, it must be observed, much more complex and never as purely economic as Marxism assumes.

If the Reformation had observed the debates and conflicts in which it was involved in the light of its own ultimate insights into the imperfect character of all human ambitions and achievements, it could have used contemporary experience to validate its doctrines and to mitigate the fury with which it supported them.

[9] J. W. Allen, *A History of Political Thought in the Sixteenth Century*, p. 209.

Perhaps it is idle to search for particular causes of the failure of the Reformation to do this; for we have previously noted that sinful pride is able to use as instruments the very doctrines which are intended in principle to overcome it. Yet it is necessary to look for particular causes of this failure; because there were other spiritual movements, both secular and religious, which did, in fact, approach a tolerance consonant with the Christian spirit of forgiveness, though they possessed less searching doctrinal insights into the contingencies of history and the sinful corruptions of culture than the Reformation.

Undoubtedly one cause of the failure of the Reformation in the field of culture was that its Bibliolatry implied "sanctificationist" principles in the realm of culture and truth, despite its generally more paradoxical conception of grace. Thomas Hobbes was one, among many, critics of the church, who observed this effect of the Reformation: "After the Bible was translated into English," he wrote, "every man, nay, every boy and wench that could read English, thought they spoke with God Almighty . . . and every man became a judge of religion, and an interpreter of the scriptures to himself." [10] The certain conviction of the faithful that the Bible gave them the final truth, transcending all finite perspectives and all sinful corruptions, thus contributed to individual spiritual arrogance, no less intolerable than the collective arrogance of the older church. This pride expressed itself despite the fact that contrary interpretations of scripture, against which the arrogance was directed, contradicted the pretension of an absolutely valid interpretation. For they proved that men interpreted Scripture variously, according to the variety of social and historical perspectives from which they severally approached it.

Though Reformation Bibliolatry (to which, as we have previously observed, Calvinism was more prone than Lutheranism) is thus one explanation of the fanaticism of the Reformers and their disciples, it is an explanation which must itself be explained.

[10] Thomas Hobbes, *Behemoth, Works*, VI, 190.

Perhaps it was possible for the Reformation to take this simple jump out of the relativities and ambiguities of history, because it did not labour with sufficient earnestness and seriousness on those ultimate problems of human culture, where both the possibiltiies and the limits of human wisdom are discovered and defined. When this is done the gospel truth, which both negates and fulfills human wisdom, cannot be claimed as a simple possession. For men are persuaded to the contrite recognition that their effort to explicate this truth by human wisdom (which is the task of theology) is subject to historical contingencies, influenced by egoistic passions, corrupted by sinful pretensions and is, in short, under the same judgment as philosophy.

Theology may differ from philosophy in that it has broken with the principle of self-centredness in culture "in principle." It has done so in principle because it recognizes that the "world by its wisdom knew not God"; that it is not possible to complete the structure of meaning from any particular human perspective, or with any finite value as the centre and source of meaning. But the whole history of theology proves that this "in principle" does not mean "in fact." When the truth which transcends all partial and particular perspectives is made relevant to the truths of history and culture (a task which theology must perform despite its perils) these applications are subject to the same contingent elements which the history of philosophy reveals. Luther's contemptuous attitude towards philosophy is therefore without justification; more particularly because in practice philosophy sometimes achieves a greater spirit of humility than theology. It is saved from *hybris* by its lack of any quick means of escape from the obvious limitations of all human knowing. It has no Jacob's ladder upon which the angels of grace rightly ascend and descend, but which is used falsely when the theological Jacob imagines it an instrument for climbing into heaven.[11]

[11] *Cf.* Genesis 28:12.

In short, the intolerance of the Reformation is the consequence
of a violation of its own doctrinal position. Its doctrine of justification by faith presupposed the imperfection of the redeemed.
Logically this includes the imperfection of "redeemed" knowledge
and wisdom. Its intolerant fanaticism sprang from its failure to
apply this insight to the cultural problem so that it would mitigate
the spiritual pride of man. Its actions thus proved its theory to be
correct; but they also revealed it to be ineffective. It is a theory
which must not only be apprehended by the mind but which must
enter into the heart and break its pride. The authority of the Bible
was used to break the proud authority of the church; whereupon
the Bible became another instrument of human pride. The secularists may be pardoned if, as they watch this curious drama, they
cry "a plague o' both your houses"; and if they come to the conclusion that all ladders to heaven are dangerous. It must be
observed, however, that these ladders cannot be disavowed so
simply as the secularists imagine. Pride may ascend the ladder
which was meant for the descent of grace; but that is a peril which
inheres in the whole human cultural enterprise. The secularists end
by building ladders of their own; or they wallow in a nihilistic
culture which has no vantage point from which "my" truth can be
distinguished from "the" truth.

3. *The Renaissance and Toleration*

The toleration, whether in religious or in socio-economic disputes,
which has made life sufferable amidst the cultural and social complexities of the modern world, and which enabled modern society
to achieve a measure of domestic tranquility without paying the
price of tyrannical suppression, is obviously the fruit, primarily, of
the movement which we have defined broadly as "Renaissance."
The heroes of science who defied religious authority and reopened
prematurely solved problems, stood in that tradition. The Renaissance generated a wholesome attitude of scepticism which made

for sanity wherever human pride had exceeded the limits of human certainty. The achievement of toleration in modern culture is sometimes regarded as due to the destruction of religious fanaticism through the destruction of religion itself.[12] In so far as this is the case modern culture solves the problem of toleration only when the conflicts were explicitly religious; and offers no antidote for the implicitly religious fanaticism generated in ostensibly secular political and social movements.

It must be observed, however, that sectarian Protestantism, which is, as we have previously noted, intimately related to Renaissance spirituality, also made very substantial contributions to the spirit of liberty and toleration.

The rationalist-humanist wing of the Renaissance made its contributions to toleration by challenging particular prejudices with the supposed universalities of reason; and by dissolving the false universalities of dogmatic religion by the force of empirical observations, proving the wide variety and relativity of all historical forms of culture. The two strategies frequently operated side by side and receive varying degrees of emphasis in the typical champions of toleration in Renaissance humanism. Bruno leans to the one, Montaigne to the other mode of attack; Descartes to the first and Locke and Voltaire to the second.

Sectarian Christianity meanwhile challenged Christian fanaticism from within the presuppositions of Christian faith. Its mystic certainties transcended the historically conditioned certainties of dogmatic faith. Its individualism challenged the orthodox passion for religious uniformity; and its social radicalism set the absolute ethical demands of the gospel against the social compromises which religious authority had prematurely sanctioned. Hans Denck, the father of Reformation pietism, in whose thought are the germs of

[12] As for instance in W. E. H. Lecky's *The Rise and Influence of the Spirit of Rationalism in Europe.* Lecky regards the religious doctrine of "exclusive salvation" as the primary, if not sole, cause of the spirit of persecution; and "rationalism" as its sole cure.

both mystic-pietistic and radical-apocalyptic sectarianism, was a champion of toleration, as was also Schwenkfeld.[13]

While the Independents and the Levellers were the particular champions of toleration among seventeenth-century English sects, all the English sects made some contribution to the ideals of liberty. Lilburne and Walwyn, Winstanley and Roger Williams, these and many lesser known champions of liberty, are equally or more important in the history of English toleration, than the champions of liberty on the humanist side of the Renaissance.

The most distinguished of all champions of toleration, John Milton, combines Renaissance humanism and sectarian Christianity in a remarkable synthesis. Less profoundly Thomas Jefferson also achieved this synthesis, though the rationalist element in his thought is more pronounced and the Christian content more minimal.[14]

Sectarianism was not, of course, universally tolerant. It had its own source of fanatic fury. Its simple perfectionism made it blind to the inevitability of the compromises in which it saw its opponents involved. It therefore poured the fury of its self-righteous scorn upon them without recognizing that their compromises were but the obverse side of responsibilities, which the perfectionists had simply disavowed.[15] Sometimes its individualism (and this applies to secular libertarianisms as well) rendered its preaching of toleration too cheap; for it assumed no responsibility for, nor understood the

[13] Denck's last words before death were: "God is my witness that I desire things to go well with me only for the sake of one sect: the communion of saints, let be where it will."

[14] In English history the only important group which does not conform to these two general categories were the Cambridge Platonists and the moderate Anglican champions of toleration, particularly W. Chillingworth and Jeremy Taylor. The latter's *Liberty of Prophesying* is a classic on the subject. These Anglicans combine Renaissance insights with more orthodox rather than sectarian-Christian conceptions. Thomas More is an earlier exponent of the same general viewpoint.

[15] The modern counterpart of this sectarian fury is the self-righteousness of some pacifists who think it easy to love a tyrant but find it hard to preserve a decent Christian charity towards fellow-Christians who differ with them on the proper method of destroying tyranny.

necessity of, social peace and order. It did not therefore recognize the necessity of minimal coercion in even the most liberal society.[16]

But despite these sectarian fanaticisms, the history of sectarianism in general is as important as the more secular movement of the Renaissance in the development of toleration in the Western world.

The agreement upon this issue between secularists and sectarians rests upon two common approaches to the problem of truth, in which other differences are transcended. Both recognize the peril to truth in the coerced acceptance of it. And both are conscious of the finite character of human perspective and the variety of human viewpoints, which make perfect agreement in the search for truth impossible.

On the first point the secularists emphasize the futility of maintaining truth by coercion. "The truth," declared John Locke, "would certainly do well enough if she were left to shift for herself. She seldom has received, and I fear never will receive, much assistance from the power of great men. . . . If truth makes not her way into the understanding by her own light, she will be but weaker for any borrowed force violence can add to her."[17] The sectarian Christians give this same idea a slightly more moral-religious content. They do not see how coerced acceptance of the truth can redeem the soul. A letter of Flemish Baptists, under persecution in Elizabethan England, was a moving expression of the idea: "We testify before God and your majesty that were we in our conscience able by any means to think or understand the contrary, we would with all our hearts receive and confess it; since it were a great folly in us not to live rather in the exercise of a right faith, than to die perhaps in a false one. . . . It is not in our power to believe this or that as evil doers who do right or wrong as they please. But the true faith must

---

[16] The conflict between Oliver Cromwell and sectarian fanatics is instructive on this point. Cromwell agreed in principle more with the spirit of Independency than with Presbyterian policy. But he understood the difficulties of maintaining social order and peace as his sectarian critics did not.

[17] From *A Letter on Toleration*.

be planted in the heart by God, and to Him we pray daily that he would give us His spirit to understand His word and the Gospel." [18]

The second point of agreement between secular and sectarian theories of toleration is derived from the appreciation and understanding by the Renaissance of the cultural task as an historical process. It understands the contingent character of all historical knowledge and appreciates the wide variety of perspectives which history and nature, geography and climate introduce into human culture.[19] Here the Renaissance is more thoroughly in agreement with the Biblical understanding of man as "creature" and the Christian appreciation of the limits of human knowledge in history than alternative and more orthodox Christian doctrines. The Renaissance had its own ways of surmounting this historical relativity, which must be considered presently. It was led into new errors by many of them. But its provisional understanding of historical relativity gave it a great advantage over Christian orthodoxy.

This recognition of the fragmentary character of all historical apprehension of the truth is superbly expressed in Milton's *Areopagitica,* though in symbolism more Biblical than modern culture as a whole uses: "Truth indeed came once into the world with her Divine Master and was a perfect shape most glorious to look upon; but when He ascended and His Apostles after him were laid asleep, then straight arose a wicked race of deceivers . . . who took the Virgin truth, hewed her lovely form into a thousand pieces and scattered them to the four winds. From that time ever since the sad

[18] Roger Williams makes the same point, as indeed it is continually made by sectarian Christianity: "The ordinances and discipline of Jesus Christ, though wrongfully and profanely applied to unregenerate men, may cast a blush of civility and morality upon them . . . yet withal I affirm that the misapplication of ordinances to unregenerate and unrepentant persons, hardens up their souls in a dredful sleep . . . and sends millions of souls to hell in the secure expectation of a false salvation." From *The Bloudy Tenent of Persecution.*

[19] This insight was Montaigne's particular contribution to modern thought but it is proliferated in many forms and varieties of thought.

friends of Truth, such as durst appear, imitating the careful search that Isis made for the mangled body of Osiris, went up and down, gathering up limb by limb, still as they could find them. We have not yet found them all, Lords and Commons, nor ever shall do till the Master's second coming."[20]

The same idea is the frequent preoccupation of sectarian and independent thought. "Let us not," wrote John Saltmarsh, ". . . assume any power of infallibility to each other; . . . . for another's evidence is as dark to me as mine to him . . . till the Lord enlighten us both for discerning alike."[21]

This provisional understanding of the relativity of human knowledge, including the relativity of various interpretations of religious revelation, is an integral part of the recovery of the sense of the historical in Renaissance thought. It is the primary cause of the ability of the Renaissance to meet one of the two tests of the problem of toleration: the willingness to entertain views which oppose our own without rancour and without the effort to suppress them.

It is in meeting the other test: the ability to remain true to and to act upon our best convictions, that modern culture most frequently fails. It finds difficulty in avoiding irresponsibility and scepticism on the one hand and new fanaticisms on the other.

Its position is safe from illusion so long as it simply seeks to preserve the free commerce of opinion, in the hope that a higher truth will emerge in the process. In the words of John Stuart Mill: "Though silenced opinion be an error, it may, and very commonly does, contain a portion of the truth; and since the general or prevailing opinion on any subject is rarely or never the whole truth, it

[20] Milton's use of Biblical and oriental symbolism is indicative of the combination of Christian and humanist elements in his thought. The statement is nevertheless a perfect expression of the Christian doctrine of history as an "interim" between the revelation of the truth and its fulfillment. It encourages the gathering up of the truth "limb by limb" on the one hand; and yet expects no completion of the truth in history on the other.

[21] From *Smoke in the Temple* (1646).

is only the collision of adverse opinion that the remainder of the truth has a chance of being supplied." [22]

The hope that fragmentary portions of the truth will finally be pieced together into the whole truth, or the belief that intellectual intercourse is a kind of competition in which the truth will finally prevail against falsehood, are admirable provisional incentives to tolerance. They are, moreover, provisionally and relatively true. The intellectual life of mankind is a process in which truth is constantly being sifted from falsehood; and the confidence that truth will finally prevail in history robs falsehood of its seeming immediate peril and mitigates the anxious fanaticism with which "our" truth is defended.

The difficulty with this solution is that it is only a provisional and not a final answer to the question of the relation of the "whole truth" to the fragmentary truths of history. Obviously this issue is a segment of the whole problem of time and eternity. The belief that history is moving towards the disclosure of the whole truth is a part of an entire conception of the relation of time to eternity, in which it is assumed that history transmutes itself into eternity, and progressively devours its own finiteness. It is typical of the combination of classical and historical viewpoints in the Renaissance, according to which the *logos* in history is not emancipated from finiteness and history but gradually prevails within history.[23]

[22] From Essay on *Liberty*.

[23] A typical modern statement of this belief and hope is to be found in Professor John Dewey's *A Common Faith*. According to Dewey the divisive elements in human culture are vestigial remnants of outmoded religious prejudices which will yield to the universal perspectives which modern education will inculcate. This education will create practical unanimity among men of good will. Modern culture was generating new and fierce ideological conflicts, not remotely connected with traditional religious concepts, while Professor Dewey was writing this book.

The hope of establishing an intellectual position free of ideology springs up eternally in modern culture and takes many forms too numerous to mention. A particularly striking form is found in Professor Karl Mannheim's *Ideology and Utopia*. His contribution is striking because his "sociology of knowledge" is so much more conscious of the all-

In so far as modern tolerance has been achieved by disavowing religion it may rest merely on indifference towards the ultimate problems of life and history, with which religion is concerned. Since religious questions have been a particularly fecund source of fanaticism and conflict, the gain in provisional toleration has therefore been great. But the weakness in the modern position is also quite apparent. Either it achieves toleration by taking an irresponsible attitude towards ultimate issues; or it insinuates new and false ultimates into views of life which are ostensibly merely provisional and pragmatic. Here are the twin perils of scepticism and a new fanaticism.

It is significant that so much of modern toleration applies merely to the field of religion; and that the very champions of toleration in this field may be exponents of political fanaticism. It is simple enough to be tolerant on issues which are not believed to be vital.[24] The real test of toleration is our attitude towards people who oppose truths which seem important to us, and who challenge realms of life and meaning towards which we have a responsible relation. Tolerance in religion, therefore, frequently means an irresponsible attitude towards the ultimate problem of truth, including particularly the problem of the relation of *the* truth to the fragmentary truths of history. In the same way tolerance in political struggles may merely reveal irresponsibility and indifference towards the problem of political justice.

This irresponsible attitude may degenerate into complete scepticism, though there are very few consistent sceptics in the world. Absolute scepticism is rare because the very lack of confidence in the possibility of achieving any valid truth in history presupposes some

---

pervasive character of ideology than most similar analyses. He nevertheless hopes to eliminate ideology by developing a high degree of consciousness of the conditioned character of human knowledge. Such a consciousness may indeed purge knowledge of many overt ideologies, but it cannot produce an unconditioned mind.

[24] "Tolerance," said Gilbert Chesterton, "is the virtue of people who don't believe anything."

The danger of toleration resulting in complete scepticism and the necessity of scepticism for toleration

criterion of truth by which all fragmentary truths are found wanting. Nevertheless, complete scepticism is always a possible consequence of the spirit of toleration; for no toleration is possible without a measure of provisional scepticism about the truth we hold.[25] The Christian position of contrition in regard to "our" truth, the humble recognition that it contains some egoistic corruption, degenerates into irresponsibility as soon as we disavow the obligation to purge the truth we hold of its egoistic corruption. The irresponsibility degenerates into more complete scepticism if we come to the conclusion, that since history contains nothing but partial perspectives and fragmentary viewpoints, there is no possibility of discerning truth from falsehood. Complete scepticism represents the abyss of meaninglessness, a pit which has constantly threatened modern culture and into which it occasionally tumbles. Frequently, as in pre-Nazi German culture, it precedes the subordination of truth to political power. Scepticism thus becomes the forerunner of cynicism.

But new fanaticisms are the much more probable consequence of the modern position than complete scepticism. In these fanaticisms an ultimate position and a final truth are implicitly or explicitly insinuated into what was provisionally regarded as a realm of partial and fragmentary truths. Thus new religions emerge in an ostensibly irreligious culture.

In the main current of Renaissance thought, the belief that the intercourse between fragmentary truths will culminate in the realization of the whole truth becomes itself a religious position as soon as it is changed from a merely provisional and tentative attitude towards the immediate problem of dealing with fragmentary truths, into an answer to the final problem of truth and falsehood. Such a religion can and does maintain tolerance towards all religious beliefs except those which challenge this basic assump-

---

[25] "The only foundation for toleration," said Charles James Fox, "is a measure of scepticism and without it there can be none."
Oliver Cromwell, facing the peril to the state of conflicting religious absolutes, expressed the same idea in religious terms: "By the bowels of Christ," he said, "remember that you may be mistaken."

tion. The idea of progress is the underlying presupposition of what may be broadly defined as "liberal" culture. If that assumption is challenged the whole structure of meaning in the liberal world is imperiled. For this reason the liberal world is intolerant in regard to this article of its creed. It does not argue about its validity, precisely because it has lost every degree of scepticism in regard to it.

The creed is nevertheless highly dubious. It is true in so far as all historical processes, including the intellectual and cultural process, are meaningful and lead to fulfillment. It is false in so far as all historical processes are ambiguous. In the field of culture this means that the realization of a higher truth can lead to a new falsehood. Penetration into the mysteries of nature, for instance, may lead to false analogies between nature and history; or the discovery of the dynamic character of history may lead to the error of assuming that growth means progress.

The erroneous belief that history is its own fulfillment has been previously considered. The very structure of the human spirit refutes confidence in history as a process of cultural fulfillment as certainly as it refutes the general confidence in history. Man being a creature who both transcends and is involved in historical process cannot find perfect fulfillment in that process. His freedom over the process can be used on any level to introduce new error into the discovery of truth. But even if this were not the case his transcendence over history makes it impossible to complete his structure of meaning within the limits of history. He must ask how historical truth is related to ultimate, that is, "eternal" truth. And if he knows that historical truth is not merely imperfect but also corrupted truth, he faces a problem for which there is no answer but a divine mercy which purges the historical of its corruptions and completes its incompleteness.

But other fanaticisms grow up on the ground of the modern position baser than the mild fanaticism of the religion of progress. All of them, despite their variety, may be defined as political fanaticisms, generated by political religions. Thomas Hobbes and the French protagonist of political absolutism, Jean Bodin, may be regarded as the most typical historical exemplars of this tendency in modern culture, which finally culminated in the Nazi creed of race and nation. The tendency begins with a sceptical and irresponsible attitude towards the religious problem and an aversion to religious controversy because it imperils the tranquility of the national state. In the case of Bodin, the fratricidal religious conflict in France persuaded him to renounce his Huguenot faith for a syncretistic religion. His new religious position nicely reveals the perils of scepticism. For his highminded effort to find the truth in all religions ends with the poorly concealed conviction that all religions are equally true and *equally false*.[26] But Bodin's real concern was the unity of France; and he solved that problem by conceiving an absolute state, which had the power and the right to suppress all opinions and vitalities which might imperil its unity. In the thought of both Hobbes and Bodin, this demand for unconditioned loyalty to the state is implicitly rather than explicitly religious. It is implicitly religious because it demands unconditioned loyalty; but not explicitly so because it does not make the overt claim that the whole meaning of life and existence is fulfilled in the individual's relation to the national community. It was left to the Nazis to illustrate one possible kind of progress in history, by developing the logic of this state absolutism to its final conclusion. Thus they achieved the final corruption of cynicism on the soil of religious scepticism.

Thomas More, who was a Renaissance nationalist when his sovereign Henry VIII imperiled the interests of England by subservience to papal politics, and who was a Catholic universalist when the king sought to establish royal supremacy in spiritual matters, proved the validity and availability of the Christian position as a resource against this new political fanaticism. Despite its own corruption of fanaticism, the Catholic version of the Christian faith is at least a bulwark against the idolatry of political and national absolutisms. Challenged by the king to submit to his

[26] *Cf.* Jean Bodin, *Colloquium Heptaplomeres.*

authority spiritually as well as politically, and presented with the futility of defiance in view of the submission of all other English leaders, More appealed to the authority of the universal church which had not submitted. "For," said he, "though some nations fall away, yet likewise as how many boughs fall from the tree, though they fall more than be left thereon, yet they make no doubt which is the very tree, although each of them were planted in another place and grew to a greater tree than the stock he came first of." [27]

This Christian universalism, despite its corruptions in both the Protestant and Catholic versions of the Christian faith, has proved as resourceful in our own day as in the day of Henry VIII. It has defied the cynical solution of the cultural problem, more successfully than any other position.

The Marxist solution of the problem of truth stands on a higher ground than the subordination of all culture to the power of the state. But it is nevertheless a political religion; and must be regarded as one of the late fruits on the soil of Renaissance thought. According to its faith the particular perspective of the proletarian class is not a relative but a transcendent vantage point for the apprehension of the truth. All truth but its own is therefore tainted with the "ideological" taint of interest. But obviously the pretension of any class or nation, of any culture or civilization, that it alone has escaped from the finiteness of human knowing. and the corruption of interest and passion, is merely another form of the taint of pride which confuses all quests for the truth. It is a secularized version of

[27] *A Dialogue concerning heresyes and matters of religion* (1528). When More was told that "the bishops, universities and best learned of this realm" had submitted to the king he replied significantly: "For I nothing doubt that, though not in this realm yet in Christendom about . . . they be not the fewer part that are of my mind therein. But if I should speak of those already dead, of whom many now be holy saints in heaven, I am sure that it is far the greater part . . . of them that thought in this case the way that I think now. Therefore am I not bound to conform my conscience to the council of one realm against the general council of Christendom." Cf. *Thomas More* by R. W. Chambers, p. 341.

the pretension of complete sanctification. The fruit of fanaticism is the natural consequence of this claim.

However we twist or turn, whatever instruments or pretensions we use, it is not possible to establish the claim that we have the truth. The truth remains subject to the paradox of grace. We may have it; and yet we do not have it. And we will have it the more purely in fact if we know that we have it only in principle. Our toleration of truths opposed to those which we confess is an expression of the spirit of forgiveness in the realm of culture. Like all forgiveness, it is possible only if we are not too sure of our own virtue.

Loyalty to the truth requires confidence in the possibility of its attainment; toleration of others requires broken confidence in the finality of our own truth. But if there is no answer for a problem to which we do not have the answer, our shattered confidence generates either defeat (which in the field of culture would be scepticism); or an even greater measure of pretension, meant to hide our perplexities behind our certainties (which in the field of culture is fanaticism).

{ very good point

tests of tolerance — ① ability to have a tolerant attitude toward those who differ, ("forgiveness") due to the half of the paradox of grace which implies we cannot have all the truth; ② the ability to maintain convictions, due to the half of the paradox of grace which implies that we can have some of the truth

CHAPTER IX

THE KINGDOM OF GOD AND THE STRUGGLE FOR JUSTICE

THE STRUGGLE for justice is as profound a revelation of the possibilities and limits of historical existence as the quest for truth. In some respects it is even more revealing because it engages all human vitalities and powers more obviously than the intellectual quest.

The obligation to build and to perfect communal life is not merely forced upon us by the necessity of coming to terms with the rather numerous hosts, whom it has pleased an Almighty Creator to place on this little earth beside us. Community is an individual as well as social necessity; for the individual can realize himself only in intimate and organic relation with his fellowmen. Love is therefore the primary law of his nature; and brotherhood the fundamental requirement of his social existence.

Since man is a unity of vitality and reason, the social coherence of life can never be purely rational. It includes an interpenetration of all powers and potencies, emotional and volitional as well as rational. But the power of rational freedom gives human communities a higher dimension than those of nature. Man's freedom over the limits of nature in indeterminate regression means that no fixed limits can be placed upon either the purity or the breadth of the brotherhood for which men strive in history. No traditional attainment of brotherhood is secure against criticism from a higher historical perspective or safe from corruption on each new level of achievement.

The indeterminate character of these possibilities of both good and evil in social and political relations justifies the dynamic interpretation of the social process. The facts of history may not support the conclusion that historical process has continually purified and perfected social relations; but they certainly prove that the breadth and extent of historical communities have been consistently increased. Every age, and more particularly the age of technics, has confronted men with the problem of relating their lives to a larger number of their fellowmen. The task of creating community and avoiding anarchy is constantly pitched on broader and broader levels.

These facts have presented modern culture with what seemed irrefutable proofs of its progressive view of the social task. The "Kingdom of God" seemed to be an immanent force in history, culminating in a universal society of brotherhood and justice. The secular and liberal-Protestant approaches to the socio-moral problem, based upon this presupposition, are too numerous to mention. Modern sociological treatises are practically unanimous in assuming this view of history. The Marxist interpretation of history deviates from it. But the deviation is only provisionally radical. Its catastrophism is finally subordinated to a progressive and utopian concept of history. The liberal-Protestant version has added little but pious phrases to the interpretation.

The definition of the Christian view of human destiny as presented must lead to other, and partly contrary, conclusions. The conclusions are not completely contrary because they do not refute the dynamic character of history or the significance of its continually expanding tasks and obligations. They do, however, challenge the identification of historical growth with moral progress. According to our interpretation, "grace" is related to "nature" partly as fulfillment and partly as negation. If the contradiction between "nature" and "grace" is not recognized, and the continued power of "nature" in the realm of "grace" is not conceded, new sins are brought into history by the pretension that sin has been progressively eliminated.

II

THE RELATION OF JUSTICE TO LOVE

If we apply this formula of the Christian interpretation of life to human society it may be well to begin by translating the terms so that they will be relevant to the socio-moral issue. "Nature" in this case represents the historical possibilities of justice.[1] "Grace" would correspond to ideal possibility of perfect love, in which all inner contradictions within the self, and all conflicts and tensions between the self and the other are overcome by the complete obedience of all wills to the will of God.

Translated into these terms the Christian conception of the relation of historical justice to the love of the Kingdom of God is a dialectical one. Love is both the fulfillment and the negation of all achievements of justice in history. Or expressed from the opposite standpoint, the achievements of justice in history may rise in indeterminate degrees to find their fulfillment in a more perfect love and brotherhood; but each new level of fulfillment also contains elements which stand in contradiction to perfect love. There are therefore obligations to realize justice in indeterminate degrees; but none of the realizations can assure the serenity of perfect fulfillment. If we analyse the realities of history in terms of this formula it will throw light on aspects of history which would otherwise remain obscure and perplexing; and will obviate mistakes which are inevitably made under alternative interpretations. Higher realizations of historic justice would be possible if it were more fully

---

[1] It may be helpful to recall that in Christian usage "nature" when set in juxtaposition to "grace" never means the finite or natural process as distinguished from rational freedom. It means the "sinful nature" of man, as distinguished from the state of emancipation from sin.

understood that all such realizations contain contradictions to, as well as approximations of, the ideal of love. Sanctification in the realm of social relations demands recognition of the impossibility of perfect sanctification.

The paradoxical relation between justice and love is expressed on various levels. We have previously explored the relation between sacrificial and mutual love.[2] In that analysis it became apparent that mutual love (in which disinterested concern for the other elicits a reciprocal response) is the highest possibility of history in the sense that only such love is justified by historical consequences; but also that such love can only be initiated by a type of disinterestedness (sacrificial love) which dispenses with historical justification. Thus the pinnacle of the moral ideal stands both inside and beyond history: inside in so far as love may elicit a reciprocal response and change the character of human relations; and beyond history in so far as love cannot require a mutual response without losing its character of disinterestedness. The love commandment is therefore no simple historical possibility. The full implications of the commandment illustrate the dialectical relation between history and the eternal.

III

LAWS AND PRINCIPLES OF JUSTICE

The relation of justice to love contains complexities analogous to the dialectical relation of mutual to sacrificial love. These complexities may be clarified by considering them in two dimensions. The first is the dimension of rules and laws of justice. The second is the dimension of structures of justice, of social and political organizations in their relation to brotherhood. The difference between the first and second dimension obviously lies in the fact that laws and principles of justice are abstractly conceived, while structures and organizations embody the vitalities of history. The contradiction between actual social institutions and arrangements and the ideal

[2] Vol. II, Ch. III.

of brotherhood is obviously greater than between love and the rules and laws of justice.

All systems, rules and laws governing social relations are on the one hand instruments of mutuality and community; and they contain on the other hand mere approximations of, and positive contradictions to, the ideal of brotherhood. These aspects of the character of rules of justice must be examined in turn.

Systems and principles of justice are the servants and instruments of the spirit of brotherhood in so far as they extend the sense of obligation towards the other, (*a*) from an immediately felt obligation, prompted by obvious need, to a continued obligation expressed in fixed principles of mutual support; (*b*) from a simple relation between a self and one "other" to the complex relations of the self and the "others"; and (*c*) finally from the obligations, discerned by the individual self, to the wider obligations which the community defines from its more impartial perspective. These communal definitions evolve slowly in custom and in law. They all contain some higher elements of disinterestedness, which would not be possible to the individual self.

In these three ways rules and laws of justice stand in a positive relation to the law of love. It is significant that the rational element is constitutive in each of them. An immediately felt obligation towards obvious need may be prompted by the emotion of pity. But a continued sense of obligation rests upon and expresses itself in rational calculations of the needs of others as compared with our own interests. A relation between the self and one other may be partly ecstatic; and in any case the calculation of relative interests may be reduced to a minimum. But as soon as a third person is introduced into the relation even the most perfect love requires a rational estimate of conflicting needs and interests. Even the love within a family avails itself of customs and usages which stereotype given adjustments between various members of the family in such a way that each action need not be oriented by a fresh calculation of competing interests.

The definitions of justice arrived at in a given community are the product of a social mind. Various perspectives upon common problems have been merged and have achieved a result, different from that at which any individual, class or group in the community would have arrived. The fact that various conceptions of a just solution of a common problem can be finally synthesized into a common solution disproves the idea that the approach of each individual or group is consistently egoistic. If it were, society would be an anarchy of rival interests until power from above subdued the anarchy.

Interests may indeed clash to such a degree that no arbitration of the conflict is possible, in which case the conflict is ended either by the victory of one side or the other, or by the submission of both to a superior coercive force. Martin Luther's and Thomas Hobbes' political views are informed by the belief that all conflicts of interest are of such a nature.

The achievements of democratic societies refute this pessimism; and with it the purely negative conception of the relation of government and systems of justice to the ideal of brotherhood. History reveals adjustments of interest to interest without the interposition of superior coercive force to be possible within wide limits. The capacity of communities to synthesize divergent approaches to a common problem and to arrive at a tolerably just solution proves man's capacity to consider interests other than his own. Nevertheless, the fact that a synthesis of conflicting interests and viewpoints is not easy, and may become impossible under certain conditions, is a refutation of a too simple trust in the impartial character of reason. It would be as false to regard rules and principles of justice, slowly elaborated in collective experience, as merely the instruments of the sense of social obligation, as to regard them merely as tools of egoistic interest.

An analysis of the development of social conscience on any current social issue, as for instance the community's sense of obligation to the unemployed, may clarify the complex factors involved in this development. The unemployment benefits which the community pays to those who are out of work is partly an expression of the sense of obligation of the more privileged members of the community towards those who are less fortunate. They find an advantage in meeting this obligation according to fixed principles instead of relying upon their own occasional feeling of pity for this or that needy person. They know furthermore that their own knowledge of comparative needs is very inadequate and that they require the more impartial and comprehensive perspective of the total community, functioning through its proper agencies. This function of principles of unemployment relief presents the most positive relation between specific rules and the sense of brotherhood.

On the other hand the benefits which are paid to the unemployed are almost always higher than the privileged would like to pay, even though they may be lower than the poor would like to receive. Some members of the privileged classes in modern communities have in fact obscured the issue of justice in regard to this problem by the most obvious and transparent of all ideologies. They have sought to maintain that the unemployed are the victims of sloth rather than of the caprices of an intricate industrial process; and that the fear of hunger might cure their sloth. The actual schedule of payments upon which the community finally decides represents the conclusions of the social, rather than any individual, mind, and is the consequence of a perennial debate upon the subject. It is probably a compromise between conflicting viewpoints and interests. It certainly is not an unconditionedly "just" solution of the social problem involved. The privileged may in fact accept it for no better reason than that they fear the revolt of the poor. This aspect of the situation proves the impossibility of completely separating the concept of "principles of justice" from the hopes and fears, the pressures and counter-pressures, of living communities, expressed below the level of a rational calculation of rights and interests.

The solution may nevertheless become a generally accepted social standard; and some privileged members of the community may welcome it, because it expresses their considered sense of social obligation upon which they would prefer to rely rather than upon the momentary power of pity. The poor as a whole may receive less from these benefits than an individual needy person might secure by appealing to a given sensitive and opulent individual. But they will certainly receive more than if all of them were dependent upon nothing but vagrant, momentary and capricious impulses of pity, dormant unless awakened by obvious need.

This positive relation between rules of justice and the law of love must be emphasized in opposition to sentimental versions of the love commandment, according to which only the most personal individual and direct expressions of social obligation are manifestations of Christian *agape*. Both sectarian and Lutheran analyses of the relation of love to justice easily fall into the error of excluding rules of justice from the domain of love.[8]

Laws and systems of justice do, however, have a negative as well as a positive relation to mutual love and brotherhood. They contain both approximations of and contradictions to the spirit of brotherhood. This aspect of their character is derived from the sinful element in all social reality. They are merely approximations in so far as justice presupposes a tendency of various members of

[8] Emil Brunner succumbs to this error when he writes: "The believer's most important duty . . . always remains that of pouring the vitality of love into the necessarily rigid forms of the order [structure of justice]. . . . The end is the personal relation itself. . . . To improve it [the order] is not a hopeless task, nor is it unnecessary but it is still only a matter of *secondary importance*. The one thing that matters is to do what can be done only from the standpoint of faith, namely, to love our neighbour 'In Christ,' and to serve him in any way we can. . . . It is supremely important to emphasize the truth that what is decisive always takes place in the realm of personal relations and not in the political sphere, save where we are concerned with preserving the whole order from a general breakdown." *The Divine Imperative*, p. 233.

Brunner's consistently negative interpretations of the political task and his idea of its secondary importance is a Lutheran heritage in his thought. He is, of course, correct in asserting that no systems and schemes of justice fulfill the law of love so that the possibility of giving them a higher content by personal attitudes and actions is obviated.

a community to take advantage of each other, or to be more concerned with their own weal than with that of others. Because of this tendency all systems of justice make careful distinctions between the rights and interests of various members of a community. The fence and the boundary line are the symbols of the spirit of justice. They set the limits upon each man's interest to prevent one from taking advantage of the other. A harmony achieved through justice is therefore only an approximation of brotherhood. It is the best possible harmony within the conditions created by human egoism. This negative aspect of justice is not its only characteristic, as has been previously observed. Even if perfect love were presupposed, complex relations, involving more than two persons, require the calculation of rights. The negative aspect is nevertheless important.

The more positive contradiction to brotherhood in all schemes of justice is introduced by the contingent and finite character of rational estimates of rights and interests and by the taint of passion and self-interest upon calculations of the rights of others. There is no universal reason in history, and no impartial perspective upon the whole field of vital interests, which compete with and mutually support each other. Even the comparatively impartial view of the whole of a society, as expressed particularly in the carefully guarded objectivity of its juridical institutions, participates in the contingent character of all human viewpoints.

Such rules of justice as we have known in history have been arrived at by a social process in which various partial perspectives have been synthesized into a more inclusive one. But even the inclusive perspective is contingent to time and place. The Marxist cynicism in regard to the pretended moral purity of all laws and rules of justice is justified. Marxism is right, furthermore, in regarding them as primarily rationalizations of the interests of the dominant elements of a society. The requirements of "natural law" in the medieval period were obviously conceived in a feudal society; just as the supposed absolute and "self-evident" demands of eighteenth-century natural law were bourgeois in origin.

The relative and contingent character of these ideals and rules of justice refutes the claim of their unconditioned character, made alike by Catholic, liberal and even Marxist social theorists.[4] Both Catholic and liberal social theories (and for that matter the Stoic theories in which both had their origin) make a distinction between "natural law" and the "positive" or "civil" law. The latter represents the actual and imperfect embodiment of the rules of justice in specific historical communities. The contingent and relative character of the latter type of law is recognized; but finality is ascribed to the former. This fundamental distinction must be challenged. It rests upon an untenable faith in the purity of reason; and it is merely another of the many efforts which men make to find a vantage point of the unconditioned in history. The effect of this pretended finality of "natural law" is obvious. It raises "ideology" to a higher degree of pretension, and is another of the many illustrations in history of the force of sin in the claim of sinlessness.[5]

There is of course a tenable distinction between ideals of justice and their embodiment in historical or "civil" law. The latter is the consequence of pressures and counter-pressures in a living community. It is therefore subject to a greater degree of historical relativity than "natural law." In so far as thought is purer than action

[4] Marxist theory as usual detects the taint of interest in theories other than its own. But it also has the equivalent of a "natural law." In that law the dominance of the ideal of equality is, for instance, clearly "ideological." It is informed by a justified resentment of the poor against inequality but fails to recognize the inevitability of functional inequalities in society.

[5] Catholic theories of "natural law" are no less pretentious than secular theories, even though they subordinate the virtue of justice, enjoined in the natural law, to the virtue of love, achieved by grace. According to Catholic theory "natural law" is the part of the "divine" or the "eternal" law which is manifested in human reason. The endless relativities of historical rational perspectives are obscured. This unconditioned claim for an essentially universal reason is the basis of the remarkable degree of certainty with which Catholic moral theology is able to define "justice" and "injustice" in every possible situation. *Cf.* Vol. I, Ch. X.

*transcendent principles of justice exist, tho'
they are not to be regarded as "realizable".*

"natural law" is purer than "civil law." Furthermore it is important
to recognize the validity of principles of justice, rationally conceived, as sources of criticism for the historical achievements of
justice in living communities. If the medieval and modern secular
theories of natural law claim too much for these rational principles
of justice, both secular and Reformation relativists frequently dismiss them as irrelevant or dangerous. Karl Barth's belief that the
moral life of man would possess no valid principles of guidance, if
the Ten Commandments had not introduced such principles by
revelation, is as absurd as it is unscriptural.[6]

The practical universality of the prohibition of murder for
instance in the moral codes of mankind is just as significant as the
endless relativities which manifest themselves in the practical application of the general prohibition. There are essentially universal
"principles" of justice moreover, by which the formulation of
specific rules and systems of justice is oriented. Both "equality"
and "liberty" are recognized in Stoic, medieval and modern theories of natural law as transcendent principles of justice; though
the modern theories (both bourgeois and Marxist) falsely regard
them as realizable rather than as transcendent principles. An
analysis of one of them, the principle of equality, will serve to reveal
the validity of both as transcendent principles of justice.

The perpetual recurrence of the principle of equality in social
theory is a refutation of purely pessimistic conceptions of human
nature, whether secular or religious. Its influence proves that men
do not simply use social theory to rationalize their own interest.
Equality as a pinnacle of the ideal of justice implicitly points
towards love as the final norm of justice; for equal justice is the
approximation of brotherhood under the conditions of sin. A higher
justice always means a more equal justice. Special privilege may be

---

[6] It is in conflict with the Pauline assertion: "For when the Gentiles
which have not the law, do by nature the things contained in the law,
these, having not the law, are a law unto themselves." Romans 2:14.
Barth's exegetical effort to eliminate the force of this Pauline doctrine is
tortuous. *Cf.* his *Epistle to the Romans*, pp. 65–68.

frowned upon more severely by those who want it than those who have it; but those who have it are uneasy in their conscience about it. The ideological taint enters into the discussion of equality when those who suffer from inequality raise the principle of equality to the definitive principle of justice without recognizing that differences of need or of social function make the attainment of complete equality in society impossible.[7] The beneficiaries of special privilege emphasize, on the other hand, that inequalities of social function justify corresponding inequalities of privilege. They may also assert, with some, but less, justification, that inequality of reward is a necessary inducement for the proper performance of social function. But they will seek to hide the historic fact that privileged members of the community invariably use their higher degree of social power to appropriate an excess of privileges not required by their function; and certainly not in accord with differences of need.

The validity of the principle of equality on the one hand and the impossibility of realizing it fully on the other, illustrates the relation of absolute norms of justice to the relativities of history. The fact that one class will tend to emphasize the absolute validity of the norm unduly, while another class will be inclined to emphasize the impossibility of achieving it fully, illustrates the inevitable "ideological taint" in the application of a generally valid principle, even if the principle itself achieves a high measure of transcendence over partial interest.[8]

[7] This is the aspect of the problem recognized in Stoic and medieval theories, according to which equality belongs to the golden age or to the perfection before the fall.

[8] The Stoic and Catholic distinction between relative and absolute natural law is a helpful recognition of the necessity of accommodating absolute principles to relative and "sinful" historic situations. But the idea that the requirements of "relative" natural law can be stated absolutely proceeds from the failure to include the human mind in the relativities of history. Here Emil Brunner's criticisms of this distinction are admirable. *Cf. The Divine Imperative*, pp. 626–632.

Brunner, however, erroneously follows the Reformation disparagement of the function of reason in the realm of social ethics and arrives

The complex character of all historic conceptions of justice thus refutes both the relativists who see no possibility of finding valid principles of justice, and the rationalists and optimists who imagine it possible to arrive at completely valid principles, free of every taint of special interest and historical passion.

The positive relation of principles of justice to the ideal of brotherhood makes an indeterminate approximation of love in the realm of justice possible. The negative relation means that all historic conceptions of justice will embody some elements which contradict the law of love. The interests of a class, the viewpoint of a nation, the prejudices of an age and the illusions of a culture are consciously and unconsciously insinuated into the norms by which men regulate their common life. They are intended to give one group an advantage over another. Or if that is not their intention, it is at least the unvarying consequence.

IV

STRUCTURES OF JUSTICE

If rules and principles of justice ideally conceived and transcending the more dubious and ambiguous social realities of living societies have an equivocal relation to the ideal of brotherhood, this twofold

---

at a consequent dismissal of the ideal of equality as merely a "rational" and therefore unchristian norm. He writes: "The egalitarian law of nature does not belong to the world of the Bible but to the context of Stoic rationalism. The egalitarian ideal does not arise out of reverence for the Creator but out of the desire to dictate to the Creator how things ought to be, or the presupposition that the Creator ought to treat every one alike." *Ibid.,* p. 407.

Any parent who has sought to administer justice and to compose childish disputes will know how spontaneously children appeal to the principle of equality as the correct principle of arbitrament, and with what difficulty they must, on occasion, be persuaded that differences of age, function and need, render the principle inoperative, or make it only indirectly relevant. The children may lack proper reverence for the Creator of inequalities; but on the other hand they have certainly never heard of, or been spoiled by, "Stoic rationalism."

character is even more obvious and apparent in the structures and systems, the organizations and mechanisms, of society in which these principles and rules are imperfectly embodied and made historically concrete. We have already noted the distinction between "natural law," as a rational statement of principle of justice, and "positive" law, which designates the historic enactments of living communities. But an analysis of the equivocal character of the "structures" of justice must include more than a mere consideration of "civil" or "positive" law. It must look beyond legal enactments to the whole structure and organization of historical communities. This structure is never merely the order of a legal system. The harmony of communities is not simply attained by the authority of law. *Nomos* does not coerce the vitalities of life into order. The social harmony of living communities is achieved by an interaction between the normative conceptions of morality and law and the existing and developing forces and vitalities of the community. Usually the norms of law are compromises between the rational-moral ideals of what ought to be, and the possibilities of the situation as determined by given equilibria of vital forces. The specific legal enactments are, on the one hand, the instruments of the conscience of the community, seeking to subdue the potential anarchy of forces and interests into a tolerable harmony. They are, on the other hand, merely explicit formulations of given tensions and equilibria of life and power, as worked out by the unconscious interactions of social life.

No human community is, in short, a simple construction of conscience or reason. All communities are more or less stable or precarious harmonies of human vital capacities. They are governed by power. The power which determines the quality of the order and harmony is not merely the coercive and organizing power of government. That is only one of the two aspects of social power. The other is the balance of vitalities and forces in any given social situation. These two elements of communal life—the central organizing principle and power, and the equilibrium of power—

are essential and perennial aspects of community organization; and no moral or social advance can redeem society from its dependence upon these two principles.

Since there are various possibilities of so managing and equilibrating the balance of social forces in a given community that the highest possible justice may be achieved and since the organizing principle and power in the community is also subject to indeterminate refinement, communal order and justice can approximate a more perfect brotherhood in varying degree. But each principle of communal organization—the organization of power and the balance of power—contain possibilities of contradicting the law of brotherhood. The organizing principle and power may easily degenerate into tyranny. It may create a coerced unity of society in which the freedom and vitality of all individual members are impaired. Such a tyrannical unification of life is a travesty on brotherhood. Again, the principle of the balance of power is always pregnant with the possibility of anarchy. These twin evils, tyranny and anarchy, represent the Scylla and Charybdis between which the frail bark of social justice must sail. It is almost certain to founder upon one rock if it makes the mistake of regarding the other as the only peril.

No possible refinement of social forces and political harmonies can eliminate the potential contradiction to brotherhood which is implicit in the two political instruments of brotherhood—the organization of power and the balance of power. This paradoxical situation in the realm of social life is analogous to the Christian conception of the paradox of history as discerned in other realms of life. In order to explore the meaning of the paradox more fully it will be well to begin with an analysis of the nature and meaning of "power" in communal life.

1. The Unity of Vitality and Reason

The perennial importance of power in social organization is based upon two characteristics of human nature. The one is the unity of vitality and reason, of body and soul. The other is the force of human sin, the persistent tendency to regard ourselves as more important than any one else and to view a common problem from the standpoint of our own interest. The second characteristic is so stubborn that mere moral or rational suasion does not suffice to restrain one person from taking advantage of another. Legal authority may be more sufficing; but there is no legal authority which does not imply sanctions or the threat of coercive action against recalcitrance. The first characteristic, the unity of vitality and reason in human nature, guarantees that egoistic purposes will be pursued with all vital resources which an individual or collective will may control. Therefore social restraints upon these anti-social purposes must be equally armed with all available resources.

Disputes may of course be composed and conflicts arbitrated without recourse to all such resources. Conscience may appeal to conscience and reason to reason. There are in fact no conflicts in which these appeals are not made, even when the conflict has become physical. But in every conflict of interest the possibility of marshalling every possible resource on either side is implied. Most human conflicts are composed, or subdued, by a superior authority and power, without an overt appeal to force or without the actual use of force, either violent or non-violent. But the calculation of available resource on each side is as determinative in settling the outcome of the struggle as more purely rational or moral considerations.[1]

The threat of force, whether by the official and governmental representatives of a community or by the parties to a dispute in a community is a potent instrument in all communal relations. It may not be frequently used in a stable and well-ordered community; but if either government, or a party to a dispute, explicitly dis-

[1] A strike in industry is a case in point. It may be arbitrated but the compromise between the two sides or the yielding of one side to the other is partly determined by the shrewd calculation of either side of the resources of social and economic power of which the other side could avail itself in case the conflict became overt, and of the possible position which government and public would take towards it.

avowed any resource at its disposal, it would upset whatever equilibrium of social forces existed at that moment; it would thereby increase the possibility of successful recalcitrance or resistance on the part of the group or interest, prepared to use every available resource. The prospect of successful resistance naturally also increases the probability that a venture in resistance will be made.[2] The rational calculation of the powers and vitalities, involved in a social situation, is thus an inevitable accompaniment of the rational calculation of rights and interests, involved in a socio-moral problem. The invariable correlation of the two is a nice symbol of the unity of vitality and reason in all social existence.

2. *Types of Power in Social Life*

The spiritual and physical faculties of man are able, in their unity and interrelation, to create an endless variety of types and combinations of power, from that of pure reason to that of pure physical force. Though reason is commonly supposed to be transcendent, rather than partial, it is hardly necessary at this point to prove that reason may be the instrument of the ego in advancing its claims against another. When it is so used it is a "power" which supports

---

[2] This is how a liberal democratic world, dreaming of progress towards purely rational and moral resolutions of all social conflicts, stumbled into a "total war." A sensitive conscience may be revolted by the tragic and brutal realities of man's social life and decide to disavow all power. But if this powerlessness is not accompanied by a concomitant disavowal of social responsibility it leads to the moral confusions in which secular and religious perfectionists are usually involved. Complete nonresistance may have moral meaning, if it is understood that unprotected rights and privileges will probably be lost and that in many social situations they are practically certain to be lost. Non-violent resistance has meaning as a pragmatic technique; for it is well to explore all methods of achieving justice and maintaining peace, short of violent conflict. But non-violent resistance as a moral or political absolute is a source of moral and political confusion. The implicit and explicit aversion of the democratic world to violent forms of dispute was a factor upon which proponents of "total war" calculated. It increased the probability of their success and therefore the certainty of their venture.

the claims of one life against another. The shrewd do take advantage of the simple. A rational solution of a conflict may be a very unjust one, if the more robust has "overpowered" the weaker intellect. But there are other spiritual faculties which may serve the same purpose. One man may keep another enslaved purely by "soul" force.[3] Such soul force may consist of spiritual vitalities of various kinds, mental and emotional energy, the possession or the pretension of virtue, the prestige of an heroic life, or of a gentle birth. Pure physical force is always a last resort in individual relations. It is determinative in these relations only on primitive levels. All civilized relations are governed more by spiritual, than by physical, facets of power. It is significant that they are not, for that reason, naturally more just.

The forms of power which are developed collectively display an even wider variety of types. On the whole social power rests upon differentiations of social function. The soldier is the bearer of physical force in advanced societies, not because he is physically strong, but because he has the instruments, and masters the techniques, of physical conflict. The priest has social power (especially potent in the organization of early empires) because he mediates the authority of some ultimate majesty and endows the political authority of a given oligarchy with this sanctity. The ownership and the control of property and economic process represents partly physical and partly spiritual power. It is physical in so far as the wealth created by the economic process is physical. It is spiritual in so far as the right to use and control this physical force is derived from law, custom, the prestige of function and other similar considerations. The modern belief that economic power is the most basic form, and that all other forms are derived from it, is erroneous. The first landlords were soldiers and priests who used military

---

[3] Gandhi's identification of "soul force" with non-egoistic motives and "body force" with egoistic ones, is almost completely mistaken. The type of power used by the will to effect its purposes does not determine the quality of the purpose or motive.

and religious forms of social power to possess and to acquire land. Economic power, before the modern period, was derivative rather than primary. It was used to enhance the comforts of the oligarchs of society and to insure the perpetuation of their social eminence from generation to generation. But it did not give them their initial eminence. In modern Germany, Nazi political oligarchs transmute political power into economic power. In the bourgeois period economic power did tend to become more fundamental and to bend other forms to its purposes. In democratic societies it was, however, always under some restraint from the more widely diffused political power of the common man, inhering in the universal right of suffrage.[4]

 All historic forms of justice and injustice are determined to a much larger degree than pure rationalists or idealists realize by the given equilibrium or disproportion within each type of power and by the balance of various types of power in a given community. It may be taken as axiomatic that great disproportions of power lead to injustice, whatever may be the efforts to mitigate it. Thus the concentration of economic power in modern technical society has made for injustice, while the diffusion of political power has made for justice. The history of modern democratic-capitalistic societies is on the whole determined by the tension between these two forms of power. In this history the economic oligarchy has sought to bend political power to its purposes, but has never done so with complete success. On the other hand the political power of the common man

---

[4] It has been an error in both liberal and Marxist social interpretations to identify ownership with economic power. The control and manipulation of economic process is also a form of economic power. It gives workers minimal power resources to set against the power of ownership; and the managers of economic process are acquiring an even larger share of power. James Burnham's *The Managerial Revolution* is a one-sided correction of the error of identifying ownership with economic power too simply. The error contributes to the political miscalculations of Marxism. For when it abolishes economic ownership it may merely merge both economic and political power in the hands of an oligarchy which controls both political and economic processes.

has been an instrument of political and economic justice; but it has also not succeeded completely in eliminating flagrant forms of economic injustice. This tension is unresolved, and may never be completely resolved. At the moment the justice achieved by this tension in the democratic world is under attack from a tyranny created by the mergence of political, economic and religious power in a Nazi oligarchy and by its more or less intimate partnership with an older military oligarchy.

Political power deserves to be placed in a special category, because it rests upon the ability to use and manipulate other forms of social power for the particular purpose of organizing and dominating the community. The political oligarchy usually possesses at least two forms of significant social power. In all early empires these two forms were the priestly and the military power, which were either merged in one class, or which were combined through intimate collaboration between the military and the priestly class. Modern democracies tend towards a more equal justice partly because they have divorced political power from special social functions. They endowed all men with a measure of it by giving them the right to review the policies of their leaders. This democratic principle does not obviate the formation of oligarchies in society; but it places a check upon their formation, and upon the exercise of their power. It must be observed, however, that the tyrannical oligarchy, which now challenges the democratic world, arrived at its eminence by the primary use of political power (the demagogic manipulation of the masses) and then gradually acquired the other forms of power: the control of economic process, the pretension of religious sanctity, and the control of, or collaboration with, military power.

The shifting interrelations of various types of power in human society are determined by a wide variety of historical developments from the technical to the religious level of social existence. Thus the development of modern commerce gave the middle classes new economic power. They used it to challenge the priestly-military oligarchy of feudal society. They undermined the power of land-

The influence of prophetic religion upon the formation of democratic & oligarchic socie[ties]

ownership with the more dynamic economic power of the ownership of bank stock. The development of modern technical industry had a twofold effect. It both enhanced the economic power and wealth of the owners and manipulators of economic process, and it gave industrial workers a form of power (exercised for instance by their refusal to co-operate in an interrelated economic process) which the common men of agrarian societies did not have. Sometimes a shift in power relations has a much more spiritual origin. Who can deny that the development of prophetic religion, which challenges rather than supports political majesty in the name of the majesty of God, helps to destroy priestly-military oligarchies and to create democratic societies? In this way the prophetic elements in Christianity have contributed to the rise of modern democratic societies, just as conservative elements in the Christian tradition have strengthened the pretensions of oligarchies by their uncritical identification of political power with the divine authority.

The complexity of the technical, rational and prophetic-religious factors which contributed to the rise of modern democracies, illustrates the complex and intimate involvement of all these factors in the whole historical process. The interweaving of these various strands in the total fabric of historical development refutes both vitalists and rationalists, who would interpret the social process either as merely a chaos of vital forces or as a simple progressive triumph of reason over force. "Reason" and "force" may be the "end terms" of human spirituality and vitality. But no sharp distinction can be made between them at any point. Nor are there absolute distinctions between any of the intermediate manifestations of human vitality, which history elaborates in endless variety. No form of individual or social power exists without a modicum of physical force, or without a narrow pinnacle of "spirit" which transcends the conflict and tension of vital forces. But the tension and balance of such forces in any given social situation include vitalities and powers which manifest the complex unity of spirit and nature, of reason and force, in the whole of human existence.

3. *The Organization and Balance of Power*

the point

Our primary concern is with the twofold relation of structures of justice or various forms of communal organization to the principle of brotherhood. These structures invariably contain, according to our analysis, both approximations and contradictions to the ideal of love. This thesis must now be examined more closely in the light of the conclusion that all social life represents a field of vitality, elaborated in many forms, which are related to each other in terms of both mutual support and of potential conflict. Since human history defies, rather than observes, the limits, in which nature confines both mutual dependence and conflict, it becomes a task of conscious political contrivance in human history to mitigate conflict and to invent instruments for the enlarging mutualities of social existence.

Human brotherhood is imperiled by two, and possibly three, forms of corruption. Will seeks to dominate will. Thus imperialism and slavery are introduced into history. Interest comes in conflict with interest and thus the relations of mutual dependence are destroyed. Sometimes the self, individual or collective, seeks to isolate itself from the community and to disavow communal responsibilities. This evil of isolationism is, however, a negative form of the evil of conflict, and therefore does not deserve a special category.

The domination of one life by another is avoided most successfully by an equilibrium of powers and vitalities, so that weakness does not invite enslavement by the strong. Without a tolerable equilibrium no moral or social restraints ever succeed completely in preventing injustice and enslavement. In this sense an equilibrium of vitality is an approximation of brotherhood within the limits of conditions imposed by human selfishness. But an equilibrium of power is not brotherhood. The restraint of the will-to-power of one member of the community by the counter-pressure of power by another member results in a condition of tension. All tension is covert or potential conflict. The principle of the equilibrium of power is thus a principle of justice in so far as it prevents domination and enslavement; but it is a principle of anarchy and conflict in so far as its tensions, if unresolved, result in overt conflict. Furthermore social life. when not consciously managed and manipulated, does not develop perfect equilibria of power. Its capricious disproportions of power generate various forms of domination and enslavement. Human society therefore requires a conscious control and manipulation of the various equilibria which exist in it. There must be an organizing centre within a given field of social vitalities. This centre must arbitrate conflicts from a more impartial perspective than is available to any party of a given conflict; it must manage and manipulate the processes of mutual support so that the tensions inherent in them will not erupt into conflict; it must coerce submission to the social process by superior power whenever the instruments of arbitrating and composing conflict do not suffice; and finally it must seek to redress the disproportions of power by conscious shifts of the balances whenever they make for injustice.[7]

It is obvious that the principle of government, or the organization of the whole realm of social vitalities, stands upon a higher plane of moral sanction and social necessity than the principle of the balance of power. The latter without the former degenerates into anarchy. The former is, moreover, a more conscious effort to arrive at justice than the latter. It belongs to the order of the historical while the former belongs, on the whole, to the order of the natural.[8]

[7] This is done in the democratic state, for instance, when the taxing power is used not merely for securing revenue but also to counteract the tendency towards centralization of power and privilege which inheres in the technical and highly centralized industrial process.

[8] Rousseau's and Hobbes' social contract theories of government have such contradictory estimates of the "state of nature" because both fail to understand the ambiguous character of social equilibrium without the interference of government. Rousseau sees only the elements of harmony within it, and Hobbes only the elements of conflict and anarchy. Rousseau on the other hand sees only the principle of domination in government and Hobbes only the principle of order.

It is nevertheless important to recognize that government is also morally ambiguous. It contains an element which contradicts the law of brotherhood. The power of the rulers is subject to two abuses. It may actually be the dominion which one portion of the community exercises over the whole of the community. Most governments until a very recent period were in fact just that; they were the consequence of conquest by a foreign oligarchy.[9] But even if government does not express the imperial impulse of one class or group within the community, it would, if its pretensions are not checked, generate imperial impulses of its own towards the community. It would be tempted to destroy the vitality and freedom of component elements in the community in the name of "order." It would identify its particular form of order with the principle of order itself, and thus place all rebels against its authority under the moral disadvantage of revolting against order *per se*. This is the sin of idolatry and pretension, in which all government is potentially involved. This evil can be fully understood only if it is recognized that all governments and rulers derive a part of their power, not only from the physical instruments of coercion at their disposal, but also from the reality and the pretension of "majesty." The uncoerced submission which they achieve, and without which they could not rule (since coerced submission applies only to marginal cases and presupposes the uncoerced acceptance of the ruler's authority by the majority) is never purely "rational" consent. It always includes, explicitly or implicitly, religious reverence for "majesty." The majesty of the state is legitimate in so far as it embodies and expresses both the authority and power of the total community over all its members, and the principle of order and justice as such against the peril of anarchy. The legitimate majesty of government is acknowledged and affirmed in the Christian doctrine of government as a divine ordinance.

[9] The Norman unification of England, the Tartar conquest of Russia and the Manchu conquest of China are a few of the many examples of foreign conquest as the agent of the unification of a society.

But there are no historic expressions of the majesty of state and government without an admixture of illegitimate pretensions of majesty and sanctity. These can be most simply defined as the tendency of states and governments to hide and obscure the contingent and partial character of their rule and to claim unconditioned validity for it.

The whole development of democratic justice in human society has depended upon some comprehension of the moral ambiguities which inhere in both government and the principle of the equilibrium of power. It is the highest achievement of democratic societies that they embody the principle of resistance to government within the principle of government itself. The citizen is thus armed with "constitutional" power to resist the unjust exactions of government. He can do this without creating anarchy within the community, if government has been so conceived that criticism of the ruler becomes an instrument of better government and not a threat to government itself.[10]

The achievements of democracy have been tortuously worked out in human history partly because various schools of religious and political thought had great difficulty in fully comprehending the perils to justice in either one or the other instrument of justice—the organization of power and the balance of power. Usually the school of thought which comprehended the moral ambiguities of government did not understand the perils of anarchy inhering in uncontrolled social life; while those who feared this anarchy were uncritical of the claims and pretensions of government. History had to stumble by tortuous process upon the proper techniques for avoiding both anarchy and tyranny, against the illusions of idealists and of realists who understood only one or the other side of the problem. In this process the Christian tradition itself seldom

---

[10] The Presbyterian constitutionalist of seventeenth-century Scotland, Samuel Rutherford, expresses the distinction in the words: "We teach that government is natural not voluntary; but the way and manner of government is voluntary." *Lex Rex* (1644), Question IX.

stated the full truth of its twofold approach to the political order in such a way that it would give guidance in the complexities of political and social life. The mistakes which were made in comprehending the paradox in the political sphere conform to the limitations of the various Christian and secular traditions, which we have examined in other spheres. They can therefore be stated fairly briefly.

v

THE CHRISTIAN ATTITUDE TO GOVERNMENT

The development of Christian and of modern secular theories of politics is determined by an interplay of one classical and of two Biblical approaches to stuff of the political order. The Bible contains two approaches, which taken together and held in balance, do justice to the moral ambiguities of government. According to the one, government is an ordinance of God and its authority reflects the Divine Majesty. According to the other, the "rulers" and "judges" of the nations are particularly subject to divine judgment and wrath because they oppress the poor and defy the divine majesty. These two approaches do justice to the two aspects of government. It is a principle of order and its power prevents anarchy; but its power is not identical with divine power, It is wielded from a partial and particular locus and it cannot achieve the perfect union of goodness and power which characterizes divine power. The pretension that its power is perfectly virtuous represents its false claim of majesty. This claim elicits alternate moods of reverent obedience and resentful rebellion in history.[1]

---

[1] It is significant that the first Biblical record of the institution of monarchy is interpreted from two perspectives according to two traditions embodied in the book of Samuel. According to the one, Samuel anointed Saul King at the behest of Yahweh (1 Sam. 8:22). According to the other the desire of the people for a king was regarded as an affront to God, who was himself king of his people: "And ye have this day rejected your God, who himself saved you out of all your adversities

The double approach of prophetic criticism and of priestly sanctification of royal or state authority, have armed both conservative and radical schools of Christian thought with plausible proof-texts for their respective positions. Only occasionally is the truth in each position properly appreciated. Unfortunately a single text from St. Paul has done much to destroy the force of the Biblical paradox. St. Paul's very "undialectical" appreciation of government in Romans 13 has had a fateful influence in Christian thought, particularly in the Reformation.[2] But its influence was fortunately never able to

---

and your tribulations; and ye have said unto him, Nay, but set a king over us." 1 Sam. 10:19.

The various expressions of these two approaches towards government cannot be fully traced here. The critical attitude of the prophets towards government has been considered in another context. On the other hand the idea that the King is the Lord's anointed runs through the whole Old Testament as does the appreciation of the necessity of government (*Cf.* Judges 17:6: "In those days there was no king in Israel, but every man did that which was right in his own eyes.").

In the New Testament Jesus on the one hand recognizes the legitimate authority of government ("Render therefore unto Caesar the things that are Caesar's." Mt. 22:21) but on the other hand he sets the dominion of kings in contrast to the mutual love and service of the Kingdom of God ("The kings of the Gentiles exercise lordship over them . . . but ye shall not be so: but he that is greatest among you, let him be as the younger; and he that is chief, as he that doth serve." Luke 22:25–26).

[2] Romans 13:1–3: "Let every soul be subject unto the higher powers. For there is no power but of God: the powers that be are ordained of God. Whosoever therefore resisteth the power, resisteth the ordinance of God . . . for the rulers are not a terror to good works, but to the evil."

This unqualified endorsement of government and the unqualified prohibition of resistance to its authority is justified by the mistaken assertion that government is no peril to virtue but only to vice. History proves that the power of government is morally ambiguous. It may on occasion imperil not evil but "good works." The best possible government cannot completely escape from such a possibility. It must be recognized that the Pauline justification of government was valid enough in the particular historical context in which it was made. It was undoubtedly a warning against the irresponsibility towards government which the eschatological mood of the early church encouraged. The fact that it

extinguish the power of prophetic criticism upon the evils of government in Christian history.

As against these two approaches to the political order in the Bible the classical world thought of politics in simpler and more rational terms. Government was primarily the instrument of man's social nature. Its function of preventing anarchy, so strongly emphasized in Christian thought, and so unduly stressed in the Reformation, was appreciated only indirectly. For Aristotle the purpose of government was fellowship (κοινωνία); and Plato studied the state in his *Republic* as a macrocosm which would reveal all the laws of harmony in larger outline relevant to the microcosm of the individual soul.

In both Aristotle and Plato the harmony of society is practically identified with the constitutional structure, the principles by which it is governed. The approach is, in the parlance of modern philosophy, "non-existential." [3] They are always looking for forms and principles of justice, for constitutions and arrangements which will bring the rough vitalities of life under the dominion of the

---

became a vehicle for a too uncritical devotion to government by its indiscriminate application in subsequent centuries illustrates one of the perils of Biblicism. Biblical observations upon life are made in a living relation to living history. When they are falsely given an eminence which obscures this relation, they can become the source of error and confusion.

[3] Aristotle declares that "the constitution (πολιτεία) is the life of the *polis*" (*Politics* VI, iv, 11). In Plato's *Laws* the Athenian Stranger declares: "When there has been a contest of power, those who gain the upper hand so entirely monopolize the government as to refuse all share to the defeated party. . . . Now according to our view such governments are not polities at all nor are laws right which are passed for the good of particular classes and not for the good of the whole state. . . . That state in which the law is subject and has no authority, I perceive to be on the highway to ruin; and that state in which the rulers are the inferiors of the law has salvation."

The idea that the practices of states must conform to rules and principles of justice is of course tenable and necessary. But both Plato and Aristotle underestimate the dynamic and vital elements in the political order. They obscure the fact that political life is a contest of power, no matter by what laws it is governed.

logos. They do not of course trust the mere force of law to do this. But when they look for the best human agencies to interpret, apply and enforce the principles of law, and try to construct some transcendent vantage point from which government may operate against the conflicts of partial interests (in the case of Aristotle particularly against the conflict between rich and poor) they find it in some class of virtuous and rational men. It is the superior reason of such men or their specialized knowledge in affairs of government, which endows them with the virtue of disinterestedness. Greek political theory believes in other words in an *élite class.* The perils of anarchy according to classical thought arise primarily from the ignorance of common citizens who are unable to comprehend the total needs of the community. Plato seeks to cultivate the disinterestedness of the rulers by semi-ascetic disciplines, as well as by rational excellency. In any case the realm of politics, as a field of vitality and as a contest of power is inadequately comprehended. The Stoic theory, particularly in its distinction between the absolute and the relative natural law, comes closer to the realities of politics. But even the Stoics, and particularly the Roman Stoics, have a too optimistic conception of the political order. Cicero gave a highly moralistic account of politics in general and of Roman imperialism in particular. He regarded the state as a compact of justice, and had little understanding of the power realities which underlie the compact.

The Christian ages, after the dissipation of the eschatological hope and the concomitant political irresponsibility of the early church, worked out a political ethic in which gospel perfectionism and Biblical realism were combined with classical (particularly Stoic) optimism. Augustine was the first to introduce a new and more Pauline note into this field of thought, as he did in so many other fields. Making the criticism of Ciceronian rationalism and optimism his point of departure he denied that the state is a compact of justice, and insisted that "there is not any justice in any commonwealth whatsoever but in that whereof Christ is the founder and ruler."⁴ He regarded the peace of the world as an uneasy armistice between contending social forces. It is "based on strife." It is not so much justice as "the harmonious enjoyment of that which they love" which holds the *civitas* together.⁵ Such a morally neutral definition of political cohesion allows Augustine to compare the harmony of the state with the harmony which thieves maintain among themselves and to suggest that there may be little difference except size, between a state and a robber band.⁶

Augustine sees the social life of man as constantly threatened either by conflict between contending forces, held in an uneasy equilibrium, or by the tyranny of the dominant power which "lays a yoke of obedience upon its fellows." This interpretation may not do full justice to the constructive elements of order in either the Roman Empire or in any *res publica* or commonwealth of history. He may

⁴ *De civ. Dei,* Book II, ch. 21.
⁵ *De civ. Dei,* Book XIX, ch. 24.
⁶ *Ibid.,* IV, 4. See A. J. Carlyle's *Medieval Political Theory in the West.* Vol. I, pp. 165–170. C. H. McIlvain is not certain that Carlyle's interpretation of Augustine's departure from the political theories of St. Ambrose and the other Fathers is correct. *Cf.* McIlvain: *The Growth of Political Thought in the West,* p. 155. However, Augustine's position is made clear in other than the particular passages in which he distinguishes between Cicero's conception of the *res publica* and his own. For instance he compares the social order of the state with the divine order, not in terms of justice but in terms of order created by power: "For herein is perverse pride the imitator of the goodness of God, laying a yoke of obedience upon its fellows under itself instead of God; thus hates it a just peace of God and builds an unjust one for itself." *De civ. Dei,* XIX, 12. This is the same point made by Biblical prophetism against the pretension of kings.

He regards the peace established in various earthly realms as good, so far as it goes, but as unstable. "Wretched are they that are strangers to God; and yet have they a kind of allowable peace, but they will not have it forever for they used it not well while they had it" (*Ibid.,* XIX, 26). It is always threatened either by civil war or by imperialistic ventures which know no limits: "For any part [of the civitas terrena] which wars against the other desires to be the world's conqueror. . . ." And if it conquer it extols itself and so becomes its own destruction." *Ibid.,* XV, 4.

have taken the conditions of a declining, rather than a more healthy, Roman Empire as definitive; and he may have sharpened the contrast too much between the *civitas Dei* and the *civitas terrena,* so as to produce a perfect antithesis between the love of God in the one and the love of self in the other. But despite these errors of overemphasis, the Augustinian conception of the political order gives a much truer picture of both the dynamic and the anarchic elements in political life than classical political theories.

Despite Augustine's great authority, his political realism had only a moderate influence on the course of medieval political theory. The latter incorporated a much larger classical element than is evident in Augustine's thought. Medieval Catholicism succeeded in fact in creating as imposing a synthesis in the realm of political theory as in other fields of thought. The synthesis is still superior to many alternative systems which have developed since the destruction of the synthesis; but it is, of course, subject to the general limitations of its larger principles of synthesis.

Medieval political theory manages to incorporate both strands of Biblical thought with classical perspectives. The prophetic-Biblical criticism upon the injustice and the pride of rulers is never lacking; but unfortunately it becomes the instrument of the papal-ecclesiastical claim of dominion. The Stoic-Christian idea that government is a requirement of the relative, rather than of the absolute, natural law, prevents the inequalities and the coercive necessities of government from being regarded as finally normative. The distinction preserves a minimal note of criticism upon government. There is thus a moderate medieval constitutionalism which makes the ruler subject to both natural law and to civil law.[7]

The authority of the ruler and the idea of necessity of govern-

[7] To civil law because the natural law implies a covenant of justice between the ruler and the people. According to Carlyle medieval constitutionalism represents an unbroken tradition until the fifteenth century and does not allow the idea of the absolute and unconditioned rights of the ruler to arise. Carlyle, *op. cit.,* Vol. VI.

ment is upheld at the same time both by Biblical authority and by the Stoic idea of government as a necessity in an imperfect world. The more classical element in medieval political thought is revealed in an essentially rationalistic approach to political problems, tending to obscure the tension of vitalities and interests as a perennial factor in all social life. The peril of tyranny, inherent in the power of the state, is not regarded as arising inevitably from its nature as a centre of power, and from the natural inclination of power, including state power, to become excessive. Instead medieval theory makes moralistic and too absolute and clear-cut distinctions between the justice and tyranny of rulers.[8] It does not comprehend that the justice and peace which the power of the state achieves is always subject to some degree of corruption by reason of the inordinate character of this power, and the particular interests of the ruler.

Medieval constitutionalism contains abundant moral justification for resistance to tyranny but the idea is not implemented politically and Lord Acton is therefore slightly extravagant in regarding Aquinas as the fountain of democratic theory.[9] Medieval theory failed to comprehend the political order as a vast realm of mutually dependent and conflicting powers and interests, and to appreciate the contingent and relative character of any "justice" which might be achieved at a given moment by the power of government and by the specific equilibria of forces existing at that moment. This failure was one cause of its inability to deal realistically with the new

[8] Aquinas defines tyranny as "ruling which is not directed to the common good of the multitude but rather to the private good of the ruler." *De regimine principum.*

[9] Aquinas did believe that the people had the right to appoint the king and therefore an equal right to depose him (*De regimine principum* I, 6). John of Salisbury even justified regicide as a remedy for tyranny. This critical attitude towards the injustices of government is far superior to modern theories of state absolutism; but it is not democratic in the sense that it provides no constitutional means of resisting the inordinate claims of government or of placing its power under continued popular scrutiny. *Cf.* McIlvain, *op. cit.,* pp. 326–28.

forces, and the consequent disbalances introduced into the medieval political economy by rising commerce.[10]

With the decay of the medieval synthesis, the various elements in the compound of political thought took their own more consistent way, as was the case in other realms of thought. Many of the new political theories may be less true, and are certainly less balanced, than the more comprehensive medieval interpretation of the political order. But most of them contain facets of truth which do more justice to the highest possibilities and the darkest realities of the political order than was possible in the medieval synthesis.

The Renaissance in its secular streams of thought developed two fundamental tendencies. The one embodied the rationalistic-optimistic approach to the problem. We cannot trace this tendency in all of its elaborations. It is expressed in the many varieties of the "liberal" approach to politics. In some of them the *laissez-faire* thesis predominates. It is believed to be a simple matter to achieve a stable equilibrium of social interests if only the inordinate power of government is eliminated. In others the power of government is regarded as a simple rational authority over rational men, which will become more just and more universal as reason is extended.

One contemporary fruit of this stream of Renaissance thought consists in theories of world government, according to which the self-will and moral autonomy of nations could be destroyed by the

[10] A modern Catholic historian regrets that Catholicism was so long in overcoming the influence of Augustinian pessimism, and thinks that the essential optimism of Thomas Aquinas came just a little too late to save the structure of medievalism (*Cf.* Alois Demph, *Sacrum Imperium*, p. 30). An absolutely contradictory thesis would come as near to the truth. The optimism of medievalism prevented it from comprehending the tendency towards decay and disintegration in any social structure. The medieval church sought, according to Troeltsch, for "a perpetuation of the relatively satisfactory situation in which the relative values of the social order are crowned by the absolute values of the institution of grace." Ernst Troeltsch, *Social Teachings of the Christian Churches*, Vol. I, p. 326.

simple expedient of depriving the sovereignty of nations of its legal sanctity.[11] Other theorists are slightly more realistic and hold that international government must be supported by predominant power. But they would create the central pool of power abstractly by some kind of social contract between the nations, without reference to the organic and vital processes through which equilibria of power and the centralization of power are actually effected in history.

The Renaissance movement, however, developed another stream of thought which appropriated some of the insights of Christian realism and pessimism. It recognized the perils of conflict in the dynamic elements of social existence; but it was prompted by these insights to elaborate absolutistic theories of the state. It failed, in other words, to appropriate any of the prophetic-critical elements in the Christian tradition. To this strain of thought we must, in cursory terms, assign Machiavelli, Thomas Hobbes, Jean Bodin, in some respects Hegel and Bosanquet, and of course a host of other lesser men. Sometimes as in the case of Machiavelli, the political pessimism degenerates into moral cynicism. Marxism has the distinction of being the only pessimistic-realistic school of thought in the modern period which directs its realism against the moral ambiguities of the power of government, rather than upon the perils of social anarchy which government is designed to mitigate.

The strong Biblical basis of sectarian radicalism makes it advisable to consider it in this context in juxtaposition to the orthodox Reformation, rather than in relation to the Renaissance movement. So conceived Protestant Christian theories of politics, in their totality, describe a full arc from the extreme pessimism of the Lutheran Reformation to the extreme optimism of the more radical sects; from the uncritical sanctification of government in Luther to the uncritical rejection of government, as such, in the anarchistic sects; from the uncritical acceptance of inequality as a consequence and

[11] Cf. *inter alia*, G. Niemeyer, *Law Without Force*.

remedy for sin in Luther, to the uncritical belief in equality as a simple historical possibility in the communistic sects. In this wide variety of thought the greatest contribution to democratic justice was made by those Protestant groups which came closest to an understanding of both the vice and the necessity of government and both the peril and the necessity of a free interplay of social forces. Among those who came nearest to this understanding were moderate Anglicans who combined Catholic with Renaissance perspectives and whose political theories are most systematically expressed in the thought of Thomas Hooker; semi-sectarian movements like English Independency; and finally the later Calvinists, who rescued Calvinism from its earlier and too consistent pessimism.

This rather sweeping judgment demands historical substantiation, though the limits of this treatise necessarily restrict the analysis of the vast historical material.

Luther's uncritical moral and religious sanctification of the power of government (particularly based upon Romans 13) has been previously considered. It prevented Lutheranism from having any vital relationship with the development of democratic justice in the modern world, with the possible exception of the Scandinavian countries.[12] The development of political theory in modern radical Reformation thought is instructive because Barth is on the whole more Lutheran than Calvinistic in his approach to political questions. He has been Lutheran, at least in his general indifference towards problems of political justice, though he has not quite shared Luther's uncritical acceptance of political authority. His strong emotional reaction to Nazi tyranny has, however, persuaded him to change his emphasis. He now criticizes the Reformation for having regarded government as an ordinance of divine providence without at the same time setting it under the judgment of God. Nevertheless

[12] I say "with the possible exception of the Scandinavian countries" because I have been unable to find authoritative material on the relation between the impressive development of constitutional democracy in Scandinavia and the dominant Lutheran religion.

the influence of Reformation perspectives is so powerful in his thought that his doctrinal justification for his opposition to Nazi tyranny is hardly sufficient to explain that opposition.[13]

As against the uncritical sanctification of established political authority, and the pessimistic acceptance of coercion, inequality and conflict as necessary conditions in a sinful world in Lutheranism, sectarian Protestantism in its many forms manages to express all the various aspects of the critical-prophetic strain of Christian thought.

In the more extreme sects this is done to the point of obscuring the other side of the truth. The perils of government are appreciated, but not its necessity. The contradiction between the majesty of government and the majesty of God is emphasized; but the legitimate majesty of government is not apprehended.[14] Usually the failure to appreciate the necessity of government is derived from per-

[13] Barth defines a just state [*Rechtsstaat*] as follows: "It will realize its own potentialities insofar as it gives the church the freedom [to preach the gospel of justification]. . . . What human justice is cannot be measured by some romantic or liberal conception of natural rights but purely by the concrete right of the freedom which the church must claim for its word, insofar as it is God's word." *Rechtfertigung und Recht*, p. 46.

This is a very minimal contribution to the problem of justice in the state. The freedom to preach the gospel of justification means of course that the state would thereby permit the word of divine judgment to be spoken against its pride and pretensions. But none of the intermediate problems of justice are illumined by this final word of judgment.

In his letter to British Christians Barth declares that "it was probably wise of the government to *allow* [*sic*] the British public to discuss peace aims" but he thinks that "British Christians should . . . take as little advantage of this *permission* as possible." *This Christian Cause*.

[14] In the "Certain Queries Presented by Many Christian People" to Lord Fairfax, Lord General of the Army of Parliament, he is warned: "not to take that honour to yourselves that is due to Christ, nor be instrumental in setting up a mere natural and worldly government . . . whereby the public interest of Jesus Christ will be banished." Quoted by Arthur S. Woodhouse: *Puritanism and Liberty*, p. 242.

George Fox's indictment of the "magistrates" as "usurpers" reveals the same uncritical lack of appreciation of the necessity of government.

fectionist illusions in regard to human nature and human society.[15] Sometimes government is accepted; but the libertarian emphasis is so strong that all coercive acts of government are morally repudiated.[16]

Sometimes the requirements of the absolute natural law, the ideals of liberty and equality, were rightly restored as principles of criticism and final judgment upon all relative justice and injustice in history; but the inevitability of relative distinctions in history is usually not understood. The eighteenth-century secular theory of equality as a simple "law of nature" is rooted in seventeenth-century sectarian theory.[17] The sect of "Diggers" anticipated, and may have inspired, the Marxist theory of government as primarily a tool of the privileged classes.[18]

Though the extremer sects always went too far in challenging either the pessimism of the Reformation or the circumspection of

[15] Many forms of American liberal-Protestant perfectionism are implicitly anarchistic in their social theories, as they are explicitly sanctificationist in their theories of redemption. *Cf. inter alia:* E. Stanley Jones, *Christ's Alternative to Communism.*

[16] This position is taken for instance by the "Leveller" sect. Its leader, John Lilburne, declared: "It is unnatural, irrational, sinful, wicked, unjust, devilish and tyrannical for any man whatsoever spiritual or temporal, clergyman or layman, to appropriate or assume unto himself power, authority and jurisdiction to rule, govern, or reign over any sort of men in the world without their free consent." From a *Freeman's Freedom Vindicated* (1646). The idea is legitimate if it means the "free" acceptance of the authority of government in general. But in sectarianism it frequently excluded the coercive power of government in specific instances, thus making for anarchism.

[17] *Cf.* Woodhouse, *op. cit.,* pp. 68–69.

[18] *Cf.* David Petegorsky, *Left-Wing Democracy in the English Civil War.* The theory is of course partly right in the sense that oligarchies tend to seek their own advantage. It is wrong, however, in the sense that the corruption of a principle cannot explain the principle. The special privileges of a ruling class were the fruits of their special power. Their special power was partly derived from the necessity of government in the community, which they supplied, however imperfectly. The necessity of government, by which special privilege is created, is antecedent to the corruption of government.

Catholic theories, they did of course provide much of the leaven of modern democratic development. But the more inclusive and comprehensive conceptions of political life were developed by the semisectarian Separatists (Roger Williams), the Independents (John Milton) and by the later Calvinists.

calvinistic political theory

The development of Calvinistic thought from a conservative justification of political authority to a living relation with democratic justice deserves special consideration because, in its final form, Calvinistic theory probably came closest to a full comprehension of all the complexities of political justice.

The earlier Calvin was almost as uncritical as Luther in his sanctification of state authority and in his prohibition of resistance to it.[19] Fortunately he permitted some exceptions to this position. He, himself, extended these to some degree under the stress of history, and later Calvinists developed them into a full-orbed democratic outlook. He allowed disobedience, though not resistance, if the political authority came in conflict with God's demands upon the conscience;[20] and he objected only to private and not official resistance to the authority of the ruler. The "lower magistrates" were not only allowed, but enjoined, to resist the tyranny of kings. It was a simple matter for later Calvinists to think of any elected representatives of the people as lower magistrates, who resisted tyranny officially and not privately.

The later Dutch, French and Scottish Calvinists distinguished

[19] *Cf. Inst.*, IV, xx. "Wherefore if we are cruelly vexed by an inhuman prince or robbed and plundered by one avaricious . . . let us remember our offenses against God which are doubtless chastised by these plagues . . . and let us consider that it is not for us to remedy these evils . . . but to implore the aid of God in whose hands are the hearts of kings . . ."

[20] *Inst.*, IV, xx, 32. "But in that obedience . . . due to rulers . . . we must always make this exception . . . that it be not incompatible with obedience to Him, to whose will . . . kings should be subject."
It must be admitted that this qualification did not have the force it might have had because it was applied narrowly. It meant that men must not allow rulers to interfere with their profession of the right religion.

between government as an ordinance of God's providence and the particular form of government which might obtain at a given moment. Thus they freed the religious conscience from undue reverence for any particular government and established a critical attitude towards it; while yet preserving religious reverence for the principle of government. They understood, as the proponents of the secular social contract theory of government did not, that it is not within the power of conscious human will to create government. The formation of government and statehood belongs to the slow processes of the ages and its roots are antecedent to any human decision. Government deserves reverence not only because it is necessary but because it is a gift which man did not consciously contrive. But unlike Calvin the later Calvinists did understand the importance of human action in the formation of particular governments and the responsibility of men for the achievement of justice.[21]

Calvin believed that kings had a covenant with God to rule justly and the people had a covenant with God to obey. But he denied that this double covenant implied a contract between the ruler and the people. It was a simple matter for later Calvinists to insist that this covenant was triangular, between the ruler, the people, and God; that it was a covenant of justice; and that if the ruler broke it by injustice, the people were absolved of obedience.[22] Thus justice,

[21] Calvin declared that "the correction of unbridled governments" is a "revengement of the Lord" and "it is not committed to us to whom is given no other commandment but to obey and to suffer" (*Inst.*, IV, xx). In contrast Samuel Rutherford, the Scottish constitutionalist, declared: "It is not in men's free will that they have government or no government . . . or to obey or not to obey the acts of the court of nature, which is God's court." But he advised that we must "distinguish between the power of government and the power of government by magistracy." The latter the people may "measure out by ounce weights . . . no more and no less, so that they may limit, moderate and set banks and marches to the exercise," . . . they "may give it out . . . upon this and this condition." *Lex Rex*, iii, iv (1644).

[22] In the words of Rutherford: "There is an oath betwixt the king and his people laying on by a reciprocation of hands, mutual civil obligation of the people to the king and the king to the people." *Ibid.*

In the important French Huguenot, anonymous tract *Vindiciae con-*

Summary of Development — early Reformation — undue/uncritical reverence for political authority; later Reformation democratic criticism as the instrument of justice —
Rom. 13 interpreted relatively

§ v]   *The Christian Attitude to Government*   283

rather than mere order and peace, became the criterion for government; and democratic criticism became the instrument of justice.[23]
The difference between the democratic temper of later Calvinism
and the undue and uncritical reverence for political authority in the
early Reformation, both Lutheran and Calvinistic, is well illustrated
in John Knox's interpretation of Romans 13. Being asked how he
could square his defiance of royal authority with this scriptural
injunction in Romans 13, he answered: "The power in that place is
not to be understood as the unjust commandment of men but the
just power wherewith God hath armed his magistrates and lieu-
tenants to punish sin." Advised that this interpretation implied
that subjects could control and judge their rulers, he replied: "And
what harm should the commonwealth receive if the corrupt affection of ignorant rulers be moderated and bridled by the wisdom
and discretion of Godly subjects so that they would not do violence
to any man?" [24]

Too much must not be claimed for either later Calvinism or *warns*
Independency in establishing democratic justice in the Anglo-Saxon
world. The vindication of the right of self-government and the
elaboration of effective constitutional forms for the expression of the
right, was the fruit of many secular, as well as religious, movements. But the secular movements were inclined to libertarianism
in their reaction to the evils of government; or to base their democratic theories upon the idea of the goodness of human nature; and

---

tra tyrannos (1579) the same argument is advanced: "It is certain that
the people require a performance of covenants . . . The people ask the
king whether he will govern justly. He promises he will. Then the
people answer, and not before, that whilst he govern uprightly, they
will obey faithfully. The king promises . . . the which failing to be
accomplished the people are quit of their promises."

[23] It is not possible in this context to trace the development of the
idea of democratic election of rulers from the idea of the right of resistance. Samuel Rutherford argues that since even royalists admit the
right of the people to elect inferior magistrates in the cities, "ergo many
cities have the power to create a higher ruler; for royal power is but the
united and superlative power of inferior judges." *Ibid.*

[24] John Knox, *History* II, 282.

a good theory for Elders of the church to go by!

consequently to underestimate the perils of anarchy, while they directed their attention to the perils of tyranny.[25]

Whatever may be the source of our insights into the problems of the political order, it is important both to recognize the higher possibilities of justice in every historic situation, and to know that the twin perils of tyranny and anarchy can never be completely overcome in any political achievement. These perils are expressions of the sinful elements of conflict and dominion, standing in contradiction to the ideal of brotherhood on every level of communal organization. There is no possibility of making history completely safe against either occasional conflicts of vital interests (war) or against the misuse of the power which is intended to prevent such conflict of interests (tyranny). To understand this is to labor for higher justice in terms of the experience of justification by faith. Justification by faith in the realm of justice means that we will not regard the pressures and counter pressures, the tensions, the overt and the covert conflicts by which justice is achieved and maintained, as normative in the absolute sense; but neither will we ease our conscience by seeking to escape from involvement in them. We will know that we cannot purge ourselves of the sin and guilt in which we are involved by the moral ambiguities of politics without also disavowing responsibility for the creative possibilities of justice.

VI

JUSTICE AND WORLD COMMUNITY

In the crisis of world history in which we stand, we have a particularly vivid example of the twofold character of all historic political tasks and achievements. The economic interdependence of the world places us under the obligation, and gives us the possibility,

[25] American constitutionalism owes more to the circumspection of James Madison's essentially Calvinistic approach to the problems of government than to Thomas Jefferson's simple libertarianism. Jefferson as a statesman more frequently acted, in fact, upon Madison's presuppositions than upon his own.

of enlarging the human community so that the principle of order
and justice will govern the international as well as the national
community. We are driven to this new task by the lash of fear as
well as by the incitement of hope. For our civilization is undone
if we cannot overcome the anarchy in which the nations live. This
new and compelling task represents the positive side of historical
development and reveals the indeterminate possibilities of good in
history.

Unfortunately, however, many of the idealists who envisage this
new responsibility think they can fulfill it best by denying the
perennial problems of the political order. They think that world
government is possible without an implied hegemony of the stronger
powers. This hegemony is inevitable; and so is the peril of a new
imperialism, which is inherent in it. The peril can best be overcome
by arming all nations great and small with constitutional power to
resist the exactions of dominant power. This is to say that the principle of the balance of power is implied in the idea of constitutional
justice. But if the central and organizing principle of power is
feared too much, and the central authority is weakened, then the
political equilibrium degenerates once more to an unorganized
balance of power. And an unorganized balance of power is potential
anarchy.

Thus we face all the old problems of political organization on the
new level of a potential international community. The new international community will be constructed neither by the pessimists,
who believe it impossible to go beyond the balance of power principle in the relation of nations to each other; nor by the cynics, who
would organize the world by the imposition of imperial authority
without regard to the injustices which flow inevitably from arbitrary
and irresponsible power; nor yet by the idealists, who are under the
fond illusion that a new level of historic development will emancipate history of these vexing problems.

The new world must be built by resolute men who "when hope
is dead will hope by faith"; who will neither seek premature escape

from the guilt of history, nor yet call the evil, which taints all their achievements, good. There is no escape from the paradoxical relation of history to the Kingdom of God. History moves towards the realization of the Kingdom but yet the judgment of God is upon every new realization.

CHAPTER X

THE END OF HISTORY

Everything in human life and history moves towards an end. By reason of man's subjection to nature and finiteness this "end" is a point where that which exists ceases to be. It is *finis*. By reason of man's rational freedom the "end" has another meaning. It is the purpose and goal of his life and work. It is *telos*. This double connotation of end as both *finis* and *telos* expresses, in a sense, the whole character of human history and reveals the fundamental problem of human existence. All things in history move towards both fulfillment and dissolution, towards the fuller embodiment of their essential character and towards death. *The problem*

The problem is that the end as *finis* is a threat to the end as *telos*. Life is in peril of meaninglessness because *finis* is a seemingly abrupt and capricious termination of the development of life before it has reached its true end or *telos*. The Christian faith understands this aspect of the human situation. It shares an understanding of the tension between time and eternity with all other religions. But it asserts that it is not within man's power to solve the vexing problem of his subjection to, and partial freedom from, the flux of time. It holds, furthermore, that evil is introduced into history by the very effort of men to solve this problem by their own resources.

The evil thus introduced by the "false eternals" of human pride complicates the problem of historical fulfillment. The culmination of history must include not merely the divine completion of human incompleteness but a purging of human guilt and sin by divine judgment and mercy.

We have previously considered the implications of the revelation of God in Christ for the interpretation of history, and sought to establish that the Kingdom of God as it *has come* in Christ means a disclosure of the meaning of history but not the full realization of that meaning. That is anticipated in the Kingdom which *is to come,* that is, in the culmination of history. It must be remembered that a comprehension of the meaning of life and history from the standpoint of the Christian revelation includes an understanding of the contradictions to that meaning in which history is perennially involved.

Such an understanding by faith means that the world is in a sense already "overcome"; for none of the corruptions of history, its fanaticisms and conflicts, its imperial lusts and ambitions, its catastrophes and tragedies, can take the faithful completely unaware.[1] The light of revelation into the meaning of life illumines the darkness of history's self-contradictions, its fragmentary realizations of meaning and its premature and false completions. But obviously such a faith points to an *end* in which history's incompleteness and corruption is finally overcome. Thus history as we know it is regarded as an "interim" between the disclosure and the fulfillment of its meaning. Symbolically this is expressed in the New Testament in the hope that the suffering Messiah will "come again" with "power and great glory."[2] Men shall "see the Son of man sitting on the right hand of power, and coming in the clouds of heaven."[3]

---

[1] *Cf.* 1 Thess. 5:3-6. "For when they shall say, Peace and safety: then sudden destruction cometh upon them, as travail upon a woman with child. . . . But ye, brethren, are not in darkness, that *the day should overtake you* as a thief. Ye are all the children of light. . . . Therefore . . . let us watch and be sober."

[2] Mt. 24:30.

[3] Mt. 26:64 and Mk. 13:26.

2nd coming – not to be taken literally – (but as a symbol.) pointing from the conditioned to the ultimate but are to be taken seriously.

§ 11]   *The New Testament Idea of the End*   289

II

THE NEW TESTAMENT IDEA OF THE END

This hope of the *parousia* in New Testament thought is sometimes dismissed as no more than a projection of those elements of Jewish apocalypse to which the first coming of Christ did not conform and for the satisfaction of which a "second coming" had to be invented. On the other hand they have frequently been taken literally and have thus confused the mind of the church. The symbol of the second coming of Christ can neither be taken literally nor dismissed as unimportant. It participates in the general characteristic of the Biblical symbols, which deal with the relation of time and eternity, and seek to point to the ultimate from the standpoint of the conditioned. If the symbol is taken literally the dialectical conception of time and eternity is falsified and the ultimate vindication of God over history is reduced to a point in history. The *[fallacy of millen-talism]* consequence of this falsification is expressed in the hope of a millennial age. In such a millennial age, just as in a utopian one, history is supposedly fulfilled despite the persisting conditions of finiteness. On the other hand if the symbol is dismissed as unimportant, as merely a picturesque or primitive way of apprehending the relation of the historical to the eternal, the Biblical dialectic is obscured in another direction. All theologies which do not take these symbols seriously will be discovered upon close analysis not to take history seriously either. They presuppose an eternity which annuls rather than fulfills the historical process.

The Biblical symbols cannot be taken literally because it is not possible for finite minds to comprehend that which transcends and fulfills history. The finite mind can only use symbols and pointers of the character of the eternal. These pointers must be taken seriously nevertheless because they express the self-transcendent character of historical existence and point to its eternal ground. The symbols which point towards the consummation from within the temporal flux cannot be exact in the scientific sense of the word.

They are inexact even when they merely define the divine and eternal ground of history in terms of contrast to the temporal. They are even more difficult to understand when they seek to express the Biblical idea of an eternity involved in, and yet transcending, the temporal.

The *eschata* or "last things" in New Testament symbolism are described in three fundamental symbols: the return of Christ, the last judgment and the resurrection. They must be considered in order.

1. *The Parousia*

The idea of the return of the triumphant Christ dominates the other two symbols. The judgment and the resurrection are a part of the vindication of God in the return of Christ. To believe that the suffering Messiah will return at the end of history as a triumphant judge and redeemer is to express the faith that existence cannot ultimately defy its own norm. Love may have to live in history as suffering love because the power of sin makes a simple triumph of love impossible. But if this were the ultimate situation it would be necessary either to worship the power of sin as the final power in the world or to regard it as a kind of second God, not able to triumph, but also strong enough to avoid defeat.[1]

The vindication of Christ and his triumphant return is therefore an expression of faith in the sufficiency of God's sovereignty over the world and history, and in the final supremacy of love over all the forces of self-love which defy, for the moment, the inclusive harmony of all things under the will of God.

This return of Christ stands at the "end" of history in such a way that it would sometimes appear to be a triumph in history and to mean a redeemed temporal-historical process. But according to

[1] In Zoroastrianism, the only other historical religion beside Judaism and Christianity, this dualistic conclusion is actually drawn and history is conceived as an equal battle between the good and evil God. But even in Zoroastrianism the good God triumphs in the end.

the final consummation lies
beyond the conditions of the temporal process
yet fulfills rather than negates, the histor-
ical process

§ 11]   *The New Testament Idea of the End*   291

other, and usually later, interpretations, the fulfillment of the historical process is also its end in the quantitative sense; and the redemption of history would appear to be its culmination also. This twofold aspect of the final vindication of Christ implies a refutation in Biblical faith of both utopianism and a too consistent otherworldliness. Against utopianism the Christian faith insists that the final consummation of history lies beyond the conditions of the temporal process. Against other-worldliness it asserts that the consummation fulfills rather than negates, the historical process. There is no way of expressing this dialectical concept without running the danger of its dissolution. The dissolution has, in fact, taken place again and again in Christian history. Those who believed in the simple fulfillment of history have been arrayed against those who believed that historical existence was robbed of its meaning in the final consummation. Both parties to the debate used Christian symbols to express their half-Christian convictions.

If we analyse the meaning of the two subordinate symbols of the "last judgment" and the resurrection it becomes clear that, according to Biblical faith, some aspects of history are refuted more positively while the meaning of historical existence as such is affirmed more unequivocally than in alternative conceptions.

2. *The Last Judgment*

The symbol of the last judgment[2] in New Testament eschatology contains three important facets of the Christian conception of life and history. The first is expressed in the idea that it is Christ who will be the judge of history. Christ as judge means that when the

[2] *Cf.* Mt. 25:31 ff. "When the Son of man shall come in his glory, and all the holy angels with him, then shall he sit upon the throne of his glory: and before him shall be gathered all nations; and he shall separate them one from another, as a shepherd divideth his sheep from the goats."

II Cor. 5:10: "For we must all appear before the judgment seat of Christ; that every one may receive the things done in his body, according to that he hath done, whether it be good or bad."

historical confronts the eternal it is judged by its own ideal possibility, and not by the contrast between the finite and the eternal character of God.[3] The judgment is upon sin and not finiteness. This idea is in logical accord with the whole Biblical conception of life and history, according to which it is not the partial and particular character of human existence which is evil, but rather the self-love by which men disturb the harmony of creation as it would exist if all creatures obeyed the divine will.

The second facet in the symbol of the last judgment is its emphasis upon the distinction between good and evil in history. When history confronts God the differences between good and evil are not swallowed up in a distinctionless eternity. All historical realities are indeed ambiguous. Therefore no absolute distinction between good and evil in them is possible.[4] But this does not obviate the necessity and possibility of a *final* judgment upon good and evil. To be sure the righteous, standing before the last judgment, do not believe themselves to be righteous,[5] and their uneasy conscience proves the final problem of history to be that, before God, "no man living is justified." There is no solution for this final problem short of the divine mercy and the "forgiveness of sins." We have already noted the import of the Christian doctrine of the Atonement. It affirms that the ultimate mercy does not efface the distinctions between good and evil; for God cannot destroy evil except by taking it into and upon Himself. The very rigour with which all judgments in history culminate in a final judgment is thus an expression of mean-

[3] Augustine interprets the idea that we must be "made manifest before the judgment seat of Christ" as follows: "God the Father will in his personal presence judge no man, but He has given His judgment to His Son who shall show himself *as a man* to judge the world, even as he showed himself as a man to be judged of the world." *De civ. Dei,* Book XIX, ch. 27.

[4] This is the point of the parable of the wheat and the tares, both of which must be allowed to grow until the harvest (final judgment) because they cannot always be distinguished from one another. Mt. 13:24-30.

[5] *Cf.* Vol I, Ch. II.

ingfulness of all historic conflicts between good and evil. Yet the necessity of a "final" judgment upon all other judgments is derived from the ambiguity of these conflicts.

The third facet in the symbol of the last judgment is to be found in its locus at the "end" of history. There is no achievement or partial realization in history, no fulfillment of meaning or achievement of virtue by which man can escape the final judgment. The idea of a "last" judgment expresses Christianity's refutation of all conceptions of history, according to which it is its own redeemer and is able by its process of growth and development, to emancipate man from the guilt and sin of his existence, and to free him from judgment.

Nothing expresses the insecurity and anxiety of human existence more profoundly than the fact that the fear of extinction and the fear of judgment are compounded in the fear of death. The fear of extinction is the fear of meaninglessness. When life is "cut off" before any obvious completion; when *finis* so capriciously frustrates the possibility of achieving *telos,* the very meaningfulness of life is called into question. But before faith can apprehend the divine mercy which completes our incompleteness and forgives our sins it must confront the divine judge. In that confrontation it is not death but sin as the "sting of death" which is recognized as the real peril. For the ending of our life would not threaten us if we had not falsely made ourselves the centre of life's meaning.[6]

[6] In one of the profoundest of the later Jewish apocalypses, the Fourth Ezra, the fear of extinction is compared with the fear of judgment. Judgment is regarded as preferable to mere extinction because it is a part of the consummation of life: "Woe unto those who survive in those days! But much more woe unto those who do not survive. For they that do not survive must be sorrowful knowing, as they do, what things are reserved in the last days but not attaining unto them. But woe also unto them that survive, for this reason, that they must see great peril and many distresses even as these dreams do show. Yet it is *better to come into these things* incurring peril, than to *pass away as a cloud out of the world* and not see what shall happen in the last time." IV Ezra 13:15 ff.

Literalistic conceptions of the allegedly everlasting fires of hell have frequently discredited the idea of a final judgment in the minds of modern Christians. But moral sentimentality in modern Christianity would have probably dissipated the significance of the idea of judgment, even if a literalistic orthodoxy had not seemed to justify the dissipation. It is unwise for Christians to claim any knowledge of either the furniture of heaven or the temperature of hell; or to be too certain about any details of the Kingdom of God in which history is consummated. But it is prudent to accept the testimony of the heart, which affirms the fear of judgment. The freedom of man, by which he both transcends and is creative in history, makes the fear of a judgment beyond all historical judgments inevitable. Many a court of opinion may dismiss us with a: "Well done, thou good and faithful servant"; but we will deceive ourselves if we believe such a judgment to be final. If men are fully aware, they will discern an accent of the fear of judgment in the fear of death. The fear of death arises merely from the ambiguity of finiteness and freedom which underlies all historical existence; but the fear of judgment is prompted by awareness of the mixture of sin and creativity which is the very substance of history.

3. *The Resurrection*

The idea of the resurrection of the body is a Biblical symbol in which modern minds take the greatest offense and which has long since been displaced in most modern versions of the Christian faith by the idea of the immortality of the soul. The latter idea is regarded as a more plausible expression of the hope of everlasting life. It is true of course that the idea of the resurrection transcends the limits of the conceivable; but it is not always appreciated that this is equally true of the idea of an immortal soul. The fact is that the unity of historical existence, despite its involvement in and transcendence over nature, makes it no more possible to conceive transcendent spirit, completely freed of the conditions of nature, than to conceive the conditions of nature transmuted into an eternal consummation. Either idea, as every other idea, which points to the consummation beyond history, is beyond logical conception. The hope of the resurrection nevertheless embodies the very genius of the Christian idea of the historical. On the one hand it implies that eternity will fulfill and not annul the richness and variety which the temporal process has elaborated. On the other it implies that the condition of finiteness and freedom, which lies at the basis of historical existence, is a problem for which there is no solution by any human power. Only God can solve this problem. From the human perspective it can only be solved by faith. All structures of meaning and realms of coherence, which human reason constructs, face the chasm of meaninglessness when men discover that the tangents of meaning transcend the limits of existence. Only faith has an answer for this problem. The Christian answer is faith in the God who is revealed in Christ and from whose love neither life nor death can separate us.

In this answer of faith the meaningfulness of history is the more certainly affirmed because the consummation of history as a human possibility is denied. The resurrection is not a human possibility in the sense that the immortality of the soul is thought to be so. All the plausible and implausible proofs for the immortality of the soul are efforts on the part of the human mind to master and to control the consummation of life. They all try to prove in one way or another that an eternal element in the nature of man is worthy and capable of survival beyond death. But every mystic or rational technique which seek to extricate the eternal element tends to deny the meaningfulness of the historical unity of body and soul; and with it the meaningfulness of the whole historical process with its infinite elaborations of that unity.[7] The consummation of life in these terms

[7] Professor John Baillie has called attention to the fact in his profound study of the Christian hope of everlasting life that the Platonic conception of immortality is but a more philosophical version of the primitive and animistic sense of a shadowy survival after death. Such a survival, according to Professor Baillie, may be convincing but not comforting. *And the Life Everlasting,* Ch. 4.

does not mean the preservation of anything significant in either the individual or the collective life of man in history.

As against these conceptions of consummation in which man denies the significance of his life in history for the sake of affirming his ability to defy death by his own power, the Christian faith knows it to be impossible for man or for any of man's historical achievements to transcend the unity and tension between the natural and the eternal in human existence. Yet it affirms the eternal significance of this historical existence from the standpoint of faith in a God, who has the power to bring history to completion.

In the symbol of the resurrection of the body, the "body" is indicative of the contribution which nature makes to human individuality and to all historical realizations. We have previously noted that human individuality is the product of both the self-consciousness of spirit and the particularity of a finite natural organism.[8] In the same way every cultural and spiritual achievement, every social and political organization in history embodies both natural conditions and normative concepts which transcend and defy the particular and unique situation in which they develop. Climate and geographic limits, poverty and plenty, the survival impulse and sexual desires, and all natural conditions leave their indelible mark upon the spiritual constructions of history. Yet historical achievements transcend these limits in varying degrees of freedom. The doctrine of the immortality of the soul implies that eternal significance can be ascribed only to that element in the historical synthesis which transcends finite conditions. If this implication is followed to its logical conclusion nothing remains in eternity but an undifferentiated unity, free of all particularity and distinctions. We have previously observed how this conclusion is rigorously drawn, particularly in Buddhism and Neo-Platonism.

The doctrine of the resurrection of the body implies that eternal significance belongs to the whole unity of an historical realization in so far as it has brought all particularities into the harmony of the

[8] *Cf.* Vol. I, Ch. III.

whole. Consummation is thus conceived not as absorption into the divine but as loving fellowship with God. Since such a perfect relation with God is not a human possibility it depends upon the mercy and power of God. Christian faith can only trust His mercy to deal with the recalcitrance of sin, even as it trusts His power to overcome the ambiguity of man's finiteness and freedom.

It is important to recognize that the rational difficulties which confront us in the doctrine of the resurrection are not all derived from literalistic corruptions of the doctrine; and they are, therefore, not all surmounted, if literalism is disavowed. Even if we do not believe that, "the earth will give back those that it treasured within it and Sheol will give back that which it had received and hell will return that which it owes" [9] we are still confronted with the formidable difficulty of asserting, what seems logically inconceivable, namely, that eternity will embody, and not annul, finiteness, or, in the words of Baron von Hügel, that the "total abidingness of God" will not destroy our "partial abidingness."

This rational difficulty partly explains the inconsistencies of Jewish apocalyptic writings, which furnished the background of New Testament conceptions. Sometimes they presented the consummation of history as something which occurred on this side of the "end of time." In that case the "resurrection of the just" was believed to usher in a millennial age upon this earth. Sometimes, particularly in the later apocalypses, the fulfillment and the end of history were conceived as coinciding; and all limitations of nature and time were believed to be transcended in the consummation.[10]

The second idea is of course more tenable than the first. But if the

[9] Similitudes of Enoch, 51:2.

[10] Edwyn R. Bevan observes: "As time went on, and the thought of the religious Jews became mature, it was largely realized that no Kingdom of God limited by the essential conditions of earthly life could satisfy the spirit of man." *The Hope of the World to Come,* p. 26.

R. H. Charles makes the same point, believing that eschatological thought gradually yielded to the conviction that "the earth, however purified is no fitting place for an eternal Messianic kingdom." *A Critical History of the Doctrine of the Future Life in Israel,* p. 220.

first had not preceded, and left its mark upon the second, the latter might well have had little to distinguish it from Greek conceptions of immortality. The whole Hebraic-Biblical conception of the unity of body and soul and of the meaningfulness of the historical process was bound to lead to this wrestling of the mind of later Judaism with this insoluble problem. New Testament thought wrestled with it too. St. Paul was convinced that "flesh and blood cannot inherit the kingdom of God; neither doth corruption inherit incorruption." [11] But this conviction did not drive him to the conclusion that everlasting life annuls all historical reality for which "the body" is the symbol. He believed rather that "it is sown a natural body and is raised a spiritual body" and that the consummation means not to "be unclothed, but clothed upon." [12] In that succinct phrase the Biblical hope of a consummation which will sublimate rather than annul the whole historical process is perfectly expressed. It is not possible to give a fuller or more plausible account of what is implied in the Christian hope of the fulfillment of life; and it is well to remember that the conditions of finiteness make a more explicit definition of the consummation impossible. It is therefore important to maintain a decent measure of restraint in expressing the Christian hope. Faith must admit "that it doth not yet appear what we shall be." But it is equally important not to confuse such restraint with uncertainty about the validity of the hope that "when he shall appear, we shall be like him; for we shall see him as he is." [13] The Christian hope of the consummation of life and history is less absurd than alternate doctrines which seek to comprehend and to effect the completion of life by some power or capacity inherent in man and his history. It is an integral part of the total Biblical conception of the meaning of life. Both the meaning and its fulfillment are ascribed to a centre and source beyond ourselves. We can participate in the fulfillment of the meaning only if we do not seek too proudly to appropriate the meaning as our secure possession or to effect the fulfillment by our own power.

[11] I Cor. 15:50. [12] II Cor. 5:4. [13] I John 3:2.

III

THE END AND THE MEANING OF HISTORY

If there are partial realizations of meaning in history, as well as corruptions and distortions, it ought to be possible to discern them from the vantage point of the true end. For this reason a Christian interpretation of human destiny requires one further view of the meaning of history in the light of what is believed about the character of the ultimate consummation. If the final consummation fulfills, rather than annuls, historical meaning, the real content of this meaning must be illumined by the light of faith. Furthermore it must be possible to gain some insight into the character of the sinful corruptions of meaning, particularly since they are mostly derived from the error of regarding partial realizations as the final fulfillment.

Such an examination of history in the light of the Christian interpretation of the end must begin with a distinction between two dimensions in the relation of eternity to time. Eternity stands over time on the one hand and at the end of time on the other. It stands over time in the sense that it is the ultimate source and power of all derived and dependent existence. It is not a separate order of existence. For this reason the traditional connotation of the concept, "supernatural," is erroneous. The eternal is the ground and source of the temporal. The divine consciousness gives meaning to the mere succession of natural events by comprehending them simultaneously, even as human consciousness gives meaning to segments of natural sequence by comprehending them simultaneously in memory and foresight.

Eternity stands at the end of time in the sense that the temporal process cannot be conceived without a *finis;* and eternity cannot be conceived as having a *finis*. Eternity outlasts time, though we know nothing about either an abrupt ending of the world or of the gradual dissipation of its natural energies. Our efforts to picture the relation in spatial terms always leads us astray and prompts us to project a particular point in future time which will also be the end of time. This effort to picture the end of time from inside the time process is the cause of most of the literalistic corruptions of the Christian conception.

The two dimensions of the relation of eternity to time result in two perspectives upon the meaning of history. From the one perspective we discern those qualities and meanings of history which seem to have absolute significance without reference to their relation to the continuum of history. An act of martyrdom or of perfect sacrifice may or may not have discernible historical consequences, and may be appreciated without reference to the consequences. It may "be recorded in heaven" without being obviously recorded on earth. There may also be a "final" judgment upon particular evils in history without waiting for a "last" judgment, *i.e.*, suspending judgment until all its historical consequences have been recorded. On the other hand a "final" judgment about any historical matter may be a judgment which seeks to comprehend a particular event, act or quality in history in the light of its consequences in history. It is not possibile, of course, for finite minds to reach a vantage point from which they could deliver final judgment from either perspective. But their effort to do so is illustrative of the two dimensions of history in its relation to the eternal.[1]

In so far as the freedom of man to be creative in history implies a freedom over history itself, there are tangents of freedom which

[1] It might be well to observe at this point that the synoptic symbol of "The Kingdom of God" is more "existential" than the Johannine and Greek conception of "eternal life." To place "eternity" and "time" in juxtaposition is to distinguish primarily between the flux of process and the principle which underlies the process. The juxtaposition of "Kingdom of God" and history implies a more religious and existential definition of the relationship. The sovereignty of God over all creaturely wills has the same two relations as eternity has to time. It is on the one hand the authority of the source of life over all life at any moment. It is on the other hand a sovereignty which is finally vindicated in "the end."

stand in direct relation to eternity. This dimension of history prompts, and would seem to justify, Leopold von Ranke's famous dictum[2] that each moment of time and history is equidistant from eternity. But the dictum is only partially justified, for it leaves the other dimension of history out of account. History is also a total process which requires understanding of its totality from some "last judgment."[3] In so far as every act and event, every personality and historical construction is immersed in an historical continuum it takes its meaning from the whole process. If we look at history only from "above" we obscure the meaning of its "self-surpassing growth." If we look at it only from a spatially symbolized end we obscure all the richness and variety which is expressed in its many parts.

IV

THE DIVERSITY AND UNITY OF HISTORY

An effort to comprehend the meaning of history from the standpoint of the Christian faith must include three aspects of it: (1) The partial fulfillments and realizations as we see them in the rise and fall of civilizations and cultures; (2) The life of individuals; and (3) The process of history as a whole. In considering these three aspects it will become apparent that the view "from above" must predominate, though it cannot be exclusive, in the consideration of the first two aspects. The view from the "end" must predominate but not be exclusive in viewing history as a whole.

[2] *Cf. Ueber die Epochen der Neueren Geschichte.*

[3] Benedetto Croce seeks to do justice to the two dimensions of the historical in the words: "Every act stands altogether in relation to itself and altogether in relation to something else; it is both a point of repose and a stepping stone; and if it were not so it would be impossible to conceive the self-surpassing growth of history." *History as the Story of Liberty,* p. 90. An act cannot stand only in relation to itself. It must be related to some realm of meaning, but it can transcend the meaning of the historical process.

1. *The Rise and Fall of Cultures and Civilizations*

History is filled with many achievements and constructions which "have their day and cease to be." The rise and fall of empires and civilizations are the most obvious examples of the pluralistic aspect of history, but they are not, by any means, the only manifestations of this aspect. The rise and fall of particular governments and oligarchies within a given civilization, the growth and decline of specific cultural traditions, or of eminent families in a community, or of various types of voluntary associations, or of even more minor historical concretions, are equally illustrative of the pluralism of history.

Whatever meaning is to be found in this pageant of recurring life and death must be discerned primarily, though not wholly, "from above." Each historical configuration may be regarded as an integral realm of meaning, for its relation to the whole historical process is minimal or, at any rate, obscure.

The pluralistic interpretation of history has received a new impetus in recent years by the work of Oswald Spengler and, more recently by Arnold Toynbee's monumental inquiry into the rise and fall of civilizations.[1] These and similar pluralistic interpretations conform to Ranke's principles of historical interpretation, summarized in his conception of the equidistance of all temporal events from the eternal. But even historical pluralism cannot escape the question of comprehensive meaning. It seeks to find some principle of coherence in the rise and fall of various civilizations. Spengler believes that the processes of nature are the only clue to the meaning of the growth and decline of various world cultures. According to his thesis there is no unity in history but the common fate of diverse and incommensurate civilizations. This common fate is governed by the laws of nature. All civilizations pass through ages analogous to spring, summer, autumn and winter; which is to say

[1] Oswald Spengler, *The Decline of the West*. Arnold J. Toynbee, *The Study of History*.

that historical organisms are equated with natural ones. Thus the freedom of history is regarded as either wholly illusory or at least as completely subordinate to nature. It cannot be denied that, since the freedom of history rises on the ground of nature-necessity, historical destiny is always partly determined by the vitality and decay of the natural factors underlying any historical achievement. Empires and cultures may "grow old"; and fail to survive perils in their age which they could have surmounted in their youth.

Yet, as Toynbee points out, the failure of civilizations always involves something more than mere weakness of age. They perish because they make mistakes in meeting some new challenge or complexity of history. Every civilization makes some fatal mistake in the end and perishes. But these mistakes are not under the law of natural necessity. Unlike individual life, the collective and social organisms of history could ideally be perpetually replenished by new life and strength. But this would require that they be perpetually adapted to new historical situations. Their final failure to do so is always a fate into which they are tempted by their freedom and is not due to natural necessity.[2] Sometimes they perish because pride of power prompts them to extend themselves beyond the limits of human possibilities. Sometimes the oligarchy which has been instrumental in organizing a society becomes purely repressive and destroys what it has created. Sometimes the strategies and techniques

[2] It is Toynbee's great merit to see this element of tragic destiny in history where Spengler sees only the organic growth and decay of historical organisms. *Cf. The Study of History*, Vol. IV, particularly pp. 260 ff. Toynbee unnecessarily emphasizes the rôle of a minority, in the period of creativity; and of the degeneration of this minority into a "dominant" minority, maintained by repression, in a period of decay. There are undoubtedly such minorities in all social and political organisms; and in so far as failure and decay is caused by errors in judgment and action they must be attributed particularly to the portion of the community in which its will and mind are articulated. But the causes of the failure are always many. Could the decay of contemporary France be ascribed to the faults of any particular minority only? Does not history point to a much more complex source of such a breakdown?

of yesterday are falsely applied to new situations and problems to which they are not relevant. This mistake may be regarded as a form of the intellectual pride which falsely raises contingent factors in history to the eminence of false absolutes.[3] Sometimes civilizations perish because they are beguiled by philosophies of "detachment." Their spiritual leaders flee prematurely to some illusory realm of supra-historical serenity and equanimity and betray their responsibilities in history.[4] Modern technical civilization may perish because it falsely worshipped technical advance as a final good. One portion of a technical society may harness techniques to the purpose of destruction and vent its fury upon another portion of the civilization, which has grown soft by regarding the comforts yielded in such great abundance by a technical age, as the final good.

If we sought to do full justice to all the various possibilities of decline and causes of decay we would find ourselves merely recapitulating the various types of human sin.[5] They would fall into the two general categories of the sins of sensuality, and the sins of pride. In the former the freedom of history is denied and men creep back to the irresponsibility of nature. In the latter the freedom of man is overestimated. Men seek to complete history without regard to the contingent and finite character of the self, individual or collective, of the culture or civilization, which they make the basis

[3] Toynbee's analysis of this "nemesis of creativity" is very convincing. He defines the confusion of the contingent and the absolute as the "idolization" of "an ephemeral self," of "an ephemeral institution" and "an ephemeral technique." *Ibid.*, Vol. IV, pp. 261 ff.

[4] The weaknesses of the rule of Marcus Aurelius in the declining days of Rome belong in this category. It is significant that the most "saintly" of Roman emperors should have hastened, though he certainly did not initiate, the decline of Rome, under the influence of Stoic idealism which made *apatheia* the final good. Some of the "Christian idealism" of our own day, dreaming of a Kingdom of God which is completely irrelevant to the tragic facts and problems of history, stands in the same relation to the decline of Western civilization. There are other, and profounder, causes of our difficulties. But modern "idealism" has certainly aggravated our problems.

[5] *Cf.* Vol. I, Chs. VII and VIII.

of their pretension. This is the sin of imperialism. Or they seek to abstract human freedom from history. This pride of mystic other-worldliness makes the human spirit, not the master of history but the agent of its own emancipation from history.

All these various forms of historical decline and destruction have one common characteristic. They are not merely biological death. The Augustinian dictum: "It is not by death that we sin but by sin that we die," may be partly untrue when applied to individual life; for individual existence is rooted in a natural organism subject to the conditions of finiteness.[6] But it is a very apt description of the death of civilizations. It is by "sin that they die." They are not determined by absolute natural necessity. Their mistakes and errors are made in the same freedom, out of which their creativity arises. The mistakes are never prompted by mere ignorance. The "vain imagination" of sin is in them.

It would be wrong, however, to view the history of the world's many cultures and civilizations with an eye only upon their decline. They die in the end; but they also live. Their life is a testimony of the creativity of history, even as their death is a proof of the sin in history. The vast variety of historic organisms, the richness of their elaborations of human potentialities, the wealth of their many cultural forms and social configurations are as certainly a testimony to the divine providence under which they have grown, as their destruction is a vindication of the eternal judgment, which they are unable to defy with impunity. In their weakness and youth, while making their way in history against all the perils of life, they are revelations of the power of God who "hath chosen . . . the things which are not, to bring to nought things that are."[7] In their glory, when the disintegration of evil is already apparent in their life and yet ultimate destruction is so long postponed, their fate reveals the "longsuffering" of the divine mercy. For God's judgments are never precipitate and the possibilities of repentance and turning from the evil way are many. According to the degree with which

---

[6] *Cf.* Vol. I, Ch. VI.   [7] I Cor. 1:28.

civilizations and cultures accept these possibilities of renewal, they may extend their life indeterminately. But at some point or other they make the fatal mistake, or a whole series of fatal mistakes. Then they perish; and the divine 'majesty is vindicated in that destruction.[8]

It is not possible to make some simple distinction between the period of creativity in a civilization and the period of decline, because every civilization and culture, every empire and nation, reveals destructive elements in its period of creativity, even as there are creative elements in its period of decline.[9] But we know that

[8] Here we must recall the relevance of the prophetic conception of the rise and fall of empires and the belief that their destruction represents a vindication of the divine majesty against the pretensions of false majesty. *Cf.* Ezekiel 28:17–18: "Thine heart was lifted up because of thy beauty, thou hast corrupted thy wisdom by reason of thy brightness: I will cast thee to the ground. . . . I will bring thee to ashes upon the earth in the sight of all them that behold thee." This and many similar predictions of doom upon the various empires is always followed with the refrain: "In that day shall they know that I am the Lord."

[9] The tendency towards nationalistic Messianism is a case in point. Every culture at some time or other makes explicit Messianic pretensions and conceives the ambition of making itself the centre of the universal community. This Messianism is the overt form of the pride which is covert in all particular human communities. Sometimes this Messianism is a last gasp of life in a decaying world. A culture seeks to obscure its mortal fate by this pretension. Thus it was a decaying Egyptian sacerdotal state (after 1600 B.C.) which made the most extravagant Messianic-imperial pretensions; and Dante's vision of a Holy Roman Empire was the swan song of Ghibelline imperialism. The Messianic pretensions of the idea of the Russian nation as "Christophorus" developed after the Russian church had ceased to exercise a decent restraint upon the political will-to-power of the state and was unconsciously intended to hide that failure.

But on the other hand a very youthful and creative American civilization compounded the Christian vision of the Kingdom of God with the "American dream." It was in the early part of the nineteenth century (circa 1800–40) that American culture expressed its contempt for a "decadent" Europe by hoping that history would be fulfilled on American soil.

In between these pretensions of youth and of age are such aberrations as Lionel Curtis' identification of the British Empire with the

there are periods in which creativity predominates; and other ages in which corruption and destruction predominates.

If the whole of history is viewed from inside a period of creativity it is given a false meaning; because the entire historical process is falsely identified with a tangent in a particular age of a particular culture. If the whole of history is viewed from the vantage point of a period of decline it is threatened with meaninglessness. For the course of history is falsely identified with the doom of a given civilization. Whatever meaning there is in the rise and fall of civilizations can be known only "by faith"; for it must be viewed from the vantage point of an eternity above history, which no man has as a possession but only by faith. From such a vantage point history is meaningful, even if it should be impossible to discern any unity in its continuing processes. It is meaningful because eternal principles are vindicated in both the life which overcomes death in rising civilizations, and in the death which overtakes proud life in dying ones.[10]

"City of God" (*cf.* Curtis, *Civitas Dei*). How can we know until we have more historical perspective whether the Messianic pretensions of Anglo-Saxon imperialism (which are frequently made more extravagantly in America than in Britain) are the swan song of a dying Anglo-Saxon world, or the egoistic corruption in the creative function of this world in organizing a world community?

[10] It is impossible to write about the life and death of civilizations in a period when it is still uncertain whether we are in the throes of death or the birth pangs of a new life in the history of Western civilization, without a special word about the relevance of the Christian interpretation of human destiny to our own situation. The genius of the Christian faith makes it impossible either to view the trials and tumults of a civilization with detached and irresponsible equanimity nor yet to identify the meaning of life with the preservation of our culture and civilization.

We are at the moment engaged in the limited task of warding off a great peril which arose when a virulent form of corruption challenged the remnants of our civilization. Our obtuseness in understanding the relation between this virulence and the more static corruption out of which it developed, our tardiness in meeting the peril, the domestic disharmonies and nationalistic prejudices which made a united action

2. *The Individual and History*

The plight of the individual in his relation to the whole process of history is derived from his twofold relation to the historical process. His creativity is directed towards the establishment, perpetuation and perfection of historical communities. Therefore the meaning of his life is derived from his relation to the historical process. But the freedom which makes this creativity possible transcends all communal loyalties and even history itself. Each individual has a direct relation to eternity; for he seeks for the completion of the meaning of his life beyond the fragmentary realizations of meaning which can be discerned at any point in the process where an individual may happen to live and die. The end of an individual life is, for him, the end of history; and every individual is a Moses who perishes outside the promised land. But each individual also has an indirect relation to eternity. In so far as he takes historical responsibilities seriously he must view the problem of fulfillment from the standpoint of the ultimate and final "end." [11]

against a common peril difficult and halting: all these weaknesses place the outcome of even the limited struggle in doubt. The outcome of the larger issues is even more problematic. We do not know whether Western civilization has the resources to transcend nationalistic parochialism sufficiently to fashion a world community, compatible with the interdependence of a technical age; or whether it can solve the domestic-economic problems, aggravated by the dynamics of a technically advanced industrial process.

Standing inside such a civilization our responsibilities are obvious. We must seek to fashion our common life to conform more nearly to the brotherhood of the Kingdom of God. No view of history *sub specie æternitatis* dare beguile us from our historical obligations. But if we should fail, as well we may, we can at least understand the failure from the perspective of the Christian faith. In so far as we understand the failure we will not be completely involved in it, but have a vantage point beyond it. We could not deny the tragic character of what we discern but we would not be tempted to regard it as meaningless.

[11] The Ezra Apocalypse (Fourth Ezra) states this problem of individual life succinctly: "But lo O Lord thou art ready to meet with thy blessing those that survive *in the end;* but what shall our predecessors

If the eternal fulfillment of individual life is comprehended merely from "above," the social and historical meaning of life is destroyed. Individual life is regarded as an end in itself. This is precisely the effect not only of mystic doctrines of fulfillment but also of many orthodox Protestant versions of eschatology, in which the "end" stands only above history and the Biblical idea of the "end" is obscured.[12]

On the other hand modern protests against these Christian (and sometimes non-Christian) forms of "other-worldliness" make the mistake of trying to fulfill the meaning of life in the historical process itself. Thereby they not only obscure the reality of individual freedom in its transcendence over history but also deny the finite character of the historical process.

In their crudest forms the purely social and historical interpretations of life bid the individual to fulfill his life in his community. The breadth of the communal life and the majesty of its power supposedly complete and fulfill the partial interests and inadequate power of the individual. The relative immortality of the community is intended to compensate for the brevity of an individual's life. The difficulty with this solution is that each individual is so much more, even while he is so much less, than the community. His years are briefer than those of his community; but both his memories and anticipations have a longer range. The community knows only of its own beginnings but the individual knows of the rise and fall of civilizations before his own. The community looks forward to the victories, and fears the defeats of history; but the individual

---

do, or we ourselves or our posterity?" (5:41). Or again: "How does it profit us that an eternal age is promised us, whereas we have done works that bring death? And that there is foretold us an imperishable hope, whereas we are so miserably brought to futility?" (7:119–20).

[12] Reformation theology is on the whole defective in failing to preserve the Biblical conception of the end; and modern Barthian eschatology accentuates this defect. It pays little attention to a possible meaning of history as a continuum and speaks of eschatology in terms of the eternity which impinges upon every moment of time.

discerns a more final judgment. If the nations stand before that last judgment too, they do so in the conscience and mind of sensitive individuals. The brotherhood of the community is indeed the ground in which the individual is ethically realized. But the community is the frustration as well as the realization of individual life. Its collective egotism is an offense to his conscience; its institutional injustices negate the ideal of justice; and such brotherhood as it achieves is limited by ethnic and geographic boundaries. Historical communities are, in short, more deeply involved in nature and time than the individual who constantly faces an eternity above and at the end of the time process.

More refined forms of social and historical schemes of redemption bid the individual to fulfill his life and compensate for the brevity of his years by his relation, not to any particular historic community, but to the historical process itself.[13]

We have previously considered the reasons why it is impossible to regard history as redemptive and why the hope of an adequate judgment and a sufficient fulfillment of the life of the individual in the historical process must lead to the most pathetic disillusionment. It may suffice at this point to illustrate and recapitulate previous analyses of this problem by the simple expedient of imagining ourselves the "posterity" to which the eighteenth century appealed

[13] An historian of the eighteenth century describes the substitution of "posterity" for eternity in eighteenth-century thought as follows: "For the love of God they substituted love of humanity; for vicarious atonement the perfectibility of man through his own efforts, and for the hope of immortality in another world the hope of living in the memory of future generations. . . . The thought of posterity was apt to elicit from eighteenth century philosophers and revolutionary leaders a highly emotional and essentially religious response." Carl L. Becker, *The Heavenly City of Eighteenth-Century Philosophers*, p. 130.
The essentially religious character of this appeal to posterity is perfectly expressed in the words of Diderot: "O posterity, holy and sacred! Supporter of the oppressed and unhappy, thou who art just, thou who art incorruptible, thou who wilt revenge the good man and unmask the hypocrite, consoling and certain idea, do not abandon me. Posterity is for the philosopher what the other world is for the religious."

and noting the incongruity of being regarded as the "supporters of the oppressed," as "holy and sacred," in short as worthy or capable of being the final judges or redeemers of those who have gone before us. We are furthermore so deeply involved in and preoccupied with our own perplexities that we are as disinclined, as we are unworthy, to act as surrogates for God.

Yet there is always an element of truth in these simple appeals to history as the fulfillment of life; for the meaning of life is to be found partly in man's involvement in historical tasks and obligations.

The New Testament answer to the problem of the individual is given from the standpoint of both the eternity which is "above" and the eternity which is at the end of history. The idea of a "general resurrection," in which all those who perished before the fulfillment of history, are brought back to participate in the final triumph, does justice to both the value of individual life, without which the fulfillment of history would be incomplete; and to the meaning of the whole course of history for the individual, without which his life cannot be fulfilled.[14]

The symbol of the resurrection of the body is, even without the conception of a general resurrection at the end of history, both more individual and more social in its connotations than the alternative

[14] The idea of a general resurrection in later apocalyptic literature in which New Testament conceptions of the resurrection are rooted, is sometimes erroneously regarded as an indication of the triumph of individualistic religion over previous tribal or nationalistic ideas of the fulfillment of life. R. H. Charles, in his otherwise authoritative work in this field, commits this error (*Cf.* R. H. Charles, *Eschatology*). The idea of a general resurrection in Jewish apocalypse which permits those who perished before the final triumph to participate in it, does of course recognize the problem of individuals who die before the social meaning of life is fulfilled. But on the other hand it also implies a mutual relation between individual and social fulfillment and makes each dependent upon the other.

The participation of individuals of all ages in the age of fulfillment is implausible when taken literally; but it is symbolically profound. It relates the eternity which stands over each moment of time to the eternity in which the time process is fulfilled.

idea of the immortality of the soul. It is more individual because it asserts eternal significance, not for some impersonal *nous* which has no real relation to the actual self; but for the self as it exists in the body. This self bears within it the anxiety and insecurity of finite existence on the one hand, and the capacity to touch the horizons of the eternal on the other hand. The hope of the resurrection affirms that ultimately finiteness will be emancipated from anxiety and the self will know itself as it is known.

The idea of the resurrection is more social because the historical constructions of human existence, the cultures and civilizations, the empires and nations and finally the whole historical process, are, just as individual life, the product of a tension between natural conditions and the freedom which transcends nature. The idea of the resurrection implies that the historical elaborations of the richness of creation, in all their variety, will participate in the consummation of history. It gives the struggles in which men engaged to preserve civilizations, and to fulfill goodness in history, abiding significance and does not relegate them to a meaningless flux, of which there will be no echo in eternity.[15]

Neither utopian nor purely other-worldly conceptions of fulfillment do full justice to the paradoxical relation of the individual to the historical process. The individual faces the eternal in every moment and in every action of his life; and he confronts the end of history with his own death. The dimension of his freedom transcends all social realities. His spirit is not fulfilled in even the highest achievements of history; his conscience is not eased by even the most unequivocal approbation of historical courts of judgment; nor need it be finally intimidated by historical condemnations. On the other hand the individual's life is meaningful only in its organic relation to historical communities, tasks and obligations.

[15] It is significant that radical sectarianism frequently recognized the relevance and meaning of the idea of the resurrection in its polemic against a too individualistic orthodox Christianity. *Cf.* particularly *Man's Mortality* by Richard Overton, the leader of seventeenth-century Levellers.

analogy of parenthood

The relation of the meaning of life to parenthood is a convenient microcosmic example of this double dimension of individual life. No individual parent fulfills the total meaning of his life in his relation to his children. There are innumerable facets of meaning which are comparatively irrelevant to the vocation of parenthood. But on the other hand it is not possible to divorce the meaning of life from the vocation of parenthood. Parents must be "justified" in the lives of their children. But children are hostages held by the future. The fulfillment of the life of the parents depends upon the realization of character in their children. Thus the present must wait upon the future for its final fulfillment.

3. The Unity of History

However meaningful life may be in the individual patterns and collective configurations which are appreciated "from above," or from the standpoint of their direct relation to the eternal source and end of meaning, history as such represents a total realm of coherence which requires comprehension from the standpoint of its ultimate *telos*.

Even without any explicit principle of comprehension, or any adequate philosophy or theology of history, the most cursory examination of history will yield certain tangents of coherence and reveal minimal relations of unity. A consistently pluralistic conception of history is not tenable, or even plausible. It may be, as Aristotle observed, that the arts are lost and found many times in the course of history. It may be that a Roman civilization must realize certain social standards completely *de novo,* without reference or dependence upon the achievement of these standards in a Babylonian or Egyptian civilization. But on the other hand there is always a residual minimum of social and cultural experience which is deposited by one civilization and used by another. The history of science cannot be traced without beginning with the mathematics and astronomy of Egyptian priests. The science and philosophy of Western civilization obviously rest upon Greek foundations; and

Western statecraft is inexplicable without an understanding of its Roman-Stoic presuppositions. The Hebraic-Christian interpretation of history, which we have sought to elucidate in these pages, has its roots in Babylonian, Egyptian and Persian forms of Messianism. There are, in short, cumulative effects in history. Even Spengler is forced to admit that, when new civilizations are built upon the ruins of old ones, their character is partly determined by the way new life absorbs, adapts itself to, and grows around the old ruins.

The inner relation of successive civilizations to each other may be described as "unity in length" or in time. The inner relation of contemporary civilizations to each other may be described as "unity in breadth" or in space. The former unity is more obvious than the latter one. The history of Western civilization is, for instance, more clearly related to Greece and Rome than it is to its own contemporary China. Yet there are minimal relations of mutual dependence even in "breadth." While the Western world has elaborated science and techniques to a greater extent than the oriental world, it would not be possible to comprehend our Western scientific development without understanding the contributions of oriental scientific discoveries towards it.[16]

Perhaps the most significant development of our own day is that the cumulative effects of history's unity in length is daily increasing its unity in breadth. Modern technical civilization is bringing all civilizations and cultures, all empires and nations into closer juxtaposition to each other. The fact that this greater intimacy and contiguity prompts tragic "world wars" rather than some simple and easy interpenetration of cultures, must dissuade us from regarding a "universal culture" or a "world government" as the natural and inevitable *telos* which will give meaning to the whole historical process.

But on the other hand it is obvious that the technical interdependence of the modern world places us under the obligation of elaborating political instruments which will make such new intimacy and

[16] *Cf.* Lewis Mumford, *Technics and Civilization.*

interdependence sufferable. This new and urgent task is itself a
proof of the cumulative effects of history. It confronts us with
progressively difficult tasks and makes our very survival dependent
upon their solution. Thus the development of unity in breadth is
one aspect of the unity of length in history.

These facts seem obvious enough to occasion some agreement in
their interpretation, even when the presuppositions which govern
the interpretations are divergent. It must be agreed that history
means growth, however much the pattern of growth may be obscured
by the rise and fall of civilizations. Though one age may have to
reclaim what previous ages had known and forgotten, history
obviously moves towards more inclusive ends, towards more complex human relations, towards the technical enhancement of human
powers and the cumulation of knowledge.

But when the various connotations of the idea of "growth" are
made more explicit a fateful divergence between the Christian
and the modern interpretation of human destiny becomes apparent.
As we have previously noted, the whole of modern secular culture
(and with it that part of the Christian culture which is dependent
upon it) assumes that growth means progress. It gives the idea of
growth a moral connotation. It believes that history moves from
chaos to cosmos by forces immanent within it. We have sought to
prove that history does not support this conclusion. The peril of
a more positive disorder is implicit in the higher and more complex
order which human freedom constructs on the foundation of
nature's harmonies and securities. The spiritual hatred and the lethal
effectiveness of "civilized" conflicts, compared with tribal warfare
or battles in the animal world, are one of many examples of the new
evil which arises on a new level of maturity.

Two other examples of this aspect of history may be cited. The
sanity of a mature individual incorporates psychic complexities and
tensions into a tolerable unity, richer and finer than the simple unity
of childhood. But it is also subject to aberrations to which children
are immune. Children may be abnormal but are usually not subject

to insanity. The political cohesion of a great national or imperial community has a breadth and extent beyond that of a primitive tribe. Furthermore it embodies social complexities of which tribal unity is innocent. The achievement of unity within this complexity represents growth toward "maturity." But every such realm of political order is filled with tensions which may become overt conflicts if not carefully "managed." The communities of history are political artifacts. They lack the security of nature and are exposed to the perils of human errors, and the aberrations of human freedom. No conceivable historical growth can therefore make a possible world government of the future as stable and secure as the order of a national community; just as no national community is as immune to disorder as the family or the tribe.

Antichrist The New Testament symbol for this aspect of historical reality, this new peril of evil on every new level of the good, is the figure of the Antichrist. The Antichrist belongs to the *eschata,* to the "last things" which herald the end of history. The most explicit denial of the norm of history must be expected in the most ultimate development of history.[17] Closely related to this idea of the final evil at the end of history, is the general anticipation of evils in the course of

[17] The specific term of Antichrist is found only in the Johannine epistles. 1 John 2:18; 4:3; 11 John 7. In these references the figure is not particularly identified with the end. But the Johannine epistles provide an explicit term for a general New Testament idea, which is variously expressed. Jesus' vision of the end includes the appearance of those who "shall come in my name, saying, I am Christ" (Mt. 24:5); and of "false Christs and false prophets" who will "shew great signs and wonders, insomuch that, if it were possible, they shall deceive the very elect" (Mt. 24:24 and Mk. 13:22). Not only the most explicit form of pride, but also final conflicts and wars belong to the end of history (Mt. 24:6).

In the apocalyptic sections of the epistles Christians are assumed to have insights into history which will make it possible for them to understand "sudden destruction" when other men say "peace and safety" (1 Thess. 5:2); and "perilous times" are predicted when "men shall be lovers of their own selves, covetous, boasters, proud," etc. (11 Tim. 3:2). *Cf.* also Revelation 16:16–18; 19:19.

history, which believers will understand but by which the world will be taken unawares.

The New Testament symbol of the Antichrist was appropriated by Catholicism primarily for the purpose of designating potent foes of the church. This polemic use of the symbol obscured the fact that the ultimate evil might be not the denial, but the corruption, of the ultimate truth. This is the point which the Protestant Reformation made in levelling the charge of Antichrist against the church itself. But neither Catholicism nor the Reformation used the symbol of the Antichrist effectively as a principle of general historical interpretation. Modern Protestantism has not understood the significance of the symbol for obvious reasons. It has, therefore, been used and misused primarily by literalists who have sought to prove that some current and contemporary Napoleon, Hitler, or Cæsar conformed to the prophecies of Antichrist or had a name, the letters of which could be tortured to yield the number 666.[18]

The inclination of contemporary millenarian literalism to identify some current embodiment of evil with Antichrist, corresponds to a recurrent tendency in all apocalypses. It is probably as natural for an age to think of the evil against which it contends as the final form of evil as to make the mistake of regarding the good which it embodies as the final good.[19] The belief of an age that it has reached

[18] *Cf.* Rev. 13:18 "Let him that hath understanding count the number of the beast: for it is the number of a man; and his number is six hundred threescore and six." The "Beast" of the book of Revelation is quite rightly related in Christian eschatology to the conception of the Antichrist for it also is a symbol of the final form of evil, demanding blasphemous worship of itself. *Cf.* Rev. 13:4.

[19] Thus the book of Daniel places the Babylonian Empire in the position of the ultimate evil, believing that, "when the wickedness of the empire has gone so far as to deify itself and deny all reverence to anything higher, it demands and brings the divine intervention. Its hour has struck and with it the hour of the world's salvation." Adam Welch, *Visions of the End*, p. 124.

In later Jewish and Christian apocalypses it is the Roman, rather than the Babylonian Empire which has this unenviable position. In the "Eagle Vision" of the Ezra Apocalypse the sins of Rome are regarded

the end of history is pathetic, even though understandable. If we must have such illusions the apocalyptic versions of it have the merit, at least, of picturing history as moving towards a climax, and of regarding the consummation not as the mere display of the triumph of the good over evil but as a desperate conflict between the two.

But an adequate Christian philosophy of history requires better use of the symbol of the Antichrist than as a polemic weapon against contemporary foes or as the bearer of inadvertent insights, scattered among literalistic illusions. In the New Testament the symbol is integral to a total and consistent view of history, according to which the future is never presented as a realm of greater security than the present or as the guarantor of a higher virtue. The Antichrist stands at the end of history to indicate that history cumulates, rather than solves, the essential problems of human existence.

This does not mean that evil has its own independent history, culminating in the final idolatries and blasphemies of the Antichrist. Both the *civitas Dei* and the *civitas terrena* grow in history, as Augustine observed. But they do not have their separate histories. The evil which appears at the end of history is either a corruption of the final good or it is an explicit denial and defiance of that good which would be impossible without the juxtaposition of the good. This is to say that evil is negative and parasitic in origin, even though its effect is positive and its power something more than inertial resistance. Modern tyrannies are not the end product of a long history of tyranny in which ancient evils have been consciously refined to their present consistency of evil. They are rather characteristic corruptions of a mature civilization in which technical instruments have become more effective tools of tyrannical purpose. Modern idolatrous religions, which conform so perfectly to the

---

as embodying and accentuating all previous evils and thus pointing to the end of history (IV Ezra 12:15).

The idea of Marxist apocalypse that capitalism is the final evil, the defeat of which will mean the destruction of evil in history, is a secularized version of this same illusion.

vision of the "Beast" who demands religious worship for himself; and of the "false Christs" who "deceive the very elect," are not the final fruit of an independent history of idolatry. They are explicit forms of self-worship which gain their power by consciously defying higher religious and moral standards. Modern international anarchy is not the fruit of a long history of anarchy. It is, rather, the corruption and disintegration of a system of order. It is so terrible because it presupposes potential or actual mutualities on a larger scale, than those achieved in previous civilizations.[20]

The final evil is thus dependent upon the final good. Either it consciously and explicitly defies the Christ, in which case it requires Christ as a foil; or it is a lesser good, claiming to be the ultimate one, in which case it requires Christ as a cloak. The one form is the Antichrist of the sinners and the other the Antichrist of the righteous. But in either case the force of the Antichrist, though parasitic and negative in origin, is so positive in effect, and so stubborn in purpose that no force, immanent in history, is capable of encompassing its defeat. The Antichrist who appears at the end of history can be defeated only by the Christ who ends history.

All the known facts of history verify the interpretation of human destiny implied in New Testament eschatology. Yet most of the philosophies of history, both ancient and modern, have sought to obscure either one or the other aspect of history which Biblical eschatology illumines. Ancient philosophies of history either denied the meaningfulness of history entirely or they saw only the limited meaningfulness of its allegedly recurring cycles. Modern philosophies have emphasized the unity of history and its cumulative tendencies; but they sought to obscure and deny the perils and evils in the cumulations of history, so that they might regard history itself as the God of redemption.

If we inquire more closely why these mistakes were made, our consideration of the end of human destiny brings us back to the

[20] Paul Althaus emphasizes the negative character of the Antichrist in relation to Christ in his *Die Letzten Dinge*, p. 273.

problems of the beginning. For the most plausible explanation of the mistakes is that they were prompted by the desire to find a way of completing human destiny which would keep man's end under his control and in his power. The ancient world sought to do this by emancipating the spirit of man from the flux of finiteness or by subordinating his freedom to that flux. The modern world has sought redemption by regarding the process of history itself as a guarantor of the fulfillment of human life.

In every case the "vain imagination" of human pride entered into these calculations and determined the result. "Honest" mistakes may account for some confusion. The freedom of man transcends the flux of nature in such a way that the hope of completely severing the spirit from the integuments of nature is an understandable illusion. The processes of growth in history are, furthermore, so obvious that the modern error of confusing growth with progress may be regarded as an equally inevitable mistake. Yet both these mistakes also rested upon a wilful disregard of some of the obvious evidences. It is obvious that man does not have the power to extricate himself from flux and finiteness, as idealists and mystics of the ancient and the modern world believed. It is equally obvious that history does not solve the basic problems of human existence but reveals them on progressively new levels. The belief that man could solve his problem either by an escape from history or by the historical process itself is a mistake which is partly prompted by the most universal of all "ideological" taints: the pride, not of particular men and cultures, but of man as man.

For this reason it is possible to make a truer analysis of human destiny upon the basis of a religious faith which has disavowed human pride in principle, though it must not be assumed that any particular Christian analysis will not exhibit in fact what it has disavowed in principle. But if the Christian faith really finds its ultimate security beyond all the securities and insecurities of history; if it is really "persuaded, that neither death, nor life, nor angels, nor principalities, nor powers, nor things present, nor things to come, nor height, nor depth, nor any other creature, shall be able to separate us from the love of God, which is in Christ Jesus our Lord," [21] it may dissuade men from the idolatrous pursuit of false securities and redemptions in life and history. By its confidence in an eternal ground of existence which is, nevertheless, involved in man's historical striving to the very point of suffering with and for him, this faith can prompt men to accept their historical responsibilities gladly. From the standpoint of such a faith history is not meaningless because it cannot complete itself; though it cannot be denied that it is tragic because men always seek prematurely to complete it.

Thus wisdom about our destiny is dependent upon a humble recognition of the limits of our knowledge and our power. Our most reliable understanding is the fruit of "grace" in which faith completes our ignorance without pretending to possess its certainties as knowledge; and in which contrition mitigates our pride without destroying our hope.

[21] Romans 8:38–39.

FINIS

INDEX OF SCRIPTURAL PASSAGES

GENESIS 28:12, 230
DEUTERONOMY 5:6–7, 26
JUDGES 17:6, 270
I SAMUEL 8:22, 269; 10:19, 270
ECCLESIASTES 3:19, 7; 3:20, 8; 9:4, 76
ISAIAH 6:9 ff., 29; 11:3–4, 19; 11:6, 28; 13:9–14:2, 27; 17:9–14, 27; 40:11, 19; Ch. 53, 44; 64:1–9, 30
JEREMIAH 13:23, 29
EZEKIEL Chs. 26–34, 30; 28:17–18, 306; 34:8, 146; 34:22–25, 28; 37:24, 19
AMOS 3:2, 24; 5:12, 28; 5:18, 23; 7:12, 24; 8:4, 28; 9:7, 23
MICAH 3:11–12, 29
FOURTH EZRA 7:45, 34; 7:116, 34; 7:119–120, 309; 12:15, 318; 13:14 ff., 293
MATTHEW 3:9, 42; 4:1 ff., 42; 5:4–6, 84; 5:20, 40; 5:27–48, 40; 7:11, 84; 10:23, 50; 13:30, 210; 15:6, 39; 15:21 ff., 42; 16:17, 53; 6:22, 47; 16:27, 48; 16:28, 50; 22:21, 270; 23:12, 44; 23:25, 40; 24:5, 316; 24:6, 49, 316; 24:24, 316; 24:30, 288; 25:24–25, 192; 25:31 ff., 43, 291; 25:37–39, 43; 26:64, 288
MARK 7:24 ff., 42; 8:31, 44; 8:31–38, 147; 13:22, 316; 13:26, 288
LUKE 4:5, 27; 4:21, 35; 10:20, 49, 88; 18:9 ff., 40; 22:25–26, 270

JOHN 1:5–11, 215; 1:12, 215; 1:17, 54, 98; 3:8, 208
ROMANS 1:21, 109; 2:14, 106; 3:20, 105; 3:22 ff., 103; 324, 105; 5:1, 103; 5:12, 76; 6:2, 126; 6:8 ff., 101; 6:22, 101; 7:18, 108; 7:23, 145; 8:6, 101; 8:35, 37, 38, 52; 8:38–39, 321; 9:18, 116; 13, 283; 13:1–3, 270; 14:8, 89
I CORINTHIANS 1:23–24, 54; 1:25, 35; 4:4, 121; 4:19, 98; 12, 145; 12:3, 52; 13:1–2, 92; 13:12, 92; 15:22, 76; 15:50, 298
II CORINTHIANS 5:4, 298; 5:10, 291
GALATIANS 2:20, 107, 119; 3:11, 105; 3:28, 85; 5:1, 40; 5:4, 104; 6:24–26, 102
EPHESIANS 2:8, 103; 4:1–10, 94; 4:17–32, 102; 4:24, 101; 5:8, 102
PHILIPPIANS 2:12, 13, 117; 3:8–11, 104; 3:12, 102
I THESSALONIANS 5:2, 316; 5:3–6, 288
II TIMOTHY 3:2, 316
HEBREWS 1:3, 55
I JOHN 1:8, 103; 2:18, 316; 3:2, 208; 3:6, 102; 3:9, 102; 4:1–2, 112; 4:3, 316
REVELATION 3:20, 117; 13:4, 317; 13:18, 317; 16:16–18, 316; 19:19, 316

INDEX OF PROPER NAMES

Adler, Mortimer, 123
Alberti, 154
Alivisatos, Hamilcar S., 133
Allen, J. W., 228
Androustos, Chrestos, 133
Anselm, 56, 59
Aquinas, Thomas, 77, 117–118, 140–141, 275
Aristotle, 82, 91, 271–272
Asmussen, Hans, 195
Athanasius, 132

Augustine, 80, 109, 115–116, 134–140, 144, 221, 272–274, 292, 305, 318

Bacon, Francis, 163
Bacon, Roger, 162–163
Baillie, John, 295
Balling, Peter, 172
Barclay, Robert, 173
Barth, Karl, 38, 64, 66–67, 116, 117, 159, 254, 279, 309

Benz, Ernest, 91, 162
Bergson, Henri, 79
Bernard of Clairvaux, 142
Bevan, Edwyn, 297
Bockelson, Jan, 177
Bodin, Jean, 241, 277
Boehme, Jacob, 90–91
Bonaventura, 162–163
Bosanquet, B., 120, 277
Bradley, Francis H., 66, 113, 120
Brunner, Emil, 64, 124, 188, 189, 191, 196, 197, 251, 255
Buber, Martin, 26
Bultmann, Rudolf, 84–85
Burdach, Konrad, 161
Burnham, James, 262

Caird, J., 120
Calvin, John, 198–203, 227, 282, 283
Campanella, 163
Carlyle, A. J., 273, 274
Charles, R. H., 297, 311
Cicero, 272
Clement of Alexandria, 58, 131
Clough, Arthur Hugh, 10
Coachman, Robert, 169
Cochrane, Charles Norris, 15
Comte, August, 166
Condorcet, 165
Cromwell, Oliver, 234, 239
Croce, Benedetto, 167, 301
Curtis, Lionel, 306

Dante, Alighieri, 163, 306
Denck, Hans, 172, 232
Denny, James, 113
Descartes, Rene, 164
Dewey, John, 237
Diderot, Denis, 310
Dodd, C. H., 48

Eckhardt, Meister, 90, 92
Epicurus, 9

Fichte, J. G., 164, 167
Ficino, 154
Florovsky, G. V., 225
Fox, Charles J., 239
Fox, George, 170, 171, 279
Francis, Saint, 161–162
Franck, Sebastian, 172
Fromm, Erich, 111

Gandhi, Mahatma, 261

Gore, Bishop Charles, 138
Gregory of Nyssa, 59, 77, 132

Harnack, A., 58, 130, 132
Hartshorne, Charles, 71
Hegel, G. W. F., 78, 164, 167
Hermas, 130
Hildebrand, 144
Hobbes, Thomas, 229, 240–241, 249, 266, 277
Hume, David, 82–84

Ignatius, 130
Irenæus, 59, 77, 132

Jefferson, Thomas, 233, 284
Jesus, 38–52, 69, 80, 87–88
Joachim of Flores, 161–162
Jones, E. Stanley, 280
Jones, Rufus M., 171, 172
Jordan, W. K., 222
Justin Martyr, 130

Kierkegaard, Soren, 38, 57, 61
Knox, John, 283
Koeberle, Adolf, 159
Kunkel, Fritz, 79

Lecky, W. E. H., 232
Lenin, Nicolai, 87
Leo II, 1, 222
Lilburne, John, 233, 280
Locke, John, 232, 234
Lucretius, 8–9
Luther, Martin, 117, 124, 185–198, 202, 226–227, 249, 277–278

Machiavelli, Niccolo, 277
Madison, James, 284
Mannheim, Karl, 237
Marcus Aurelius, 304
Maritain, Jacques, 93–94
McIlvain, C. H., 273
Mercier, Sebastian, 165
Mill, J. S., 236
Milton, John, 192, 233, 235–236, 281
Moberley, Robert, 143
Montaigne, M. E. de, 235
Montefiore, C. G., 46
More, Thomas, 163, 233, 241–242
Mumford, Lewis, 314

Narborough, F. D. V., 48
Newman, Cardinal, 143

Niebuhr, H. R., 219
Nietzsche, F. W., 91
Norris, John, 173
Nygren, Anders, 84

Oesterley, W. O. E., 48
Origen, 58, 131
Otto, Rudolf, 45, 46

Parsons, Robert, 222
Paul, 11, 37, 40, 41, 62, 100–105, 115, 123, 127, 195, 270, 298
Perrault, Charles, 168
Petrarch, 163
Plato, 11–13, 271–272
Plotinus, 3, 13, 135
Polycarp, 130
Porphyry, 58
Przywara, Erich, 221–222

Ranke, Leopold von, 302
Rashdall, Hastings, 59, 132
Rousseau, J. J., 266
Russell, Bertrand, 7

Saint John of Chrysostom, 133
Saint John of the Cross, 92–93
Schleiermacher, F. D. E., 73
Schweitzer, Albert, 50
Seneca, 14
Spengler, Oswald, 302, 314
Sterry, Peter, 172

Tertullian, 131
Tillich, Paul, 2, 217–218, 226
Tolstoi, Leo, 134
Toynbee, Arnold, 302–304
Troeltsch, Ernst, 276

Virgil, 10, 17
Voltaire, 165

Wernle, Paul, 101
Wesley, John, 173–175
Wiesner, H., 86
Williams, Roger, 235
Winstanley, Gerrard, 178–179

Zinzendorf, N. L. von, 174

INDEX OF SUBJECTS

Absolute, 12
Adam, 77–78, 91, 93
Agape, 71, 74–75, 76, 81–86, 88–90, 96, 123, 186, 187, 189, 204, 251
Alexandrian, 131–132
American Dream, 306
Anabaptists, 176–177
Anarchy, 194, 195, 258, 271, 285, 319
Anglican, 158–159, 225
Antichrist, 49, 129, 177, 316–319
Antinomian, 174–175, 190, 193, 198
Apocalyptic, 27–28, 33–34, 36, 37, 39, 41, 43, 47–48, 154, 172, 172–178, 289, 297, 311, 316–318
Apostolic Fathers, 130
Atonement, 46, 53, 55–60, 67, 147, 211, 212, 292

Babylonian, 16, 21, 313, 314, 317
Baptism, 130, 133
Becoming, 12, 37
Being, 12, 37
Bibliolatry, 152, 202, 229, 231
Body, 258, 296, 298, 311

Brotherhood, 79, 85, 95–96, 182, 244–256, 258, 265, 267
Buddhism, 13–14

Calvinism, 116, 180, 198–203, 204, 278, 281–283
Catholic, 59, 73, 93, 105, 117–119, 123, 133, 134–156, 161, 168, 169, 183, 199, 203, 207–208, 211, 216, 220–225, 227–228, 253, 255, 274, 317
Chalcedon, 60
Christ—divinity of, 61, 70, 72, 73; as essential man, 76; as expected, 4–5, 15–34, 53, 54, as "foolishness," 6, 11, 16, 35, 37, 54, 67, 97, 115, 121, 126; as fulfillment of history, 36–37; as fulfillment of self, 108–114; as God-man, 74; as head of Church, 145; humanity of 61, 70, 72, 73; as judge, 290–291; perfection of, 70–95; as second Adam, 68, 75, 76–77, 80, 91, 95; second coming of, 47–48, 51, 288–294; as Son of Man, 55; as "stumbling-block," 16, 31, 35, 37, 54, 59; as

suffering Messiah, 55, 127, 288, 290; two natures of, 60–61, 70, 72; as unexpected, 6–15, 58; as unique revelation, 16; virgin birth of, 73; as wisdom and power, 55, 57, 61–62

Christ-Mysticism, 185

Christological controversy, 60, 70

Church, 42, 138–139, 144–148, 150–152, 208, 224–225

Civilization, 302–307, 314–315

Civitas dei, 138, 274, 318

Civitas terrena, 138, 274, 318

Conscience—easy, 141, 192; uneasy, 85, 97, 117, 185, 190, 196–197

Contrition, 56–57, 61, 63–64

Creation, order of, 197–198

Cromwellian, 176–179, 233, 234, 280

Cross, 6, 36–37, 45, 53, 62, 68–75, 81–82, 86–89, 96–97, 104

Culture, 16, 67, 191, 205–210, 214, 217, 219, 231–232, 235, 237, 240, 296, 302–317

Day of the Lord, 4, 20, 24

Death, 1, 7–10, 51–52, 58, 293–294, 305, 307, 311

Democracy, 249, 260, 266, 268, 278, 283

Demonic, 110–112

Despair, 56–58, 207

Determinism, 115–116

Dialectical, 123, 204, 218

Egyptian, 16, 21, 313, 314

Empire, 306–307

Enlightenment, 85, 86, 158, 164–165

Equality, 254–255

Eros, 82, 84, 123

Eschatology, 47–48, 131, 162, 163–164, 166, 176–180, 196, 291–299, 300

Eschaton, 4, 28, 43, 50, 290, 316

Eternal life, 37

Eternity, 2–5, 7, 9–10, 13, 36, 37–38, 41, 46, 50, 58–59, 69, 91, 128, 131, 134, 164, 167, 247, 289–290, 292, 296, 299–301, 308–309, 311, 312

Evil, 10, 19–20, 32, 40–41, 43–46, 49, 68, 123, 155, 177, 197, 198, 211–212, 290, 292–293, 316–319

Existential, 112, 174, 300

Faith, 25, 52, 54, 57, 60, 63–64, 73, 75–76, 99–100, 103, 118, 120, 186, 287, 293, 295–296, 307, 320–321

Fall, 77–78, 179

Family, 83, 124, 313

Fanaticism, 231, 233–234, 239, 240, 241

Finis, 287, 293, 299

Finitude, 2–5, 8, 28, 37–38, 51, 53, 57, 58–61, 63, 74, 117, 120, 124, 128, 134, 144, 151, 167, 173, 214–215, 218, 219, 252, 292, 294, 295, 312, 320

Freedom, 1–2, 3, 5, 14–15, 40, 78, 80, 91, 95, 116–117, 124, 151, 152, 214, 244, 295, 300–301, 303, 304

Gnostic, 91–92, 129, 132

God—his forgiveness, 56–57, 98, 100, 104–105, 130–131, 135, 150, 174, 187, 196–197, 292; as hidden, 35, 65–66; his immanent relation to world, 66, 94; as judge, 23–26, 30, 31, 55, 68, 109, 127, 139, 145, 209, 211–212, 278, 286, 292–294, 305; his justice, 55–56, 131; his Majesty, 71, 167, 306; his mercy, 29–31, 32–33, 46, 55–57, 60, 67, 68, 71, 104, 109, 114, 116, 135, 211–212, 292, 297; as person, 66–67; as power, 22, 99–100, 109, 150, 184, 204; his providence, 166, 278; his sovereignty, 15, 18, 23, 35–36, 45–46, 47, 49, 52, 57, 290, 300; his suffering, 46, 55–56; as transcendent, 66–67, 94; as wisdom, 63, 99; his wrath, 30–31, 55–56, 60, 193, 211

Good, 10, 12–13, 19–20, 32, 40–41, 43–46, 49, 68–69, 155, 177, 197, 198, 211–212, 290, 292–293

Government, 21, 194–195, 197–198, 266–269; as ordinance of God, 269, 282; Christian attitude toward, 269–284; order of, 195, 267; world government, 284–285

Grace, 54, 57, 61, 64, 98–100, 100–107, 107–126, 127–129, 129–133, 134–148, 150–153, 170, 175, 184, 186, 187, 191, 202, 204, 207–208, 211, 213, 216–218, 226, 245–246, 321

Greek Orthodox, 133, 224–225

Hebraic, 16, 21, 37, 298
Heilsgeschichte, 62–63, 152, 162
Hellenism, 17, 37, 58–60, 72, 103, 130–133, 135
History—as beginning, innocence, 76–81, 90, 95; as end, 47–48, 50, 76, 154, 162, 166, 254, 287–321; as fulfillment, 15–31, 35–67, 99, 160–161, 211, 213, 240, 288, 291; growth in, 315–316; as incomplete, 3, 4, 67, 99, 211, 321; meaning of, 2–6; as substance, mutual love, 76, 81–90, 247; transcended, 3, 10, 35–37, 68–69, 75, 90–92
Holy Spirit, 99, 110–112, 162, 170, 187

Idealism, 11, 14, 99
Ideology, 214, 238, 320
Immortality, 296, 312
Immaculate Conception, 73
Imputation, 103–104, 114, 119, 187
Incarnation, 55, 59, 91
Individual, 79, 161, 232, 233, 296, 308–313
"Inner light," 172–173, 176
Interim, 49–51, 213, 288

Jesuit, 222
Johannine, 37, 54, 103, 300
Judaism, 40
Judgment, last, 43, 50, 51, 291–294, 300–301, 310
Justice, 21–22, 84–86, 138, 192–197, 203, 213, 244–269, 282–284, 284–286
Justification by faith, 103–105, 120–121, 124–125, 132, 135, 143, 148–149, 174, 185, 186, 188, 189, 196, 197, 200, 226
Justitia originalis, 64

Kingdom of God, 35–36, 47–49, 83–87, 138, 144, 161, 178–180, 192, 204, 244–286, 288, 300, 308

Law, 39–41, 91, 105, 106–107, 166, 188–192, 196, 197, 202, 247–248; civil, 253–254, 257, 274; natural, 197, 253, 254, 257, 274, 280
Legalism, 39–41, 106, 190–191, 198, 202
Liberalism, 45, 49, 53–54, 73, 85, 86, 158, 159, 240, 253, 260

Logos, 11, 14–15, 71, 91, 164–166, 176, 215–216, 237, 271–272
Love—law of, 56, 96, 180, 201, 244; mutual, 68–70, 78, 81–87, 92, 96, 247; sacrificial, 68–72, 78, 80–86, 86–90, 96, 247; suffering, 49, 51, 92, 290
Lutheran, 180, 184–198, 202, 204, 278

Man—as creature, 1; as creator of history, 1, 8, 80–81; as image of God, 139, 171; his mind, 14; his nature, 68, 171; his pretension, 113, 144, 214, 216; his self-love, 135–139, 140; as self-righteous, 44, 140, 200–201; his self-transcendence, 3, 5, 8, 10, 11–12, 38, 40, 63, 74–75, 128, 142, 153, 214; his will, 20–21, 135; his will to power, 165–166
Marxism, 86–87, 160, 166, 178, 179, 181, 245, 252–253, 277, 280, 318
Materialism, 7, 11, 14
Methodism, 170
Messianism, 5, 16–34, 35–38, 39, 41–48, 65, 81, 147, 163, 306–307, 314
Monasticism, 161–162
Monogamy, 197
Moravian, 174
Mysticism, 11–14, 25, 37, 70, 90–94, 99, 112–113, 141, 161, 162, 170–173, 185, 187, 188

Nation, 18, 30, 32, 43–44, 62, 124
Nationalism, 23–27, 41–42, 111
Nature, 1–5, 7–10, 14–15, 64, 74–75, 90, 95, 97, 139–140, 151, 165, 245–246, 294
Naturalism, 5, 7–11
Nazism, 18, 262, 263, 278
"Negation of negation," 114–115, 119
Newness of life (*see* self, reconstruction of in grace)
Nicene Creed, 60
Nomos, 257
Non-resistance, 72, 194–195, 260
Nous, 13, 312

Optimism, 164–165, 181–182, 205
Original sin, 29, 108, 131, 134

Pacifism, 177, 233

Papacy, 144–146
Parousia, 50, 289, 290–291
Pelagian, 135, 139, 158, 175
Perfection—Catholic, conception of, 133, 136, 138, 141, 150, 161, 162, 163, 185; Divine, 68, 72–75, 76–77, 81, 86, 89, 91–92, 94, 95, 104, 272; as innocency of pre-fallen man, 77, 78–79, 80, 81, 90, 93, 95, 218; Reformation, conception of, 194–195; Sectarian conception of, 87, 125, 134, 154, 169–176, 178, 233, 279–280
Pessimism, 164, 277, 285
Pharisees, 39, 41, 44
Pietism, 154, 161, 170–176, 177
Platonism, 11–13, 91
Pluralism, 302–313
Power, 20–22, 57–58, 60–61, 110, 132, 135, 177, 186, 208, 257–269
Predestination, 116
Presbyterian, 227
Pride, 30, 40–41, 43–44, 104, 110, 122, 125–126, 137, 144, 147, 201, 229, 231, 287, 304, 320
Progress, 7, 49, 154, 164–166, 168, 206, 240
Prophetism, 18–20, 23–31, 31–34, 35–36, 38–53, 55, 65, 148, 180, 211, 264, 270–271, 274
Protestant, 64, 73, 157–158, 169–180, 210, 232, 245, 277–280, 309, 317
Puritanism, 198, 201, 227

Quakers, 177

Ransom, 46, 53
Reason, 6–7, 12–15, 58, 147, 150–151, 164–165, 173, 258–260
Redemption, 5, 46, 118, 209, 213, 217, 310
Reformation, 101, 116–117, 119, 137, 148–156, 157–159, 171, 174–175, 179–181, 183, 184–212, 219, 220, 226–231, 255, 270, 277–279, 283, 309, 317
Regeneration, 108, 125
Religion—natural, 26, 75–76, 120; revealed, 26, 75–76
Renaissance, 149–156, 157–183, 191, 204–212, 216, 231–243, 276–277
Repentance, 100, 121–122, 189–190
Resurrection, 36, 48, 69, 114, 294–298, 311, 312

Revelation, 5, 15, 25–26, 35, 45, 47, 52–54, 60, 67, 71, 96–97, 98, 99, 128, 217, 288
Righteous, 10, 43–44, 46, 127

Sacrament, 133, 225, 226
Sacramentalism, 160, 208
Salvation, 5, 130, 132
Sanctification, 101–102, 105, 135–136, 153, 155, 156, 159, 188–189, 197, 199–200, 216, 220, 225, 226, 229, 247
Sarx, 123
Scepticism, 238–239
Sectarian, 86–87, 92, 154, 169–180, 203, 221, 228, 232–236, 251, 280, 312
Secularism, 86–87, 157–158, 234, 235, 280, 283, 315
Self, reconstruction of in grace, 98–103, 105, 107–118, 121–124
Self-consciousness, 13, 25, 64–65, 80, 172
Sermon on Mount, 40, 84, 187, 194
Shepherd King, 17, 19, 22, 28
Sin, 3, 30, 32, 56, 58, 80, 98–99, 100–102, 104–105, 113, 115, 117, 120, 125, 130, 134, 135, 136, 137, 141, 143, 144, 145, 171, 175, 179, 188, 199, 200, 214–215, 218, 220, 299, 304
Son of Man, 28, 44–45, 48, 55–56, 288
Soul, 258, 298, 312
Spirit, 3, 8, 11, 74–75, 95, 110–111, 164, 171, 264
Stoicism, 14, 253, 256, 272, 274–275
Suffering servant, 44–49, 55–56
Synergism, 118
Synoptic, 37, 300

Telos, 287, 293, 313–314
Time, 50, 129, 289–291, 299–300
Tolerance, 220–243
Trent, Council of, 142
Truth, 63, 98, 100, 213–243

Unconditioned, 70, 218
Utopian, 163

Vitality, 91, 258–259, 261

Wisdom, 11, 54–55, 57–63, 99–100, 230–231